EUROPEAN STUDIES

Understanding Europe
The Council for European Studies book series

This series of books in association with the Council for European Studies publishes research-based work that contributes to our understanding of contemporary Europe, its nation states, institutions and societies. The series mirrors the CES's commitment to supporting research that plays a critical role in understanding and applying the lessons of European history and integration to contemporary problems, including those in the areas of global security, sustainability, environmental stewardship, and democracy.

Published

European Studies: Past, Present and Future
Edited by Erik Jones

EUROPEAN STUDIES

Past, Present and Future

EDITED BY ERIK JONES

agenda
publishing

First published in 2020 by Agenda Publishing

Agenda Publishing Limited
The Core
Bath Lane
Newcastle Helix
Newcastle upon Tyne
NE4 5TF
www.agendapub.com

ISBN 978-1-78821-282-3 (hardcover)
ISBN 978-1-78821-283-0 (paperback)

British Library Cataloguing-in-Publication Data
A catalogue record for this book is available from the British Library

Typeset by JS Typesetting Ltd, Porthcawl, Mid Glamorgan
Printed and bound in the UK by TJ International

CONTENTS

Part II Lessons from Europe

Part III The changing face of Europe

CONTENTS

Part VI Final thoughts

PREFACE
Erik Jones

The study of Europe has never been more active. Whether the conversation turns to populism, Brexit, immigration, or austerity, Europe is at the forefront. The same is true when scholars debate the future of democracy, the stability of North Atlantic Treaty Organization (NATO), efforts to combat climate change, or the struggle to maintain a multilateral world order. Europe may be the "old" continent, but it is a constant source of interest, inspiration, innovation, insight, and hope for the future.

Research on Europe has continued to grow as well. You can see this progression in the page budgets, citations, and download statistics for the major European journals. You can also see it in the length and breadth of the publishing lists on Europe from the major university and commercial presses. The professional associations that focus on Europe have widened their memberships, multiplied their conferences and workshops, and expanded their remits. Meanwhile, the range of scholars involved in this activity extends ever more widely beyond the core group that straddles the North Atlantic to a dynamic new community of scholars in Central and Eastern Europe and beyond into China, South and South East Asia, Africa, and Latin America.

From research to engagement

The study of Europe has also never been more important. You can see this importance in the wide-ranging misperceptions of Europe that are held on both sides of the Atlantic, in the polarizing debate that surrounded the British referendum on European Union (EU) membership, in the divisions that emerged across the European continent during the recent economic and financial crisis, and in the reaction of many Europeans to the sudden upsurge in migration from Africa, the Middle East, and Central Asia. Misperceptions often reveal themselves in European relations with China, Russia, and the United States. Caricatures tend to predominate over subtlety or nuance; increasingly, moreover, both popular discourse and public policy-making seems to bend to stereotypes and away from substance.

The challenge now is to take advantage of this new dynamism in the study of Europe to strengthen and inform popular perception and public policy – not just within Europe and among European countries, but throughout Europe's relations with the outside world (and particularly in the United States and China). By implication, scholars who study Europe need to find more robust channels for engagement with a wider, global audience. They have to learn to shape their analysis in terms that can be widely understood and to make the insights they generate both accessible and attractive. This kind of engagement does not always come easily for academics, particularly when they work at the boundaries of multiple scholarly disciplines to address real-world problems in particular regions or countries. Nevertheless, it is vital that the insights such scholarship has to offer are not locked away from wider conversation about Europe.

Fifty years in the making

The Council for European Studies (CES) exists to foster this kind of engagement – by promoting research, organizing networks, hosting conferences, publishing commentary, and building bridges between academics and the policy community. The CES started in the United States; now it works equally on both sides of the Atlantic. As it celebrates its fiftieth anniversary, moreover, the work of the CES has never been more important.

This collection of short essays illustrates the kind of insights on Europe that the wider community of scholars has to offer. The contributions touch on the study of Europe, the lessons of the past, the changing present, and the prospects for Europe's future both as a political project and as an actor in the global arena. The contributors represent a wide diversity of opinion. Some are leading members of the academic community who have guided the CES in the past; others are new to the profession. More importantly, not all contributions agree with one another. The contrasts are sharpest on the "changing face of Europe" and Europe's future (including its world role), but there are lines of tension that run across the lessons of the past and the study of Europe as well.

The structure of the volume follows this list of themes, offering clusters of short reflections about Europe's past, present, and future. Within each cluster, you will find a mix of contributions – some that raise broad claims about what we can learn from Europe and others that focus more narrowly on how Europeans hope to tackle specific problems. Invariably, these contributions run across scholarly disciplines. What unites them is their focus on Europe. The volume concludes with a pair of final reflections. One of these offers a sense of cultural perspective, drawing connections to one of the great works of European music. The other relies on a famous piece of popular literature to frame the encompassing narrative.

The goal of the collection is to provoke thought, conversation, and interest. The best way to celebrate the fiftieth birthday of the CES, is to remember the importance of studying Europe. Looking ahead, however, the CES has broader ambitions. One of the most important of these is to use this volume as the starting point for a series of books to be produced by Agenda Publishing that will push forward the conversation on major developments in Europe. The goal with these books is to create a new form of engagement that combines depth of insight with accessibility and relevance.

Another ambition is to widen the conversation. The American Century has waned, and China has risen. Other parts of the globe are also asserting their influence and importance. What happens in Europe is already a focus for attention. The challenge is to make sure that the insights of this wider scholarly community are accessible to researchers and policymakers across the globe. The CES plans to widen its networks and deepen its strategy for engagement in response; it has had a very successful half-century, but remains committed to an even more successful future.

ACKNOWLEDGMENTS

This project was developed within the publications committee of the CES. The original members of the committee – Erik Bleich, Jan Willem Duyvendak, Karl-Orfeo Fioretos, Evelyne Huber, and Nicole Shea – each played important roles in conceptualizing the volume, formulating the strategy for soliciting the papers, reviewing those contributions that were received, and making suggestions for how to widen involvement from the membership of the organization. Previous chairs of the CES generously agreed to share their insight, as did the directors of the council's 15 research networks. Nicole Shea introduced this project to the World Society Foundation, which was crucial not only in providing much needed financial assistance but also in encouraging us to look for non-traditional voices to add into the conversation about Europe. The contributors were all very flexible with any suggestions and very responsive to any questions or queries. Zoë Strauss, a student at the Johns Hopkins School of Advanced International Studies in Bologna, played an important role in helping to organize the sections and to identify the key themes that emerged across the essays. In short, this was not only a team effort, but also a very large and cooperative team.

Finally, and perhaps most important, Alison Howson and Steven Gerrard at Agenda Publishing were enthusiastic and understanding supporters of the project, providing much needed encouragement as I missed one editorial deadline after another. Organizing a celebratory project like this is not a standard publication venture. I am very grateful that Agenda has agreed to take this on – not only as a way of celebrating the fiftieth anniversary of the CES or even as a vehicle to launch the new publication series that the CES will produce with Agenda, but also and more importantly to open up a global conversation about the future of Europe. The CES is celebrating 50 years of excellence in fostering European studies in North America and across the Atlantic. That kind of inquiry has never been more important. With partners like Agenda Publishing and the World Society Foundation, I am confident that the CES will continue to flourish and to widen the conversation for the next 50 years and more.

Erik Jones
Bologna

ABBREVIATIONS

CES	Council for European Studies
EC	European Community
ECB	European Central Bank
ECSC	European Coal and Steel Community
EDC	European Defense Community
EEC	European Economic Community
EHEA	European Higher Education Area
EII	European Intervention Initiative
EMS	European Monetary System
EMU	Economic and Monetary Union
EU	European Union
GDP	gross domestic product
IMF	International Monetary Fund
LGBT	lesbian, gay, bisexual, and transgender
NATO	North Atlantic Treaty Organization
NGO	non-governmental organisation
OECD	Organisation for Economic Co-operation and Development
SEA	Single European Act
SPD	Social Democratic Party of Germany
URBAN	Urban Communities Initiative

CONTRIBUTORS

Guya Accornero, University Institute of Lisbon

Marcos Ancelovici, Université du Québec à Montréal (UQAM)

Veronica Anghel, Stanford University and European University Institute

Lisa A. Baglione, Saint Joseph's University

Gregory Baldi, Western Illinois University

Beverly Barrett, University of St Thomas

Benjamin Bennett, University of Virginia

Sheri Berman, Columbia University

Erik Bleich, Middlebury College

Ludmila Bogdan, Harvard University

John R. Bowen, Washington University in St. Louis

Joel Busher, Coventry University

Fabio Capano, independent researcher

Josep M. Colomer, Georgetown University

Sarah Cooper, University of Exeter

Patricia W. Cummins, Virginia Commonwealth University

Sonia De Gregorio Hurtado, Universidad Politécnica de Madrid

Juan Díez Medrano, Universidad Carlos III de Madrid

William Collins Donahue, University of Notre Dame

Shawn Donnelly, University of Twente

Hélène B. Ducros, North Carolina State University

Jan Willem Duyvendak, University of Amsterdam and Netherlands Institute for Advanced Study in the Humanities and Social Sciences (NIAS-KNAW)

Jennifer Elrick, McGill University

Anlam Filiz, independent researcher

Simon Fink, Georg-August University Göttingen

Justin Gest, George Mason University

Catherine Guisan, University of Minnesota

Peter A. Hall, Harvard University

Randall Halle, University of Pittsburgh

Dermot Hodson, Birkbeck, University of London

Alma Jeftić, International Christian University

Steven Johnson, Brigham Young University

Alison Johnston, Oregon State University

Erik Jones, Johns Hopkins University

Martin Kagel, University of Georgia

Lars Klein, Georg-August University Göttingen

Michèle Lamont, Harvard University

Willem Maas, York University

Cathie Jo Martin, Boston University

Paul Marx, University of Duisburg-Essen and University of Southern Denmark

Matthias Matthijs, Johns Hopkins University

Harris Mylonas, George Washington University

Csongor István Nagy, University of Szeged and Hungarian Academy of Sciences "Lendület Federal Markets Research Group"

Twamanguluka N. Nambili, Birkbeck, University of London and Pheora Rucci Ltd

Erin O'Leary, University of Chester

Craig Parsons, University of Oregon and University of Oslo

George Ross, University of Montreal

Vivien A. Schmidt, Boston University

Oliver Schmidtke, University of Victoria

Koen Slootmaeckers, City, University of London

Alberto Spektorowski, Tel Aviv University

Karen Umansky, Tel Aviv University

Mare Ushkovska, independent researcher

Louie Dean Valencia-García, Texas State University

Shengqing Zhang, Leipzig University

PART I

THE STUDY OF EUROPE

1

THE COUNCIL FOR EUROPEAN STUDIES AT 50: LOOKING BACK AND LOOKING AHEAD

Erik Bleich

The Council for European Studies (CES) has changed a great deal since our 25th anniversary celebration in 1995. In its earliest years, the CES was supported largely through one major funder, and it held a relatively small biennial conference exclusively in the United States. The primary participants were US-based scholars of European politics and society, their graduate students, and a small number of intrepid Europeans willing to travel to Chicago in March. These gatherings were intimate affairs, counting roughly 500 participants, all of whom stayed in the conference hotel.

Since that time, the CES has grown. Although we still receive support for graduate student dissertation completion grants, the CES does not rely heavily on foundations to carry out its mission. It now organizes conferences every year, with even-year meetings typically held in North America and odd-year conferences in Europe. We have built a wider base of targeted grant-funded projects that integrate individual and institutional members on both sides of the Atlantic.

This transition has proven phenomenally successful for broadening the number and types of people that connect through the CES. Approximately 800–1,000 participants attend our North American conferences and 1,200–1,500 gather in the European years. Our attendees come from traditional areas of strength such as political science, sociology, history, and anthropology, but also from fields like law, communications, economics, geography, cultural studies, urban studies, the humanities, business, and the arts.

Research networks have become hubs of activity for most of our members. They foster interdisciplinary approaches to the study of pressing issues such as immigration, social movements, the welfare state, or gender and sexuality. Our research networks nurture intellectual and social ties that help stitch CES members together. They host mini-conferences, work on collaborative projects, draw on CES resources when applying for grants, and publish collections of their work in our online platform *EuropeNow*. They allocate funding toward graduate student participation at the annual conference, bestow prizes, hold receptions, connect members with scholarly journals, and much more. Research networks thus often create the intimacy that marked the earliest years of the CES, while simultaneously drawing in new scholars, graduate students, universities, and foundation support.

The CES has evolved quite a bit over the past two and a half decades, and it is still an object in motion. Looking ahead, our goal is to build on the strength of our conferences to expand the role of the CES, the core mission of which is to "produce, support, and recognize outstanding, multidisciplinary research on Europe through a wide range of programs and initiatives". We see challenges and opportunities in several areas.

Students

To understand Europe over the long term, we have to support undergraduate and graduate students who have a deep and abiding interest in the continent. In some fields, a focus on Europe remains central and strong. In others, however, the commitment to area studies has waned. In my own discipline of political science, for example, it is rare that graduate students think of themselves as "Europeanists" and even rarer that there are job opportunities for candidates specifically identifying as European specialists.

Studying Europe in a global context is a welcome development, as is the comparison of European countries to societies elsewhere in the world. Yet the trade-off for many North American students may be a shallower understanding of Europe, disincentives to invest in mastering European languages, and less time spent in Europe itself. European students naturally have easier geographic access. They also benefit from programs that incentivize time spent outside of their home countries. Yet for a British citizen who loses EU scholarships or a Hungarian student unable to pursue gender and sexuality studies a home, it will be harder now than in previous years to delve deeply into the study of Europe.

Encouraging undergraduate and graduate education is critical. To maintain this commitment, the CES sponsors undergraduate project prizes, graduate training, and dissertation completion grants, and spotlights teaching and education through a section of its online platform called the *EuropeNow Campus*. The CES has developed partnerships with institutions committed to the teaching of Europe and has sponsored a new European pedagogy research network that supports teaching and learning about Europe. Ensuring a pipeline of students is particularly important given the dramatic transformations taking place on the continent. We need the study of Europe in all its facets to remain robust in North America, Europe, and beyond.

Diversity

Any well-rounded understanding of Europe depends on integrating diverse perspectives. Our traditional disciplinary strengths are political science and sociology, as well as history and anthropology. This is logical given the CES's focus on contemporary problems and how such challenges are shaped by historical developments. At the same time, we have made a conscious effort to seek out scholars from a wide variety of other fields. This diversity of backgrounds enriches our research networks, our panels, our collaborative projects, and the CES as a community. If we want to understand the origins and consequences of the refugee flows of the mid-2010s, we have to analyze not only the political decisions, but also how media portrayals affect national discussions, how refugees change the neighborhoods where they settle, and how their presence influences local economies and cultural production that subsequently affects politics and society.

The CES is increasingly attentive to the geographic diversity of our members. Since 2000, we have seen a dramatic growth in the number of European scholars, to the point where Europeans now constitute approximately half of our membership. This has been a boon to the organization and to all participants who now have broader networks for sharing ideas, launching projects, and cross-training students. Yet we have not had comparable success in encouraging participation from all areas of the globe. Since the early 1990s, our conferences have increasingly covered Eastern Europe in an explicit effort to overcome the Cold War mentality of a divided continent. Yet, even among our European members, we still have more to do to enable researchers from Eastern Europe to attend our meetings. In addition, we want to build ties with centers for the study of Europe based outside North America and Europe, and with scholars from the developing world who may provide new perspectives that spark innovative research agendas. For this reason, we are especially pleased to team up with the World Society Foundation to cover the full cost of participation at the fiftieth anniversary conference for 15 scholars, three each from Eastern Europe, the Middle East and North Africa, Sub-Saharan Africa, Asia, and Latin America.

One of our primary goals moving forwards is to institutionalize additional funding for access to our conferences. This will help scholars for whom travel to Europe or North America is structurally more expensive; we will also expand our travel grants for graduate students and for scholars from resource-constrained institutions in Europe and North America. To this end, we have established a 50th Anniversary Access Fund, which will provide grant funding to enable conference participation among a more diverse set of scholars and students.

Multidisciplinary and interdisciplinary research

The pressing problems of the present and future of Europe require multidisciplinary attention. Given the CES's longstanding emphasis on applying a historical lens to understand contemporary Europe, this perspective has deep roots within the organization. As we assemble the conference program each year, we often get most excited about panels involving scholars from a variety of disciplines. When we work with members to develop research networks or pursue programmatic funding that supports connections across universities, we do it with an eye toward community building that transcends traditional disciplinary divides.

To give one concrete example of this approach, the CES recently endorsed a proposal from our members for a new research network focused on health and well-being. These are cross-cutting themes of growing attention in Europe because of their political, societal, and cultural significance. The network conveners are interested not only in the provision of health care, but also in how broader structural inequalities shape health outcomes across societies. Network participants come from the disciplines of sociology, political science, history, anthropology, social epidemiology, demography, and public health. This array of experts will help us understand how Europeans live – and how some manage to live well – through their multidisciplinary research.

Looking ahead, two of the biggest challenges facing Europe over the next few decades are the spread of populism and the deterioration of the environment. Far-right political parties, anti-European movements, and sentiments based on xenophobia, homophobia, or other axes of difference have existed in Europe for decades, but they are rising in support and show no signs of abating. There are many existing CES research networks centrally concerned with these challenges. Our networks on immigration, gender and sexuality, social movements, political parties, territorial politics, radicalism and violence, transnational memory and identity, European integration, and European culture analyze these topics from the widest variety of perspectives. While we are especially good at examining key issues within these clusters, we may learn even more by encouraging collaborative work across our research networks.

The withdrawal of the United States from the Paris climate accord and the progression of climate events from superstorms to the rapid melting of the polar ice caps provide nearly constant reminders of the urgency of environmental concerns. These are challenges that invite scholars with backgrounds in political science, pedagogy, sociology, communications, history, and science – and more – to coordinate across their disciplines to understand their effect on Europe and the world. The CES has not traditionally been a hub for the study of environmental issues, but this must be a priority going forwards. Climate change is quite simply an existential threat.

The CES is an entrepreneurial institution. Our members mobilize around pressing problems and coordinate colleagues to address them. The director and the executive committee work with scholars to identify researchers in different disciplines who share common interests, to launch new research networks, to apply for funding for programmatic initiatives or network-building, and to facilitate publication through *EuropeNow* or our new book series (the first contribution to which is this volume itself). The CES aims to provide an organizational base for producing knowledge both at our annual conference and beyond. This is true with regard to subjects like populism or the environment, but we will also support scholars interested in topics like the changing European media landscape, corruption, foreign and security policy, or indeed any subject our members view as an important issue in contemporary Europe.

Public engagement

Addressing the critical challenges of the present and future of Europe requires the sustained attention that academics bring to the table. It also requires engagement with decision-makers. Many of our members produce policy-relevant research. Through their contacts, they also influence outcomes in their home countries or in European or transnational institutions. Some share dual roles as affiliates of think tanks or non-governmental organizations (NGOs), are seconded to the government for short stints, submit legal briefs, write for the media to help shape public opinion and political decisions, or – on rare occasions – run for office.

In the coming years, the CES aims to be a focal point for sharing information about policy engagement along all these lines. We are a scholarly organization and our mission is centered around supporting the production and dissemination of research. Yet we live in an era where deep knowledge of factors that affect the lives of Europeans is sometimes brushed off as tangential or even irrelevant in the political sphere. Many of us see our scholarship as inherently related to public policy. The CES will therefore foster links between members who have experience in the policy realm and those who want their knowledge to impact public decisions. To this end, we are launching a policy forum in 2020 that we hope will facilitate this kind of exchange.

Europe in transformation

Both Europe and European studies are undergoing significant transformations. The 50th anniversary celebration of the CES provides an opportunity to reflect on how the we can help facilitate connections among our members to address the challenges of our era. We will continue to organize world-class conferences that draw scholars and students from Europe, North America, and beyond and that serve as incubators for scholarship and teaching about Europe. We will foster research networks that create more tightly knit communities within our midst. We will help our colleagues seek and obtain project-based funding and provide them with outlets for their research through our book series or by way of our more public-facing *EuropeNow* online platform. These efforts are designed to make the CES a home for initiatives aimed at understanding and addressing the complex problems of the continent's past, present, and future. We have enjoyed 50 years of success so far, and we look forward to at least 50 more.

2

EUROPEAN STUDIES AS AN INTELLECTUAL FIELD: A PERSPECTIVE FROM SOCIOLOGY

Michèle Lamont

The place of European studies in the landscape of North American social sciences has faced serious challenges since the seventies (Lamont 2013). The general decline of area studies after the transition away from a colonial, and then Cold War-inspired, geographical organization of knowledge production has meant a redefinition of the position of European studies within the social sciences field over the past several decades. This trend has materialized in a highly regrettable decline in funding from some of the main American supporters of independent social science research on Europe, most notably the Ford Foundation and the German Marshall Fund (both following earlier signals from the Mellon Foundation).

Concomitantly, the Global South has come to exercise a growing and powerful attraction on our undergraduates, due to shifts in what it means to be progressive for today's young, the intensification of globalization, and the booming economic and political importance of countries like Brazil, Russia, India, China, and South Africa (BRICS). This trend is affecting academic hiring patterns, including the turn of history departments toward global history and the accelerated hiring of experts in areas other than Europe. Although itself a positive change, such a disciplinary shift is not without consequence for European studies.

Similar transformations operate in other disciplines (Lamont 2009). To simplify greatly, within political science, an American politics-based methodological push which went hand in hand with the adoption of economics as a reference point has transformed and challenged European comparative politics, a field with a long lineage of Weberian-inspired qualitative analysis. For its part, US-based anthropology of Europe prospered for a while, albeit just when the discipline itself went into a state of decline. At the same time, macroeconomics continued to veer away from country-based analyses, to focus more exclusively on theoretical innovation and modeling. As for sociology, research endeavors in my field were never firmly grounded in geographic divisions, and very few of my contemporaries have developed intellectual identities as proper "Europeanists". Instead, while a number of sociologists are serious regional experts, it is not unusual that members of my tribe take on regional topics in a more superficial fashion: they aim to make theoretical or substantive contributions by drawing on evidence that "happened" to be gathered in Europe. The result of these converging changes can easily be interpreted as a general weakening of European studies in North American social sciences.

Complexity beneath the surface

Yet, the situation may be far more nuanced and complex than one would be led to believe at first glance. This is certainly the case if one considers the current state of the study of Europe and of European countries in sociology. With the appeal of globalization, the programs of professional meetings, such as those of the CES and the American Sociological Association, suggest that a sizable number of sociologists have been attracted by the study of Europe considered in a comparative, transnational, or global perspective. The extension and consolidation of the EU has opened a whole new field of inquiry which was simply not on the horizon 40 years ago.

In the last ten years, we have also seen the publication of important collections of articles that explicitly aim at consolidating our sociological knowledge about Europe, bringing together excellent contributions dealing with a broad range of topics including identity, inequality, and mobility. Moreover, while sociologists working on European countries had typically specialized in fields such as comparative historical sociology, labor, political sociology, and the sociology of social movements, in recent years we have seen a diversification of foci, manifested in what appears to be a rapid growth in the number of publications on a wide range of topics that include income inequality, exclusion, immigration, racism, race and ethnicity, identity, knowledge, gender, and institutions and organizations. Much of this work is comparative, as researchers aim to illuminate the American, or colonial or post-national experiences, by looking at Europe through contrasting lenses. This has also meant the emergence and diffusion of a profusion of competing new research agendas and lively transatlantic conversations.

Of course, the research landscape in Europe has expanded and changed as well, and the overall quality of social science research has improved (as it has in North America). This means that North American sociologists are now in a better position to draw on the work of their European counterparts (and vice versa) when researching a topic than was the case 40 years ago. There remain important cross-national differences in the degree of familiarity that social scientists have with US-based social sciences, from the most English-speaking countries (Scandinavia, the Netherlands, Germany, and the UK) to the less bilingual ones. But in many countries, France standing as a prime example, the younger generations of sociologists are much more aware of, and engaged with, US and international literatures than was the case when I was a graduate student in Paris in the late 1970s. While sociologists such as Pierre Bourdieu have gained enormous influence in North America, the transmission of his work has helped the diffusion of a shared sociological language and sets of questions that have been generative from the perspective of theory building (Lamont 2012).

The success of historical institutionalism has played a parallel role for political science, with considerable intercontinental interchange among researchers who are pursuing overlapping sets of questions. Completing the picture, the effect of the EU, and of other EU-based research funds in transforming European social science, cannot be overestimated, especially when it comes to the creation of an abundant (some would say overabundant) number of collaborative European research networks. These in turn have greatly benefited US sociologists working on Europe, both because of the improved quality and sheer quantity of data and knowledge on Europe being produced, and of its overall greater visibility to North American researchers.

Today's North American-based experts on Europe have many more play mates and play dates than they had a few decades ago, and the increased popularity of comparative research encourages more theory building, away from descriptive case studies with little theoretical reach or scaling-up potential. In this sense, the sociology of Europe is now more in sync with disciplinary developments than was the case 30 years ago.

In the context of these broad developments, the CES has played a pivotal role. Thirty years ago, relatively few sociologists attended the biannual meetings of the association, and most of those who did were "quasi-political scientists", working on topics that pertained to political economy, labor, political institutions, and related topics. The contemporary landscape is quite different, given the proliferation of new topics (mentioned above) which adds to the earlier strengths in the field (most of which have been maintained). There have also been rapprochements between the CES and sister learned societies such as the Society for the Advancement of Socio-Economics, whose faithful members and leadership overlap in part with those of the CES.

How about the horsepower of the field? All in all, I would venture to state that sociologists working on Europe make up a fairly remarkable group, as the subfield has attracted a number of talented individuals across the generations (while I do not risk providing names for fear of omitting meritorious figures, I am certain that readers will have their own personal "best of the best" list).

MICHÈLE LAMONT

Room for improvement

Nevertheless, despite a clear push in theory building, there is still considerable room for improvement. To mention only one area which I know well – the sociology of racism and anti-racism – researchers on both sides of the Atlantic often proceed in parallel fashion, due in part (paradoxically) to the overabundance of information and problems with the circulation of information about who does what. In fact, the relevant research communities often do not read the same journals or books and do not define the same problems as "interesting".

The result is a somewhat chaotic research area that offers more than its fair share of case studies that are developed without a clear vision of accumulated knowledge. A few topics, such as immigration, have been the object of more integration, thanks in part to the vast amounts of funds that have been made available for its study by supra and national funding organizations in the United States and Europe, as well as through foundation and non-profit funding agencies. I believe this to be an exception, and even there, European researchers on immigration to Europe tend to be somewhat more theoretically motivated than their American, more often descriptive, counterpart (at the very least, what counts as "theoretically motivated" differ across contexts).

Obviously, it should also be mentioned that the conditions of intellectual production vary enormously across European countries and that this influences the type of research that can be conducted across national contexts. The Berlin Wissenschaftszentrum, Sciences Po, the Max Planck-Cologne, and the Max Planck-Göettingen have means that are rarely matched in the social science communities of Spain and Portugal. And it is not random that the departments that are most internationalized in their hires (the Amsterdam Institute for Social Science Research comes to mind) are also institutions that have been particularly well funded in the past and where personal networks extend across the Atlantic divide. The investment of the German government in the creation of centers of excellence (for instance, the Research Center in Social and Cultural Studies in Mainz) is paying off and confirms the value of pursuing such strategies, even if they are sometimes decried as creating (what are already existing) inequalities within academic fields. The alternative is the stagnation of talents, and eventually, the intellectual and institutional decline of fields of study.

This brings me to the touchy issue of peer review, which European academics often associate with neoliberalism and which has generated much condemnation in Europe while being entirely taken for granted in the North American context. Nowhere are the pressures toward the standardization of national academic practices more visible than where and when this topic is raised. Several European countries have joined forces in the NORFACE (New Opportunities for Research Funding Agency Cooperation in Europe) network to adopt similar practices, and some, like Switzerland, have created organizations charged solely with evaluating evaluative practices, but with mixed results. For example, the French Agence d'évaluation de la recherche et de l'enseignement scientifique, was predictably abolished shortly after the Socialists came to power in 2012. While the verdict is still out about the relative success of these enterprises, I believe there may be an emerging consensus that too often European institutions have recourse to quantitative measures to assess quality (the infamous H-index which measures citation rates being the prime example), in a meaningless effort to make evaluation more "objective".

Healthy but evolving

In conclusion, despite a marked decline in the resources put at the disposal of sociologists working in Europe, most importantly by the German Marshall Fund and the Ford Foundation, I would venture to offer that the overall health of the study of Europe by sociologists remains stable. By some measures, at least, that health has even increased thanks to the creation of more intense transnational ties between North American and European professional circles, and to the accelerated development of scholarship in Europe, due to the input of considerable resources by the European Research Council, the Marie Curie Program, and other European sources. Even if our undergraduates are turning their eyes toward the Global South in growing number and fewer students of comparative politics are interested in Europe, in sociology at least we still face a relatively healthy situation.

A final provisional prediction is that the future of North American European studies is likely to depend largely on the capacity of concerned knowledge producers to reinvent their field in unpredictable ways, to the extent that the current state of affairs could not have been foreseen by extrapolating a linear evolutionary model in the production and diffusion of knowledge. Unexpected turns of events and forks in the road, such as Brexit and the rise of populism, are likely to continue to feed interest for years to come.

3

FROM WESTERN CIVILIZATION TO CRITICAL EUROPEAN STUDIES

Hélène B. Ducros and Louie Dean Valencia-García

To better envisage what European studies entails as a field of inquiry, it is useful to delve into the history of area studies and more generally into the ways in which interdisciplinarity has been advocated for and practiced. Buzzword? Field in its own right? Practice? Method? Genre? Discourse? Institutional framework? Subdiscipline? Ideology? Paradigm? Metaphor? Often considered an elusive and undertheorized pedagogy until a few decades ago, today interdisciplinarity has come to feature at the forefront of scholarly endeavors as grantors have increasingly encouraged collaborative projects. Many "area studies" emerged in the post-World War II era, but did not gather full momentum until the 1960s and 1970s when researchers started looking for alternative structures to organize knowledge and knowledge production to create participatory spaces of increased diversity within the university, with a focus on developing social capital as well as bridging the university with society.

To understand the draw toward interdisciplinarity, the latter must be replaced in the context of the compartmentalizing of the academe and disciplinary epistemological commitments that had existed for centuries. An examination of interdisciplinarity also brings the challenging responsibility of defining it. Theorists generally agree about what it is not. Rather than "pluri" or "multi" disciplinarity, which signifies a juxtaposition of the disciplines, "inter" disciplinarity developed into a critical tool to investigate scholarly expertise and offer new knowledge brought about through encounters between various disciplines. The disciplines have emerged over centuries, producing their specific methodologies, objects of studies, scopes, analytical lenses, and values. Likewise, interdisciplinarity produces specific types of knowledge, methods, and scholarly cultures, yielding collaborative networks and communities of practice that rely on social over economic capital. "Studies" can defragment the university, debalkanize departments, and are unbounded, offering needed alternative models and structures to solve complex contemporary problems.

European studies, as a discipline, developed out of the ruins of Western civilization. In the protests of the late 1960s, Western civilization courses largely fell out of fashion because of their often-explicit Eurocentrism – there was a whole world outside of Europe that had largely been ignored. As students and activists of the 1960s called for the end of Western imperialism abroad, and as the United States pushed its interests through a "containment" strategy, which supported the studies of countries outside of Western Europe, scholars of Europe found themselves adrift. What did it mean to study Europe in a postcolonial world embroiled in a cold war?

The CES: a network for knowledge production

The CES was founded in 1970 in response to this disciplinary crisis. The CES promised to serve West European study programs and "encourage wider interests in Western Europe, and particularly in those problems and themes ... common to the advanced industrialized nations of Europe and North America, rather than to encourage the sense of separateness which seems to be an inevitable concomitant of an area approach" (Blank 1974a: 36). In 1974, Stephen Blank, the founding executive director of the CES, published a book-length report titled *Western European Studies in the United States* for the US Department of Health, Education and Welfare's National Institute of Education, in which he described "the 'Eurocentric' character of American higher education" having been "sharply diluted." Despite this, Blank found there was an "extremely fragile" revival of interest in Western Europe (Blank 1974b: i). Furthermore, after the Second World War,

> [n]ew frontiers of research shifted away from Western Europe; resources were mobilized to support new research efforts and to train younger scholars to be specialists on the non-Western world. Existing resources followed new interests in the less known areas of the world and new resources – specifically, those created by the National Defense Education Act – specifically excluded Western Europe.
>
> (Blank 1974b: 5)

Of course, US government support of programs studying the non-Western world was a direct result of the Cold War. However, the creation and growth of the then-European Community (EC) necessitated focusing on the continent; the CES saw Europe as providing "the best laboratory for studying problems associated with the future development of advanced industrial societies" (Blank 1974b: 8).

In November 1974, the *European Labor and Working Class History* newsletter reported the creation of the CES to its readers. Formed by a consortium of US universities with commitments "to bring American students into the study of European society and politics as they are formulating their research interests," the CES intended to "assist and encourage researchers to utilize in comparative studies the wealth of knowledge about Europe, and to help them make contacts with scholars of other disciplines who may share their interests" (Council for European Studies 1974: 40).

From early on, European studies was meant to cultivate new scholars of Europe and to encourage transdisciplinarity. Today, European studies finds itself somewhere between the study of the EU and cultural studies approaches to the continent. However, over the *longue durée*, there still is no consensus as to what constitutes Europe and the precise object of study. Given Europe's history of colonization and the current tensions around global migration, scholars are trying not only to assess how European studies can better incorporate transdisciplinary approaches, but also how more pluralistic attitudes toward what it means to be European can help address those tensions.

Diffusing European studies through public writing

Over the years, the CES has diffused its action through an array of publications – some made available exclusively to its members, others open to anyone with an internet connection. The electronic *CES Newsletter* updates members about CES activities. It diffuses via the CES listserv and constitutes an efficient way to keep abreast of how the institution is evolving, the partnerships being established, the activities of the Research Networks, and other important news from the European studies community.

Wider in its scope and reach, *EuropeNow* has become the CES's flagship online journal. It has come to represent the public face of the CES's mission of interdisciplinarity and represents a clear effort at concretely bridging the disciplines across borders. When *EuropeNow* came about with its first issue in November 2016, it replaced and greatly expanded on *CritCom*, a previous online publication, which had been devoted to "Reviews & Critical Commentary" and was meant as a "forum ... to facilitate the dissemination and assessment of high-quality research on Europe".

EuropeNow's project was founded on the desire to create multidirectional and multiqualitative bridges across the disciplines. But it has also explicitly strived to connect the humanities with social sciences and foster exchanges that may not easily occur across departments and colleges. Its structure also lends itself to the improbable blend between intimate liberal art institutions and large research institutions, especially as it effectively links research with pedagogical methods via its "Campus" section. Further bridges have been built to reach alternative and non-academic sources of knowledge through visual art exhibits. Additionally, *EuropeNow*, in its functioning, has sought to soften academic hierarchies, by encouraging all university constituencies to work together, whether junior or senior academics, students, or administrators, as all play a part in teaching and learning about Europe.

EuropeNow participates in reconfiguring knowledge production about Europe and in drawing in growing numbers scholars who value public writing to give their research a purpose past the "ivory tower". While traditional peer-reviewed journals are uncontestably still of the essence, increasingly researchers look for outlets to reach people more directly and more broadly. *EuropeNow* holds its contributors to academic standards while simultaneously emboldening them to write for a broader public. Reaching a large number of non-specialists enhances research impact and the shared value of universities and substantiates meaning-ful societal engagement. Public writing is not only about reaching communities, but also about including communities in the production of knowledge, especially when the latter is precisely about them.

Keeping it REAL

In his 2019 address to the American Association of Geographers, Derek Alderman – a fervent supporter of hybrid fields such as geo-humanities – proposed to place storytelling at the heart of academic professional responsibility. This would allow researchers to "keep it REAL" (responsive, engaged, advocating, life-improving) in a post-truth world, in which the denial of scientific evidence and the rising cynicism toward universities as institutional centers of knowledge have intensified social vulnerabilities, discriminatory abuses, exclusions and disempowerment.

The CES and *EuropeNow* partake in changing these dynamics, anchored in the vision for an integrated academe around salient European issues and answerable to the call for a reassessment of who we are as intellectuals and more generally of the role and methods of knowledge production in the twenty-first century, whatever our respective discipline or object of study. They provide ways to tell stories, blending genres and approaches to topics with universal human value. They help increase our scholarly footprint, retool our craft, assert our role as public intellectuals, and reposition ourselves as part of the public. Alderman asks us to consider the cost of not telling our story and that of others. In the current European context, these words resonate particularly loudly.

As the CES seeks to inform policy, its core mission has been oriented toward inclusion and collaboration, as well as enhanced and shared pedagogies. The fiftieth anniversary of the CES coincides with both discourses around what it means to be European and the exit of Britain from the EU. Now is a good time to evaluate what the study of Europe has been, and what we mean by "European studies." Today, we need European studies to evolve. We must ask: what might critical European studies look like both pedagogically and as research practice?

4

BEYOND EXCEPTIONALISM IN EUROPEAN STUDIES

Catherine Guisan

Political understanding, which Hannah Arendt defined as the attempt to make oneself at home in the world, has a foundational role for the health of democratic political orders. Being at home in the EU appears a far-fetched idea today. One reason, I argue, is that the EU has experienced multiple founding moments since 1952, reflecting contradictory and ambiguous impulses. Such tensions have not been fully faced even by the founders, hence their inability to explain them.

The field of European studies could do a better a job in helping EU citizens feel at home in the world by drawing from comparative politics and historical approaches. Comparing the EU with other large polities across time and space more systematically would show that setbacks, contradictory moves, and ambiguities are part of political development, and thus need not provoke the castigation of the European project, nor portend its imminent demise. In order to make my case, I need to provide a brief review of European constitutional history before I give a few examples of the comparative approach in this essay's third part.

Historical ambiguities

The 1958 Treaties of Rome establishing the European Economic Community (EEC) and Euratom are regarded as the founding documents of the European integration process. However, little notice is taken of the extent to which these treaties diverge from the principles of the first European Treaty on the European Coal and Steel Community (ECSC) ratified six years earlier. Robert Marjolin, the senior French negotiator of the Rome Treaties, stressed his agnosticism regarding the tension between intergovernmentalism and the so-called Community method, which prioritized shared European interests in the ECSC treaty. The European founders had not been quite as agnostic a few years before.

The 1950 Schuman Declaration proposed that French-German production of coal and steel be placed under a common High Authority, within the framework of an organization open to the participation of the other countries of Europe. On specific policy areas, the ECSC High Authority's decisions would "bind France and Germany and other member countries". In the 1950s, ECSC member states, from France to Italy, were willing to limit their sovereignty in their national constitutions in favor of the Community in order to protect peace. When the ECSC founders decided they wanted more federalism rather than less to master their own security, they proposed a European Defense Community (EDC), flanked by a democratic and representative political community.

After the French National Assembly defeated the French-initiated EDC project in 1954, the chastened leaders of the ECSC member states reopened negotiations: the outcome was the Rome Treaties. The goal of peace remained in the new treaty's preamble. But this time there would be no High Authority, rather a Commission whose ability to impose its decision was much more limited. The Council of Ministers, a powerful intergovernmental legislative body, which had only been added as an afterthought in the ECSC treaty, became the main decision maker. Rather than reconciliation and federalism, the operative word became "compromise", the capacity to understand and accommodate diverse points of view and interests that would inhibit attitudes of isolationism, and domination by force, albeit in a mode which had ceased to be heroic.

The first ECSC secretary-general, Max Kohnstamm, found that the principle of compromise moving Europeans to action during the negotiations over the Treaties of Rome was "horrible", precisely because this term evoked for him the unsuccessful European attempts at balancing power during centuries of war. If there were compromises, they must be institutionalized, he said, otherwise concessions may fall prey to changes in mood. But Kohnstamm was only a silent observer at the negotiations. The EEC treaty's four annexes, 12 protocols, one convention and nine declarations were the legal expression of compromise, an exercise which brought Roberto Ducci, chair of the Institutional Committee writing the treaties, "close to a nervous breakdown", by his own admission. Another 30-hour long discussion decided on the sites of the EEC/Euratom institutions and who would occupy key posts (Guisan 2011: 66–76).

Aspiration for a simpler and more understandable order never vanished, however. The third founding started in earnest in 2001 when the Convention on the Future of Europe and its 105 members, including Turkish representatives, gathered to draft a European Constitutional Treaty. The first 60 pages of the new treaty defined EU norms, institutions, and policies clearly; after reading them, my 25 US honors students drew beautiful multicolored posters, which could be put up on the streets of Europe to inform citizens. Part II, the Charter of Fundamental Rights, was readable as well. Part III, which codified all past EU legislation, was a challenging 200-page text, which excited much controversy in France especially, although its content had long been ratified.

Negative French and Dutch referenda stopped the ratification process in 2005. Yet, rather stealthily, the EU and member states' parliaments succeeded in ratifying the Lisbon Treaty in 2009. Substantially similar in content to the Constitutional Treaty, this latest European treaty constituted a move toward more efficiency in order to accommodate an increasing number of member states, but not toward equality. The word constitution disappeared, and the EU rotating presidency was severely curtailed. Because it consists of amendments to previous treaties rather than a new codification, the Lisbon Treaty is an unreadable text. It was quickly posted on the internet in a "consolidated" form (i.e. rewritten for legibility), but the consolidated text has no legal force.

So, after 60 years of work, successive enlargements to 28 member states, and the near completion of the four freedoms of movement, European integration still rests on an opaque document, which only legal experts can interpret. This has done little to increase political understanding. EU citizens wonder: is the EU a budding federal order, or is it a large trade association? Who should decide on immigration and asylum policies, and on eurozone policies and national budgets?

Comparative politics and historical approaches for more understanding

Approaches developed in comparative politics and in historical research would enhance understanding of the bold European integration project, which was complex from the start and has experienced several founding acts. It is widely acknowledged that looking at one's own situation from an external point of view can bring new insights. But the discipline of European studies has been loath to do this, preferring to discuss the EU as a single case study, with plenty of comparisons within, but few with other large polities. Moreover, the message transmitted by EU public figures is that the EU is "unique", in some cases uniquely undemocratic (understand "bad"), in other cases uniquely peace-making (therefore exceptionally "good"). Rhetoric of the unique and exceptional tends to heat up emotions and undermine possibilities for rational exchanges; the American citizen knows this only too well.

Interestingly, there is a movement in US academia to "de-exceptionalize" the study of American politics and to introduce more comparative studies with other parts of the world. Kathleen Thelen's presidential address to the 2018 American Political Science Association annual meeting, entitled "The American Precariat: US Capitalism in Comparative Perspective", illustrates this trend with a comparative argument relying on Organisation for Economic Co-operation and Development (OECD) statistics on employment and policies in Europe and the US.

European studies would benefit from a turn to more comparative approaches. All 12 chapters of *Europe 2025: A New Agenda*, authored by 12 well-known scholars, discuss the EU as a single case study (Bekemans *et al.* 2019). Is there no way to learn from non-European experiences? One obvious case for comparison is the US. More sustained exchanges between European studies scholars and scholars of Indian and Chinese politics may also be fruitful for all concerned, although this is not an argument I have the space or expertise to develop here. But why not ask the following questions, and more.

Is the disaffection of European citizens, as manifested in the low turnout for elections to the European Parliament, unusual? Or is it quite typical of large democracies? What can be learned from what other large polities do, from the US to India, to address popular lack of engagement?

Is it abnormal or normal for a complex political constellation to undergo several founding moments? Eric Foner discusses the Thirteenth, Fourteenth, and Fifteenth Amendments to the US Constitution as a "second founding" (Foner 2019). Some US commentators even write of a third founding in the mid-1960s. Should the EU be critiqued because it failed to found itself once and for all, or are successive founding acts typical of most contemporary democracies? How have other polities overcome constitutional ambiguities and contradictions? At what cost? With what benefit?

In conclusion, exchanging best and worst practices matters, and it need not involve only scholars specialized in policy-making. For bold new ideas, let's move beyond the single case study and European exceptionalism.

5

DIVERSITY OR UNITY? THE ROLE OF CULTURE IN EUROPEAN STUDIES

Simon Fink and Lars Klein

If we follow the Humboldtian ideal, then teaching should derive from research. Our chapter argues that one of the reasons that Europe and the EU are hard to communicate to students is that we have a violation of this Humboldtian ideal. We have a mismatch between teaching and research in European studies, especially as concerns the role of culture. We take the notion of culture as our starting point, because it is a "softer" notion than, for example, economic or political institutions. While there are ample debates about the working of European economic or political institutions, at least for the most part, scholars agree on their basic properties. Not so with culture. Culture is an interdisciplinary topic that attracts many students to European studies programs, but it is even harder to pinpoint and research than economic or political institutions. Culture has long been understood as a difficult phenomenon. Some scholars understand culture to be made, claimed for political reasons, changing, and hybridized. Others consider it as fixed, or at least as a common basis for actions, motivation, and communication.

We argue that in European studies teaching, culture is often used to denote commonalities among European societies. Many master's programs emphasize (and advertise) that they teach a "common European culture". European studies scholarship, however, often emphasizes and researches variation between different national cultures. Our chapter explores this phenomenon and offers advice on how to deal with the paradoxical mismatch between teaching and research.

Teaching: one European culture, source of unity

Many European studies programs have the idea of one European culture in their title or in their teaching program. A quick browsing of the relevant websites is instructive: The Ruhr-Universität Bochum offers the Master's in European

Culture and Economy that sees Europe "as a cultural space". Similarly, the Master's of European Culture at Kent University "makes it possible to study the history, literature, and political philosophies of the continent" and has modules like "The Idea of Europe". The Master's in Cultural History of Modern Europe at Utrecht University conceptualizes European history as one shared cultural history. The Erasmus mundus Master's in European Literary Cultures at Bologna has a unit called "European History and Civilization" and one of the program's main educational goals is that a graduate "know[s] the history and culture of Europe in order to contextualize the literary production in the broader context of European cultural history". The Master's program *Interdisziplinäre Europastudien* (Interdisciplinary European Studies) at the University of Augsburg serves as a last example to support our argument. As elective part students can choose the track "European Cultural History", which includes seminars like "Europa: Idee und Geschichte eines Kulturraums" (Europe: Idea and History of a Cultural Space).

There are plausible reasons for this focus. First, the normative idea is appealing. If Europe wants to build a peaceful and prosperous continent, it needs citizens who have a pan-European outlook. The universities – and European studies programs – are one of the major places where these citizens may form. That is also one of the reasons why the European Commission funds several of these study programs with its Erasmus mundus program. The whole idea is to weaken national worldviews, or at least complement them with pan-European perspectives. Second, the European-culture-idea is appealing for students from outside Europe. In terms of marketing a program, it is a good selling proposition to offer "the whole of Europe" to students from, for example, the US or China. Third, the idea of a common European culture can also give coherence to interdisciplinary programs. Academia is a highly specialized endeavor, and if an interdisciplinary program is to work, it needs some "glue" to keep the different disciplines together. The idea that different disciplines work – at the end of the day – on the same cultural entity, is an attractive kind of glue.

In sum, European studies teaching often emphasizes a common European history and identity, a common purpose, and cultural commonalities. Further political and economic integration, then, seem to be the logical consequence.

Scholarship: many cultures, source of conflict

However, in scholarship there is currently very little emphasis on cultural commonalities. This is partly because of the crises that hit Europe: Brexit, the strains to European solidarity during the financial crisis and the refugee crisis, and the rise of populism in many member states demonstrate that the EU is built on a technocratic compromise, but not supported by a strong common European identity. The "permissive consensus" that has long fostered European integration has broken down. For a long time, European integration was an elite project, not much politicized in domestic debates. This has changed – for the good, as many analysts argue. Empirical analyses point out that in many European countries cultural issues now form the most salient cleavage. Today, questions of European integration, often framed as "European integration versus national identity and national sovereignty" dominate domestic debates.

In European studies, culture is seen as a distinctly national phenomenon. For much of scholarship, European culture is "the cultures of Europe", only very seldom a "common European culture". To some extent, this may be a sign of methodological nationalism. The EU is often analyzed in its own right. If we zoom out, commonalities of European culture might be more readily discernible. However, painting with a very broad brush, for mainstream European studies, the EU is a project of political and economic harmonization, built upon a culturally heterogeneous continent. More and more, different national "cultures" are politicized, often to the detriment of European integration. From the perspective of European studies – which have had an integrationist bias since their inception – culture is thus something that has only recently been put on the table as a major force threatening European integration.

Conclusions: how to bridge the divide?

Our analysis started from the argument that the Humboldtian ideal does not apply to the role of culture in European studies. Teaching is concerned with the unity of a European culture; research is concerned with the diversity of European cultures. While there may be some hyperbolism in the argument – not all studies programs emphasize a common European culture, not all research is only concerned with variation – we think we have put our finger on a major phenomenon.

Is this discrepancy between research and teaching a problem? We think, yes. If students witness a discrepancy between the marketing claims that advertise European studies programs, and the research papers that they read, they may become disengaged and question the purpose of their studies.

The first obvious solution to this problem is to market European studies programs differently. If there currently is no common European identity to research, then study programs cannot claim to teach about this common European identity.

The second solution is to redirect research efforts. If the alleged lack of a common European identity is caused by the limited research perspective (for example, by a lack of studies researching Europe in comparison to other world regions or taking small scale and bottom-up perspectives), then reorienting research practices might find the European identity that the study programs purport to teach.

The third solution – which is our favorite – is to use this tension between teaching and research to start a fruitful dialogue between research and teaching. The research perspective – different domestic cultures as a problem for integration – seems to have diagnostic power to explain what is currently happening. The array of crises that have hit the EU and its reaction to them – or rather the different national reactions to them – have demonstrated that we indeed lack a European identity or norms of European solidarity. Thus, the research perspective may explain why Europe is in crisis, and why political and economic integration at once seems so fragile, given the lack of a cohesive culture.

The perspective taken in teaching, on the other hand, may be better suited to show us a way out of the crises and to shape the future of Europe. A more cohesive European identity might not be the precondition for a more stable and crisis-proof European political project, but broadening perspectives on culture is one way to challenge ideas of national cultures understood in exclusive ideological ways. It also helps to problematize rather than presuppose cultural underpinnings of Europeanization processes. If this tension is highlighted in European studies programs – empirical research results meeting more or less implicit normative aspirations – both European studies teaching and research can only profit.

6

THE HORIZONS OF EUROPEAN CULTURE
Randall Halle

Cultural union, along with economic and political union, is one of the aspirations of the EU. From the first gatherings in Switzerland to the Cultural Resolution, with which the 1948 Congress of Europe in The Hague ended, discussions of cultural unity and cultural renewal dominated the postwar European project. In these considerations, the "founding fathers" of the EU were anything but the small-step bureaucrats they are often painted to be. In 1958, looking back on his first year as the first president of the Commission of the EEC, Walter Hallstein set forward his vision for the EC. In "The Unity of European Culture and the Policy of Uniting Europe", he presented a clear statement on the role of culture in the European project, placing a commonality of culture as the foundation for political and economic aspirations.

In fact, Hallstein suggested that the question of culture is more important than the aspirations of the ECSC or Euratom, which had no possibility of inspiring the populace to commit to the common European project. He echoed in this speech ideas expressed similarly by Robert Schuman, Paul-Henri Spaak, Alcide de Gasperi, Altiero Spinelli, and Winston Churchill. Jacques Delors in 1985, following in Hallstein's footsteps, set forward a cultural policy agenda during his first speech as the head of the European Commission:

> The culture industry will tomorrow be one of the biggest industries, a creator of wealth and jobs. Under the terms of the Treaty we do not have the resource to implement a cultural policy; but we are going to try to tackle it along economic lines ... We have to build a powerful European culture industry that will enable us to be in control of both the medium and its content, maintaining our standards of civilization and encouraging the creative people amongst us.   (Shore 2000: 46)

Yet culture, European culture, and the processes of European cultural unionization have received relatively little attention. The focus on European politics and economics has overshadowed research on European culture.

The importance of culture

A focus on culture is important at this moment during which the European project is fractured: the UK is heading out into the Atlantic, Turkey is aimed eastward, a Eurasian geopolitical trench opens up from the Baltics to the Bosporus, and an EU border regime turns the Mediterranean into a mass grave. It seems to be a moment of disorientation and drift in which culture and cultural difference seem to counter any ideals of European union. We need critical histories and cultural analysis that remind us that the European project has never been one of unanimity but one of fits and starts. The consolidation and expansion of the EU from 1992 to 2008 has led many to forget that long periods of stagnation and Eurosclerosis preceded the happy decade.

Scholars trained to study culture largely receive that training in national disciplines with roots in nineteenth-century nation-building projects. And in some ways "Europe" does not help overcome the national focus. It is not easily possible to identify a common European culture; the cultures of Europe have remained largely organized by often contradictory parcels of national, regional, and local identification. Hence the EU has come to focus on a shared production of culture, and increasingly at the EU level the project of cultural Europeanization has fulfilled Delors' vision, constituting a conscious political or policy project to produce a common European cultural industry.

In 2013, the EU rolled out the Creative Europe Program as the centerpiece of this initiative. The Creative Europe Program received an initial budget of €1.46 billion, representing a 9 per cent increase in cultural funding combined. The new program set out to employ 300,000 artists across the EU, publish 5,500 books, distribute 1,000 films, and benefit 2,500 cinemas. This project could appear as a grand European-scale undertaking, but precisely the people who research culture generally approach such models with critical skepticism, seeing them as part of a neoliberal model of the culture industry: culture for profit and not for a critical public sphere.

To be sure Europe is not the EU. The idea of Europe has a longer history than the 60-plus years since the founding of the Commission. And importantly, historians have developed a new approach to Europe as a result of the turn to transnational and global historiography. In attending to a *long durée* they have learned to separate the European project from the specific institutional and party configurations of the EU. Historians like Konrad Jarausch, Tony Judt, Sharon Macdonald, Klaus Kiran Patel, or Kaja Širok have moved from older models that treated European history as a history of European states and have come to approach Europe as a dynamic discourse, not a place but a process – Europeanization. They reveal Europeanization as a long history. It is a history inflected by specificities of place and socio-cultural questions in which the nation state has been a central actor, but along with forces distinct from the nation state and from the EU, a greater complexity of connections on global horizons. They show the European ideal as a complex ideal that is as much a vector for domination as for unification. But at this moment of European disunion these historians note that, just as Europeanization has "outlasted" various empires, states, and wars, Europe will surely outlast crises in the EU's institutional-political formations. Looking back, we can look forward and rest assured that if the EU ceased to exist tomorrow, Europe would not, and the European project would continue.

Humanist research has further underscored how cultural union has played an important but rather varied role in the strivings toward greater European union. In 1799, Novalis's speech "Christendom or Europe" set the tone for considerations of a new form of what we could describe as cultural union on the European continent, part of a process which Paul Michael Lützeler has described as continentalization, the coming into self-awareness of Europe as a continent. But to this we can add that European culture extends well beyond the borders of the EU and well beyond the borders of the continent.

The extent of Europe

The project of Europeanization that emerged in the postwar period is one of a long, varied, broken, and contested set of European projects, including imperial and colonial domination of vast parts of the globe. If the EU ceased to exist, Europe and European culture would continue to exist, and would exist without regard to the borders drawn by Frontex or nationalist-populist politicians. If we point here to horizons of cultural complexity beyond the Schengen Zone, nevertheless the EU has transformed the meaning of Europe and the significance of European culture inside and outside its borders. And the EU's efforts to rethink national relations have actually called forth exactly those new European histories, drawing out new assessments of the age of empire, the history of global migration, the dynamic of bourgeois revolutions, the industrial age, the age of enlightenment, and the like.

Looking back over the long history of theoretical and practical debates around European integration, we note that they extend well back before the interbellum and go well beyond the need to integrate peoples in polities or open tariff boundaries in Europe; and that cultural production and criticism were central to the transformations in that long history. Indeed, the very name Europe, with its roots in mythology, points to the centrality of creative imagining in the production of a European cultural collective. European artists and cultural producers like Novalis have been intimately involved in Europeanization, even before there was even a scientific concept of continents. With *Le patrimoine littéraire européen*, Jean-Claude Polet has produced a 17-volume collection covering three millennia with over 1,400 authors and 5,300 texts, a project understood as testifying to this progressive synthesis of European culture. Bożena Chołuj has charted how in the modern era the European ideal inspired Central and Eastern European authors in a long struggle against feudalism, absolutist imperialism, and totalitarianism for a liberal middle-class political order.

The strivings for Europe inspired Polish and other Central Europeans in their own struggles. Names like Czesław Miłosz, Vaclav Havel, Milan Kundera, and Györgi Konrád represented during the Cold War Polish, Czech, and Hungarian authors who turned to a European continent as aspirational unity. Their work asserted a belonging of their nations to the culture of Europe that sublated the East and West divides. Europe was for them an ideal of national self-determination – a point well worth recalling in the current East–West divide. What we see in these projects is that Europe – the discourse of Europe – moved forwards over long centuries, not primarily as a political or economic project in clear continental borders, but as an idea and ideal of cultural producers, contested and conflictual.

Europe beyond the EU

While it may be possible for social scientists and economists to consider European economies and polities through the constrictions of the Schengen Zone borders, a narrow focus on this EU would force us to approach European culture within untenable constraints. Would we exclude Russia as a part of European culture? Would Algeria, once a department of France, a founding territory of the EEC well before Spain and Portugal joined, suddenly drop off a European cultural map? Or in reverse, what about French Guiana or Réunion, distant from the European continent but nevertheless EU territory? Do we exclude from considerations of European culture a world shaped by European colonialism: the US, Australia, India, South Africa, Hong Kong, the Dutch Antilles, the Philippines, and on and on? And how would we incorporate the Treaty of Rome's plan for Eurafrica into our understanding of European culture (Hansen & Jonsson 2014)? Europe's complex connectivity would be lost from our consideration of Europe's cultures. The European project urgently requires scholars who explore Europe not as (only) the EU, nor as a given place, but rather as a historical discourse, a contested space, a debated term, an idea with ideal goals and often fatal consequences.

What direction does European culture take in the future, in this moment of disunion and particularity? From the perspective of cultural producers, the contemporary EU Creative Europe Program can seem largely an economic project that leaves them behind. This obtains as much for cosmopolitan internationalist authors who experienced themselves as left out of the postwar West European project, as it does for once pro-European Central European authors. Many of them after the Cold War and after ascension similarly switched to EU-skeptical work. Still, in the midst of economic crisis and political disunion, some authors and artists like writer Robert Menasse, poet Yannis Stiggas, or filmmaker Maren Ade are ready to operate in the space the transnational union has opened up for cultural production. These artists are able to address the negative impacts of European unionization and voice a demand for a different European culture. Such work points most importantly toward European culture enjoying a critical coming into its own on horizons that go well beyond the borders of the EU and well beyond the borders of the continent; a critical coming into its own based in the fullness of historical contestations, struggles of territory, discourses of domination, and an appreciation of the complex connectivity that is European culture.

7

WELCOME TO THE "FAMILY": INTEGRATION, IDENTITY, AND INCLUSIVITY IN EUROPEAN STUDIES

Sarah Cooper and Koen Slootmaeckers

The semi-centennial anniversary of the CES provides an exciting moment to take stock of 50 years of cutting-edge work and illuminates a particular success story for the ever-expanding field of gender and sexuality research. Arriving to the scholarly party far later than areas concerned with integration or political economy for example, and frustratingly still perceived in some quarters as a highly specialized, or more dismissively "niche", denomination of the social sciences, the abundance of activity in this area is now undeniable and a vibrant academic community prevails.

Established in 2011, the CES's very own Gender and Sexuality Research Network (GSRN) is just one example of this. With a membership spanning all stages of academic careers, from doctoral candidates through professors, the scholarship in this network provides a vibrant range of insights to European studies. Topics covered in our network are too many to list but include gendered+ approaches to European integration and disintegration; lesbian, gay, bisexual, transgender (LGBT) equality; the intersections between race, religion, and sexuality; and European reproductive health policies. Among a variety of endeavors that are fostered throughout the year across the network, the CES's annual conference showcases this growing presence, as was demonstrated in the 2019 conference in Madrid where no fewer than 32 panels in one way or another engaged with gender and sexuality research. The pathway to acceptance of activities with such a focus has been a long and often fractious road, however, and while it is a pertinent moment to join in the momentous celebrations for CES, the development of research and teaching in this domain must be duly noted to ensure positive growth. The arduous process of integration is a helpful point at which to begin this reflection.

The rebellious step-child

Gradual reconstitution of familial norms that erode the dominant heteronormative, two-parent family, and challenge the established binary, is a creeping and ever-evolving societal trend, and one that provides a helpful and appropriate analogy for this burgeoning research agenda. The study of gender first pervaded the academic landscape as a rebellious step-child of European studies and the social sciences, keen to challenge the patriarchal values entrenched in academia to that date. Unsurprisingly encountering teething problems around integration at this beginning stage, scholarship that sought to use gender as an analytical tool faced conservative backlash, and the academic pursuit of feminism waged a tough battle for respect from its newly acquired siblings. This attempted marginalization of gender studies to the edges of the discipline is perhaps mostly clearly elucidated by the scarce opportunities to publish gender work, and limited engagement of the mainstream discipline with insights originating from gender studies more generally; such astute observation was importantly published in a recent editorial for the *European Journal of Politics and Gender* (Ahrens *et al.* 2018). There are, however, also many encouraging steps worthy of note and signal new skills of cohabitation.

Home to the *European Journal of Politics and Gender*, the European Conference on Gender and Politics, for example, is now in its tenth year and proudly fosters attendance from over 40 countries, spanning five continents. Similarly, institutions globally have established interdisciplinary research units to promote such work "in-house" and integrate these issues into undergraduate and postgraduate teaching; Cambridge University fosters a collaboration across 20 of its departments through its Gender Research Centre, for example, with Bristol, Edinburgh, and Essex similarly endorsing such projects across the UK. Furthermore, the Vilnius University Gender Studies Centre is the first of its kind in the Baltic States, and the Czech Centre for Gender and Science has strong advocacy engagement at the EU level, to name just a few examples.

Encouraging response to these gender-centric initiatives has also been elicited from more mainstream avenues, and journals with a broader discipline approach have followed suit with the commissioning of special issues concerning gender and sexuality. A few instances across international journals include *Public Money and Management*'s forthcoming "Gender in an Uncertain Public Sector" (2020) edition, and *Social Science*'s "Gender and STEM: Understanding Segregation in Science, Technology, Engineering and Mathematics" (2016). A need to remain vigilant to the continued success of this family unit is, however, constant, and contemporary threats have emerged from powerful, external quarters.

Opposition and identity

Unsettling challenges which threaten to undermine and halt (if not destroy) the momentum of gender and sexuality studies is certainly a worrying trend to arise in recent years. The strengthening of anti-gender mobilization which seeks to demonize gender studies in order to oppose LGBT and gender equality and reinforce their heteronormative worldviews clearly demonstrate these efforts (Kuhar & Paternotte 2018). Such opposition does not only come from civil society and some far-right political parties, but also from some state institutions. In 2018, for example, the Hungarian government announced its intention to abolish accredited gender studies programs in the country. Although agreeing that current activities at this level would last the duration, it was later confirmed that no state-funded social gender programs would be launched moving forwards. In defense, the government expressed its belief that their actions would not restrict freedom of academic expression, but rather that gender studies could find a place in other academic fields or be taught in universities operated by foundations.

To a network such as ours, and undoubtedly finding support beyond our members, this suggestion that gender studies move elsewhere appears a clear retrograde step for the discipline, however, and relegates the distinct stream of study to an inferior denomination of adjacent academic clusters. Furthermore, the nurturing of the next generation of gender and sexuality scholars is directly impinged, with the ability to experience specialized and often research-led teaching in the area heavily restricted. Although the severe action is as of yet confined to a handful of countries, it is an example, although directed at the specific family unit of gender and sexuality scholars, of a much wider trend in which right-wing populist or (semi-)authoritarian regimes seek to limit the freedom of academic expression and thus silence dissident voices.

While gender studies therefore continues to develop and defend its bond within the family of European studies – albeit as one of a disruptive, vocal and, at times, rebellious teenager – it has additionally faced internal questions surrounding its own identity. The first of these challenges involved the scope of intended inquiry within the subdiscipline and was presented alongside the arrival of sexuality studies. Promoting the study of a range of diverse topics, and the addition of new scholars with differing perspectives, the meshing of these two overlapping areas is not always entirely smooth, and a co-productive conversation can be difficult to achieve. Yet, one can also observe a growing recognition of their mutual interests in challenging the dominant power structure in society, as is clearly shown by the composition of the GSRN and, more acutely, in the running of panels.

The inclusive nature of gender and sexuality research has been further criticized, however, for a problematic binary preoccupation of self-identified feminists who seek to exclude trans* experiences and voices. Reported in the media as a "bitter feud", the internal factions garner much zealous attention from outside and serve to cause attrition to the united family front. Such displays of transphobia and exclusionary practices must be resisted if we want to succeed in building our alternative, blended, and non-normative family. As such, important lessons of equality and respect must be drawn (including for our own research network), so that the gender and sexuality research community can embrace and respect the important diversity of the work of its members.

Inclusivity as priority

Thus, despite the notion of family traditionally envisaged along heteronormative, binary, and conservative lines, its analogous value for us lies in the slow erosion of this perception and the evolving priorities of inclusivity. The challenge for society is not to disband the positive relationships and interconnections that can flourish within the created title of "family", but to expand beyond the harmful, exclusionary, and limited categorization that the term often represents. This has been mirrored in the field of European studies, and gender and sexuality, although confrontational, abrasive, and even rowdy across its members, is quietly pleased to sit with its academic relatives. And while the gender studies community continues its mission to challenge the normative preconceptions on the composition of what a family entails, it has been encouraged by growing acceptance, support, and interdisciplinary projects across its siblings and a fruitful and an important knowledge base is growing as a result. Despite outside attacks of its continued viability in higher education, therefore, the bonds that have been created in the scholarly landscape happily retain the familial value of loyalty, and the flourishing CES gender studies research network is a clear product of the desire of researchers in this field to push the agenda forwards for the next 50 years, but also their ability to successfully do so when supported by peers.

8

UNEXPECTED EUROPEANISTS: BUILDING A NEW CADRE FOR EUROPEAN STUDIES

William Collins Donahue and Martin Kagel

It is no secret that European studies has suffered a setback in the academy. Maligned in some quarters as the superannuated practice of "Eurocentrism", or glibly sidelined in others as mere "area studies", the field has clearly slipped from its once prominent place among institutional priorities. How can we revive and sustain a vibrant interest in European societies among those in higher education who have, over time, succumbed to the notion that Europe is passé? The answer, in our opinion, lies not only in making the ongoing argument for the topicality of Europe – which is implicit in all our work – so much as in developing institutional strategies that provide concrete incentives for students and faculty to engage with it.

The "unexpected Europeanists" of our title are, on the one hand, faculty whose research interests include unlikely or unacknowledged investments in European studies, and on the other, students who may be eager to include European studies in their curriculum, but have not yet been offered flexible curricular options that draw meaningful connections to their primary disciplines. Thus, while we would always welcome new faculty hires and fully declared undergraduate majors in the area of European studies, we focus here upon raising interest in Europe among current colleagues and students whose primary interests lie – or appear to lie – elsewhere.

Recognizing that without students there is little point to an enhanced European studies faculty, we propose a two-pronged approach. To cultivate the undergraduate base at both Georgia and Notre Dame, we have in collaboration with other colleagues created new and flexible undergraduate curricula featuring "transnational European studies". At the University of Georgia, Benjamin Ehlers and Martin Kagel introduced a transnational European studies minor; at the University of Notre Dame, Heather Stanfiel, and William Donahue have introduced a transnational European studies major with multiple points of entry. To foster broader-based faculty interest, we offer an annual interdisciplinary,

Berlin-based seminar that convenes a vertically integrated group of scholars ranging from advanced graduate students to established senior scholars. The structure of this seminar is distinctive in that it is not built around the traditional presentation of papers or lengthy lectures by invited speakers; rather it takes the form of collective inquiry requiring all participants to engage guest presenters as well as each other. Weeks before hitting the ground in Berlin, participants receive books and online material to prepare for the seminar, a prerequisite that both facilitates substantive discussions and creates common reference points.

Interdisciplinary experiential learning

The Berlin Seminar in transnational European studies, which we have together with our colleague Nicholas Allen jointly hosted since 2018, is a week-long residential summer seminar that brings together a total of 20 faculty and graduate students from our two institutions, the University of Notre Dame and the University of Georgia. Participants hail from many different disciplines, including language and culture (English, French, German, Russian, Italian), the social sciences (history, psychology, political science, international affairs), and the so-called area studies units (such as Latin American studies and Africana studies), as well as fields such as architecture and journalism. The breadth and variety are deliberate, signaling an inclusive strategy meant to broaden the base of European studies faculty and to promote both the importance of the immediate subject matter and strengthen longer-term institutional support for European studies.

In addition to drawing upon site-specific activities in Berlin, the seminar, which is structured largely as an extended conversation, explores a variety of perspectives on European politics and culture. The opportunity to spend a fully funded week in one of Europe's liveliest capitals with colleagues from diverse fields of study, confronting topics that range widely from juridical to environmental to the fine arts, has had the distinct effect of energizing European studies on our home campuses, where conversations and activities continue well after the conclusion of the week in Berlin.

In our seminar, the concept of the transnational, which principally refers to the migration of ideas, people, goods, capital, and services across national boundaries, as well as to national identities and literatures that are constituted by (and constitutive of) more than one culture, replaces a traditional comparative approach to understanding European societies with a relational one. Admittedly, the term has sometimes been criticized for concealing negative developments often attributed to "globalization" by substituting it with the ostensibly less offensive, and more objective-sounding "transnational." To us, however, the concept of the transnational functions as an emancipatory notion – crucial to our outreach to diverse faculty – signaling an interest in dynamic cultural relation-ships. Furthermore, it calls attention to the presence of Europe outside European borders and to "non-European" people and cultures within Europe.

The concept of the transnational is, finally, a shorthand way of capturing both the constant and dynamic aspects of European studies: "Europe" is both bounded by and in constant, animated dialogue with non-European cultures. It is precisely this dynamic quality at the core of the seminar that makes it rele-vant to scholars who may not have understood themselves as "Europeanists." As one colleague put it: "The Seminar's transnational methodology demonstrated to me that the boundaries of modern Europe, as in the early modern period, have been permeable and open to debate and disputation, cutting across lines of race, religion, language, ethnicity, identity, and geography." Looking at the flow of Turkish immigrants to Germany – and Syrian refugees to Europe more broadly – one scholar of American studies, for example, found in Europe an essential case study on ethnic minorities. Another participant, a scholar princi-pally of hemispheric American studies, learned that the largest economy in the world (the EU free trade zone) can well "serve as a template for engaging other regions of the globe."

Unexpected Europeanists

Recognizing the transnational in European studies is thus central to our effort to build broader faculty interest both in the annual seminar and in the field itself. By highlighting such dynamic cultural exchanges, we are better able to make clear to our colleagues how their current work may connect to Europe in mean-ingful ways. To illustrate the point, one participant, a sinologist by training, has discovered he has to think in a more deliberate manner about European studies than he has thus far in his career because of the scale of Chinese investments in Europe. Another, a specialist in Latin American literature and culture, noted that "it is too easy to conceive of your area studies in isolation", looking to Europe solely for historical connections, when, in fact, following the seminar, he is now able "not only to appreciate, but also to articulate the many points of contact between Europe and the Americas".

It is not only the case that participants in the seminar discover unexpected connections to their own, ostensibly non-European research. The opposite is true as well: colleagues drawn to transnational European studies because of apparent commonalities (such as the rise of populism and migration "threats" both in the US and Europe) learn in the course of our discussions to make important distinctions, and to resist easy equations and projections from the ostensibly familiar (the US case) to the less well known about Europe.

Examples of "unexpected Europeanists" can be found easily on both our campuses. For some colleagues – such as the young theologian who recently completed a dissertation on ancient forms of rhetoric (comparing the parable to the fable) – the attraction to transnational European studies was the opportunity to move out of a specialty field and connect to larger, topical issues that will equip them to teach more broadly in an undergraduate humanities curriculum.

Our Berlin Seminar has the explicit ambition of cultivating this practical dimension: faculty and graduate students are given the opportunity to place their research and teaching in a broader context and are then asked, at the conclusion of the seminar, how this interdisciplinary community may have altered their practice. One participant, a historian of contemporary Ireland, reports that her teaching on public memorials, informed originally by Irish and US-American examples, benefited immensely from an array of cases originating in Central and Eastern Europe. She is now in the process of developing a new course on "public memorials as sites of contested histories" that will take Hungary and Lithuania as her case studies. It is fair to say the seminar has had its greatest immediate impact in the area of teaching, as is the case with one of the PhD student participants about to go on the job market. He noted that the seminar has helped him "to rework various phases of the survey course" he was teaching that fall, and to sharpen his "comprehension of Transnational History, a talent [he is] already putting to use as [he hits] the job market this year".

A new sense of community

The seminar has already fostered a new sense of community and scholarly solidarity on both of our campuses. Alumnae of the program meet spontaneously or in new study groups and are more willing to offer courses in the area of transnational European studies, or to include transnational European studies within current offerings. As one alumnus commented, "what surprised me the most was how many people from different departments at my home institution [Georgia] and from Notre Dame I was able to connect with, which I believe will lead to international collaboration going forward". In the respective transnational European studies undergraduate offerings at each of our institutions, this enhanced faculty engagement with Europe finds a welcoming student audience. While space does not permit further discussion here, it is crucial that returning faculty have an infrastructure on their home campus that provides a curricular framework for their new or revived interest in Europe. In this way – one that we think may be replicable at other colleges and universities – we have set out on the long-term journey of reviving European studies by creating a new cadre of unexpected Europeanists.

9

EUROPE PAST, PRESENT, AND FUTURE: CHANGING GOVERNANCE IN HIGHER EDUCATION

Beverly Barrett

Launching the Bologna Process in 1999 was a significant moment or achievement for Europe that continues to impact the present and future of the EU, and beyond, including 48 total participating countries. When this momentum jump-started on 19 June 1999 in the medieval university city in Italy, it was a year after the Sorbonne Declaration meeting of France, Germany, Italy, and the UK's ministers of education in Paris on 25 May 1998. At the time, there were 15 members of the EU, and the Cold War had been over for nearly a decade. A driving purpose of the Bologna Process and the European Higher Education Area (EHEA) was to complement the economic opportunity provided by the EU single market, as the EU would expand to the east in the next two decades. By providing a harmonized structure for academic degrees, quality assurance, and a framework for recognition of qualifications, the creation of an EHEA facilitates the mobility of graduates and researchers across the region of Europe.

This chapter sketches the historical evolution of higher education policy in Europe since the origins of integration in forming the EU following World War II. An assessment of higher education policy in Europe through the years provides a launching point from which to analyze the political and economic dimensions in the global governance of knowledge as well as the soft power influence of this initiative. Despite the differences in their economic, political, and social circumstances, the 28 countries in the EU and the 20 additional countries that have become participating members of the EHEA share educational values inherent in the Bologna Process. Each country must adopt the European Cultural Convention, which was ratified by the Council of Europe in 1954, to accede to the Bologna Process. The internalization of policies has led to new institutional frameworks, at the national and regional levels of higher education. Since the EHEA, created by the Bologna Process, is the largest regional integration scheme for higher education in the world, there are lessons to apply to higher education coordination efforts in other regions of the world.

Three periods of historical analysis in regional integration

This history of integration in European higher education can be broken into three periods: from the Treaty of Rome to the launch of the Bologna Process (1957–99); from the launch of the Bologna Process to the creation of the EHEA (1999–2010); and from the creation of the EHEA into the second decade of the Bologna Process (2010–present). The six original countries of the EU – Belgium, France, Germany, Italy, Luxembourg, and the Netherlands – that signed the Treaty of Rome propelled the regional integration that has enlarged over decades. Walter Hallstein, then West German foreign minister and later the first European Commission president, led the dialogue in the 1955 meeting at Messina (Corbett 2005: 17, 25). The European University Institute (EUI) was founded in 1972, the first action program in higher education was announced in 1976, and the Erasmus program was inaugurated in 1987.

The links between Erasmus and the 1986 Single European Act (SEA) are close in time and in supporting the notion of a single Europe. The SEA set the European common market in motion, establishing the single market in by 1993. Among the four freedoms of the common market, for goods, services, capital, and movement of labor or people, the movement of labor has particular relevance for graduates and for higher education policy in the single market and neighboring countries. The same year that the SEA was ratified, the Mediterranean countries of Portugal and Spain joined the EC. Greece had joined five years prior, and there were 12 total EEC countries by 1986. These three Mediterranean countries were emerging from four decades of authoritarian rule. Their educational systems gained greater institutional autonomy as the countries democratized across functions of domestic policy. Erasmus complemented and strengthened that evolution.

Between 1999 and 2010, attitudes shifted from optimism for European integration to skepticism for the grand experiment of European integration; that process accelerated further owing to the global financial crisis from 2007 to 2009. The introduction of the Bologna Process in 1999 occurred the same year that 11 countries in Europe formed an Economic and Monetary Union (EMU). Both developments created a sense of anticipation and enthusiasm about the European project (Cappano & Piattoni 2011). This enthusiasm spread rapidly from west to east, particularly in the context of higher education. The post-communist countries that joined the EU in 2004, 2007, and 2013 were eager to join the knowledge society (without restrictions on areas of academic inquiry) that was being constructed by the Bologna Process. The educational values and practices of Western Europe were attractive to the aspiring member states.

By 2010, the EHEA had been established legally, with national legislation having ratified the new three-tier degree structure of bachelor, master, and doctoral degrees. The national quality assurance agencies were established in the participating countries. This expanded the opportunities for educational exchanges and recognition, moving beyond the academic semester or a year in Erasmus to the recognition of the entire academic degree as indicative of the internationalization in effect.

The Bologna Process also provides the background for understanding the emphasis on indicators for higher education attainment in the Europe 2020 economic growth strategy. In 2010, the European Commission announced, as part of Europe 2020, the benchmark objective of 40 per cent higher education attainment for those between 30 and 34 years old. Additional indicators and benchmarks in the economic growth strategy have been developed in research innovation, employability, social cohesion, and climate sustainability. The Bologna Process provides a new architecture for governance of higher education, and it challenges and expands traditional notions of the state role in knowledge policies (related to research and development and innovation) in the region of Europe and beyond. According to the European Commission, approximately 9 million people have been served in Erasmus through the 2014–20 multiannual financial framework (MFF). The commitment will endure through the next MFF budget 2021–7 with additional funding support for up to 12 million total students through that period.

Global model for internationalization of higher education

The Bologna Process is large enough, in the ideological sense, to accommodate various higher educational traditions from across countries and leaves prerogative on content with the institutions. The criteria put forward by the Bologna Process – on harmonizing credits and degree structure, quality assurance, and recognition across countries – while demanding, are not as stringent as to restrict higher education institutions from continuing to develop in line with national traditions and objectives. The Maastricht Treaty, Article 23 Chapter 6, recognizes, "the responsibility of the member states for the content of teaching and the organization of education systems and their cultural and linguistic diversity". The Bologna Process continues to impact the region of Europe and other world regions that can learn from its example of international cooperation and institutional change in establishing a common framework for the mutual recognition of higher education qualifications.

Higher education institutions have evolved as agents for change in the global economy as well (Barrett 2017). The 1972 founding of the EUI in Fiesole near Florence, Italy is an example of European policy entrepreneurship in higher education (Corbett 2005). The purpose has been to establish a world-class institution to study the region's history, its integration through the years, and its future in world affairs. Biannually the ministers of education meet to review and to establish further objectives at the EHEA Ministerial Conferences. Invited observer participants, including from countries in the Association of South East Asian Nations, Mercosur, and the Pacific Alliance regional trade areas, learn from the progress in the forums. This ongoing interaction in the Bologna Process supports cooperation across Europe, which has positive spillover effects into economic and political dimensions and is in the spirit of the European project.

10

THE FUTURE OF EUROPEAN STUDIES AND HIGHER EDUCATION REFORM IN AFRICA

Patricia W. Cummins

European studies in the next 50 years will see humanities and social studies scholars working with colleagues in professional schools to bring more Bologna Process reforms to Africa. Africa has already adapted the Bologna-style bachelor's, master's and doctoral degrees. Reforms of Francophone Africa's *grandes écoles* in business and engineering have added doctoral and bachelor's programs to the traditional master's degrees, and they are expanding to continuing education, online degree programs, and English-only programs and tracks. The future of European studies in Africa will expand applied research and applied teaching, learning, and assessment with African partners. Faculty and students interested in European international business, health care, sustainable development, and peacebuilding will engage in public–private partnerships where Africa serves as a laboratory. Making Africa a more prosperous, healthier, and stable continent will also help to reduce migration and improve social justice in Europe.

Bringing the Bologna Process to Africa

As an expert on France, I summarized French successes and challenges in developing the Bologna Process in higher education in earlier publications. French Presidents François Hollande and Emmanuel Macron successfully expanded interdisciplinary master's degrees delivered in more than one language. They launched online education initiatives and encouraged public–private partnerships. The greatest challenge was the inability to serve all qualified students seeking university admission. A cumbersome centralized system for faculty recruitment still poses obstacles to allowing competitive international salaries. A centralized Ministry of Higher Education awards tenure (*titularization*) and approves endowed chairs.

Francophone Africa admits an even lower percentage of qualified students, and recruiting and retaining faculty stars are beyond reach. Europe's goal to climb university rankings resulted in new centers of excellence, in funding reforms that create tiers of institutions based on mission, and new funding sources to support the highest levels of international research. My work in Francophone Africa, where higher education follows a French model, encountered even greater obstacles to building a strong and independent university system. In the future, European studies scholars with the right political, linguistic, and intercultural expertise will have opportunities to transform African higher education using models that worked in Europe.

African higher education will help to promote political stability, economic prosperity, and social cohesion. European studies experts and their students will not only create new joint and dual degrees, but we will co-sponsor or participate in more international conferences focused on results. My university hosted the 2013 Women, War, and Peace in Africa conference in partnership with our Sister Cities Commission, the Richmond Peace Education Center, Virginia Friends of Mali, and a US Department of Education grant. That conference resulted in university partnerships and community engagement opportunities for students majoring in French, international studies, and political science to interact with health care providers and nonprofits who were helping victims of war in West Africa. In 2017 we hosted the Eighth Africa Business Conference in which 40 per cent of the program participants came from French-speaking institutions. Students in French, international studies, and international business interacted with scholars, practitioners, and local businesses interested in Africa. French and American companies, US government agencies, representatives of the French government, and the Malian embassy were present.

From 2016 to 2019, as an expert having had grants and contracts with France and French-speaking Africa, I brought together researchers from Côte d'Ivoire and my university to sign an agreement to create an African Medicines for All Institute in Côte d'Ivoire. Virginia Commonwealth University would train the initial doctoral students and postdocs, and the Houphouët Boigny National Polytechnic Institute would become a center of excellence that would train future researchers from Africa. A public–private partnership was to create a new factory where even the highest salaries were to go to African scientists and business leaders. Europe does not exist in a vacuum, and European countries today want to strengthen their existing political, socioeconomic, and cultural partnerships in Africa. Politically stable and economically healthy African economies with a high degree of social cohesion will make Africa a place where Africans and Europeans will both want to live. The roadmap to get there will go through European studies and those with the right cultural and linguistic expertise.

Focus on language and culture

Respect for languages and cultures is critical to assuring political stability, economic prosperity, and social cohesion in Europe. Experts in European education (both schools and universities) have experience introducing language policies tied to employment throughout a region. They have experience building regional school and university systems that award both national and regional degrees. They know how to assess student-learning outcomes across a region.

Like Europeans, Africans must work beyond their own borders, in countries where another language is spoken and where job qualifications must have equivalencies. With the help of European studies specialists, bilingual French and English programs will become commonplace in West Africa, North Africa, and Central Africa. Opportunities to integrate Arabic, Spanish, and Portuguese components will be identified in appropriate settings. Africa's local languages may follow models from Europe's regional languages.

The Common European Framework of Reference for Languages is already recognized in Africa, and the development of an African equivalent to Europass and the European Language Portfolio may soon follow if European experts help pave the way. Creating an African equivalent of the Erasmus program will require expertise from those who know the Erasmus program firsthand. US and European universities' international business centers can help develop university business centers in Africa so that African entrepreneurs have the expertise to increase investments in the local economy. Creating African university grants offices where grants, contracts, and patents can be encouraged and facilitated will have the best chance of success with European and North American partners whose economies are tied to Africa. European studies experts in Europe and the US will probably play a major role in this endeavor. What role will the CES itself play in the coming decades?

The contribution from European studies

European studies in the US is a subset of international studies. What is its future? As individual humanities and social science disciplines decline in the US, an interdisciplinary European studies focus is broadening to include social justice, sustainable development, and international collaboration focused on health care, scientific research, and entrepreneurship. Although Americans are largely monolingual today, the US government promotes language acquisition, and international studies programs are currently expanding their language requirements so that American experts on Europe will be able to work better internationally.

As an expert in business French, I have students take Paris Chamber of Commerce exams where they demonstrate they can function at the B2 level. They understand that for their future roles as leaders in business, government, and nonprofits in French-speaking countries, they cannot be monolingual, and they will compete for jobs with Europeans who speak two or more languages at the B2 level. Study abroad, service learning, internships, and other experiences with speakers of other languages now provide American students with real-world language experiences. The European Language Portfolio and the Common European Framework's language rating scale have US equivalents, but it is through our professional organizations that in 1999, US language teachers agreed to common standards of foreign language learning known as the five Cs: communication, culture, connections to other disciplines, comparisons across languages and cultures, and communities at home and abroad.

Europe and the US also have similar definitions of cultural competence. Both promote curricular and co-curricular experiences. My French students have conversation partners in Paris and West Africa. They do internships with a French film festival or with bilingual conferences on campus. They have had service-learning classes celebrating Mali's national independence day with a display of their Francophone cultural projects when the Malian ambassador and Malian musicians came to campus. Through a US Department of Education grant, six students went to Côte d'Ivoire, and upon their return they gave a professional meeting workshop in French on Ivorian music, cuisine, fashion, artwork, and geography. Hands-on bilingual experiences across the disciplines build communication skills and appreciation of other cultures. European studies in the US will involve both language learning and partnerships with Europe and Europe's diaspora in Africa.

Future prospects

Interdisciplinary initiatives for European studies programs working in Africa will build on the experiences of a strong multilingual and multicultural Europe. Language and business degree programs and networks of international business centers will become a bigger part of Africa's regional and national efforts to create jobs through public–private partnerships. European studies scholars, nonprofits, United Nations offices, and African regional entities recently came together to promote West African health care at the 2019 Africa Santé Expo conference in Abidjan. The Ivorian Ministry of Health and the African Development Bank were the principal funding agencies. European and North American standards for business development, oversight of health care, and international standards for medicines and pharmaceutical practices permeate the 2019 Declaration of Abidjan, where there is a solid plan to assure quality health care in West Africa. The transformation of European studies over the next 50 years will include many more examples of European studies researchers like myself promoting EU and international models of success in Africa and elsewhere.

PART II

LESSONS FROM EUROPE

11

STUDYING EUROPE AS A PATH TO UNDERSTANDING THE STATE OF DEMOCRACY TODAY

Sheri Berman

Pessimism about democracy is pervasive. Freedom House's most recent survey of the state of democracy in the world is entitled "Democracy in Retreat". Even in the West, where democracy has long been taken for granted, scholars and observers wonder whether it will survive assaults from within by populists and from without by resurgent authoritarianism. Reflecting these trends, scholarship and commentary is consumed by debate about illiberal democracy, global authoritarianism, and democratic backsliding. Summing up what has become a widespread view, Viktor Orbán, Hungary's current prime minister, recently proclaimed: "The era of liberal democracy is over."

How can we understand the state of democracy in the world today? What makes liberal democracy work well in some places and times and not others? These are questions of the utmost theoretical and practical import. But as I found when writing *Democracy and Dictatorship in Europe: From the Ancien Régime to the Present Day* (Berman 2019), studying Europe is the perfect way to begin answering them. European history makes clear that much contemporary commentary on the state of democracy is implicitly based on mistaken assumptions about how political development unfolded in the past as well as a warped understanding of what it takes to make democracy work. If we do not study democracy's past, it is hard to fully understand its present.

Painful transition, difficult consolidation

An examination of European history reveals, for example, that quick, painless transitions to democracy are extremely rare. Europe's struggle for democracy began in 1789 with the French Revolution. During the next 150 years, many transitions to democracy occurred in France and other European countries. Most failed, many spectacularly and violently, as in Italy, Germany and Spain during the interwar period. Even the few European countries that had relatively peaceful paths to liberal democracy – Britain being the prime example – took an extremely long time to get there, from the 1688 Glorious Revolution until the extension of universal male suffrage in 1918. (The same could be said of the United States, by the way, which required an immensely bloody civil war and then another hundred years of struggle before it could be considered a full liberal democracy where all citizens had access to their political rights.)

Another crucial lesson a study of European political development reveals is how much it actually takes to make liberal democracy work. It was only after 1945 – more than 150 years after the French Revolution – that liberal democracy became the norm in Western Europe, and this accomplishment required much more than merely eliminating existing dictatorships and replacing them with democratic political institutions and procedures. After the tragedies of the interwar period and World War II, Europeans understood that finally achieving successful liberal democracy would require avoiding the economic crises, inequality, and social divisions that had generated the socioeconomic and communal conflicts and political extremism that had undermined democracy in the past. However, in order to do this, great transformations at the domestic, regional, and international levels would be necessary. And so, with the help of the United States, a multifaceted and ambitious program of democracy promotion and stabilization occurred in Western Europe during the postwar period.

A supportive context

The United States took the lead in constructing new international security and economic arrangements to tie Western countries together and provide a context within which democratic consolidation could occur. In particular, triggered by fears that democracies in Western Europe could not alone protect themselves from Soviet aggression, President Truman committed the United States to defending them with the "Truman Doctrine", and in 1949 NATO was formed, linking these countries to each other and the United States, and eventually integrating Germany into the Western security bloc. The United States also helped construct international economic institutions, including the Bretton Woods system, the General Agreement on Tariffs and Trade, and the International Monetary Fund (IMF), designed to jump-start postwar economic reconstruction, promote growth, and avoid the economic conflicts and depressions that had aggravated tensions among European nations as well as contributed to democratic collapse during the interwar years.

These new American-led international security and economic arrangements were designed to undergird the peace and prosperity that were an essential pre-requisite for successful liberal democracy and also, along with the Marshall Plan which required recipient nations to decide together how aid was to be used, contributed to the formation of the regional pillar of the postwar order: European integration. Fundamentally, European integration stemmed from the recognition that successful liberal democracy would require overcoming challenges too great to be achieved by the uncoordinated efforts of individual governments acting alone. In particular, the linked challenges of reconciling Germany with Europe and ensuring postwar economic reconstruction and growth would necessitate cooperation and coordination among European nations. This led to the formation of a series of agreements and institutions, beginning with Council of Europe (1949) and the ECSC (1951), which gradually propelled the process of European integration forwards.

The contribution of social democracy

The final pillar of the tripartite foundation upon which consolidated liberal democracy was built was a new "social democratic" domestic political order. After 1945, West European political economies were reconstructed in a novel way. They were capitalist, but it was a different capitalism than existed before the war (Shonfield 1969). Democratic states now tempered or limited capitalism in order to avoid the economic crises, inequality, and social divisions that undermined democracy in the past.

This new social democratic order not only generated unprecedented prosperity – the 30 years after 1945 were Europe's fastest period of growth ever – but by spreading the benefits of capitalism more widely, it helped eliminate the belief, prevalent among liberals, Marxists, fascists, and others throughout the nineteenth and first half of the twentieth centuries, that liberal democracy could not or would not respond to all citizens' interests, rather than merely a subset of them. By showing how broadly responsive liberal democracy could be, the postwar order helped undercut the appeal of anti-democratic extremists on the left and right who claimed only non-liberal democratic regimes could truly represent "the people". As a result, during the decades after 1945 the centrifugal political dynamics of the interwar years were transformed into centripetal ones, as good times brought parties and voters back toward the political middle.

A sense of perspective

What an examination of Europe's political development in general and the post-war period in particular reveals is that building successful liberal democracy has always been a long and arduous process that requires much more than getting rid of an old dictatorial regime and putting in place new democratic institutions and procedures. These and other lessons from Europe's past can help us better understand the state of democracy today.

For example, when we look at today's relatively new democracies in Eastern Europe and elsewhere, we should not be surprised that they face significant problems. Europe's political development makes clear that toppling dictatorships is easier than building stable democracies; European history is littered with examples of the former, but the latter only become commonplace in Western Europe after 1945. To expect countries like Hungary or Poland that had only recently gained their independence (having been part of the Habsburg empire until the early twentieth century and then being integrated into the Nazi and then the Soviet empires for much of the rest of the twentieth century) and had almost no experience with liberalism or democracy, to relatively quickly and easily construct stable, well-functioning liberal democracies, would be historically unprecedented.

Indeed, given Eastern Europe's "backstory", and once we understand how long and arduous the process of constructing liberal democracy in Western and southern Europe was, we might even say there are some reasons for optimism. Anti-democratic efforts by Poland's current government to purge its Supreme Court and weaken constitutional checks and balances, and corruption and illiberalism by politicians and elites in Slovakia, Romania, and elsewhere, have generated spirited protest and opposition, revealing that many more citizens than in the past are able and willing to stand up and fight democratic backsliding. Moreover, authoritarian-inclined rulers in the region have not been able to cast aside elections as their interwar and communist predecessors did, and elections, even when flawed, can provide opposition groups with chances to mobilize, as we saw recently with mayoral elections in Turkey.

With regard to long-established democracies in the West, studying European political development should remind us of how recent an achievement successful democracy actually is and how much it took to achieve, therefore perhaps providing a greater appreciation of how fragile it can be. It was only after the tragedies of the interwar years and World War II that European and American elites fully recognized that avoiding economic crises, inequality, and social divisions was necessary to avoid the communal conflicts and political extremism that had undermined democracy in the past. Perhaps if more people study European political development, we will not need to experience another tragedy before we begin focusing more intently on what it will take to revitalize democracy today.

12

ECONOMIC CHALLENGES AND ELECTORAL POLITICS IN EUROPE

Peter A. Hall

At the heart of the challenges facing modern governments are the intertwined tasks of devising policies to deliver economic prosperity and of mobilizing popular consent for them. The importance of economic policy was noted in the nineteenth century by William Gladstone, the British prime minister renowned for his fiscal acumen, who observed that "budgets are not merely matters of arithmetic, but in a thousand ways go to the root of prosperity of individuals, and relations of classes, and the strength of Kingdoms". The importance of mobilization is manifest in democracies, where economic policy-making is always also coalition building.

Few can doubt the magnitude of those challenges in Europe today. Many countries that could once reliably command 3 per cent rates of annual economic growth now struggle to secure 1 per cent. More than 15 per cent of young people in the EU are unemployed, and the vast majority who do find work are being forced into temporary jobs lasting only months if not weeks. Moreover, the adjustment of most European countries to a technological revolution marked by the advance of digital technologies lags well behind parallel movements in the US and even China. To cope with the technological revolution of the twenty-first century, the nations of Europe need new modernization strategies.

Political will

Part of the challenge, of course, is to identify such strategies. Finding an effective strategy is not a simple task because every country starts with a different set of institutional endowments. Thus, approaches that might work in one will not necessarily succeed in others. There are no magic bullets here. However, the process of implementing new economic strategies has also been complicated by the disintegration of longstanding electoral alignments and the fragmentation of European party systems. There is some truth to the old saying that "where there is a will there is a way", but in democracies the relevant "will" emerges out of party politics and it is uncertain whether partisan competition in Europe today is capable of generating the will to implement policies that will promote prosperity in the coming years. Why not?

For a reference point, we can look to the modernization policies pursued in Western Europe over the two decades after 1945. Those were policies that transformed national economies into "managed economies" in terms that received wide popular assent. Based on a determination to avoid the mass unemployment of the 1930s, policy-makers deliberately broke with the approaches of the interwar years that had pitted advocates of laissez-faire against proponents of large-scale nationalization. They deployed the ideas of John Maynard Keynes and others who argued that activist governments could secure full employment without nationalizing the means of production, thereby reconciling socialists and conservatives alike to modest levels of state intervention, while building a new welfare state to cushion the impact of profound economic adjustments.

If new ideas supplied the means, the electoral politics of the 1950s and 1960s supplied the motor behind this movement toward new economic strategies. The key feature of that politics was the centrality to electoral competition of cleavages based on social class and religion. In 1967 Peter Pulzer could write, "Class is the basis of British party politics: all else is embellishment and detail." That was true elsewhere in Europe, if to a lesser extent, where religious affiliation also provided a base for Christian democratic parties. The class cleavage mattered because it pushed issues of full employment and social justice to the top of the agendas, forcing parties toward modernization strategies that also compensated those bearing the burdens of economic adjustment. Most party platforms moved to the left around policies that could also be described as a class compromise. Even Christian democratic parties built cross-class compromises into their platforms. As a result, for more than 30 years European electoral systems were dominated by political parties of the center right and center left which put their electoral weight behind modernization of the economy.

Politics without class

Today, similar conditions no longer prevail. The European party systems are deeply fragmented. If mainstream center-right and center-left parties had about two-thirds of the European vote in 1980, they now secure barely half of it in the face of a host of challenger parties. Populist parties of the radical right attract about a fifth of the electorate in many countries, while green parties and radical left parties approach that strength in some. In the Netherlands, admittedly an extreme case, ten parties currently have the support of at least 5 per cent of the electorate while only one party is supported by 15 per cent of voters. Even in Britain, where majoritarian electoral rules favor two large parties, deep fissures have opened up in the middle of the Labour and Conservative parties.

In East Central Europe, electoral fragmentation can be ascribed partly to the difficulties of establishing stable party systems in the wake of a transition to democracy. What accounts for the weakening of mainstream parties in Western Europe? Three sets of factors have contributed to it, each operating in a different realm. In the economic realm, many of the developments that have created new policy challenges also alter electoral politics in ways that make it more difficult for governments to cope with those challenges. In the political realm, three decades of neoliberal policies may have advanced the European economies, but they have also driven many voters, who bore the costs of those policies, away from the mainstream parties responsible for them. In the social realm, the decline of churches and trade unions has weakened two of the principal organizations once mobilizing support for Christian democratic or social democratic parties, while the rise of new social media has made it easier for challenger parties to mobilize against them.

Several economic developments matter. The movement of manufacturing out of Western Europe to emerging economies in Eastern Europe or Asia decimated manufacturing sectors that were once bastions of working-class solidarity and prime sites for trade union organization. New technology has transformed manufacturing into an enclave for skilled labor, pushing the semi-skilled workers who once found employment there into more precarious jobs in a low-wage service sector. The impact of these developments has been magnified by firm strategies which took advantage of new technology and the opening of global markets to contract out many components of their operations, often to overseas supply chains. As a result, skilled production workers no longer share the same set of economic interests as their less skilled counterparts in services, driving a wedge through the working-class solidarity on which social democratic parties once depended.

As skill-biased technological change increased the demand for well-educated workers and their wages, economic opportunity has come to depend on education, and enrollments in tertiary education have grown accordingly. But tertiary education changes the outlooks as well as the job prospects of those who experience it, often conferring the cosmopolitan values associated with support for ethnic diversity, immigration, gender equality, and environmental protection that contrast with the traditional values held by many people with less education. As a result, the class cleavage, once largely congruent with income, is being replaced by a cleavage rooted in education, because education now confers *both* economic opportunities and worldviews. Moreover, the educated can now be found in many walks of life: as tertiary enrollments approach 50 per cent of the age cohort, the days when a college education meant you were rich are over.

A more complicated electoral agenda

Of course, the votes of citizens are influenced by more than their socioeconomic positions. They also respond to the appeals of parties, and this is where political developments enter the picture. Inspired by a wave of enthusiasm for neoliberal policies during in the 1990s and early 2000s, both center-right and center-left parties embraced policies designed to intensify market competition, turn welfare into workfare, privatize or contract out public services, and restrain public spending. They gave warm support to reforms that turned the EU into a vehicle for economic liberalization.

Two sets of effects followed. Many of the people more exposed to market forces began to believe that governments were making their lives worse rather than better. Longstanding party loyalties began to dissolve. At the same time, because their economic platforms were so similar, in order to offer the electorate something distinctive center-left and center-right parties began to give more prominence to values issues. Social democratic parties, for instance, embraced cosmopolitan values to draw people in the middle class into their electoral coalition; and many of these parties now draw more votes from the middle class than the working class. In much the same way, because voters found it increasingly difficult to choose between parties on economic issues, many began to accord values issues more weight in their electoral decisions. As a result, electoral competition in Europe now turns as much on values issues as on economic issues.

The decline of the social organizations on which mainstream parties once depended is linked to these developments. Deindustrialization and globalization hit the trade unions hard: union membership has fallen by half since 1980 in countries such as Germany, France, Britain, the Netherlands and Austria. And, in the face of many secularizing pressures, less than 15 per cent of West Europeans now attend church regularly.

Today, Europe has a fragmented electoral map that reflects these developments. Working-class voters are less attached to social democratic parties. Some who care most about economic issues turn to parties of the radical left such as Die Linke or Podemos, while many who attach importance to values issues are attracted to parties of the radical right, such as the Rassemblement National, or Swedish Democrats. By linking anti-immigrant positions to calls for more social protection, the populist right now draw votes from both the center left and center right, while resurgent green parties and new liberal parties such as Macron's La République en Marche drain the votes of a cosmopolitan middle class.

Implications for Europe

Why might these electoral developments matter for the economic future of Europe? Timid economic reforms based on muddling through are not likely to accomplish the major adjustments necessary for Europe to prosper in the context of a new technological revolution. Bold new initiatives will be required. But it is difficult to assemble strong electoral coalitions capable of mounting such initiatives out of a fragmented party politics. In many countries it is taking longer even to form a governing coalition, and the coalitions that emerge often bring together parties with such different platforms that they are unable to agree on more than minimal responses to emerging challenges. These types of domestic political constraints also limit what governments can agree at the EU level.

Second, the experience of the 1950s and 1960s suggests that, if they are to be successful and sustainable, modernization strategies must be grounded, not simply in good economic ideas, but in broad-based social compromises that instantiate principles of social justice. Forging such compromises was possible when governments emerged out of electoral competition between social democratic parties speaking for an encompassing working class and conservative parties speaking on behalf of the middle class. Today, however, there are no European parties with parallel remits. An electorate that is splintered in occupational and attitudinal terms is now represented by a plethora of political parties speaking with multifarious voices. In some respects, this development may have made European electoral systems more representative. But mobilizing consent for wide-ranging economic reforms is more difficult in such a context and finding the basis for an overarching class compromise is a Herculean challenge.

In this setting, the technocratic temptation – to leave the important decisions to experts ensconced in agencies far removed from electoral politics – is omnipresent. But the EU has already tried that only to evoke a populist backlash of significant proportions. Other means of making policy will have to be found, but whether the result will be economic strategies adequate to the challenges facing Europe remains uncertain. The one point on which we can be sure is that the solution to Europe's dilemmas does not rest solely on figuring out what policies will promote economic prosperity. It also depends on finding ways to mobilize consent for those policies within a fissiparous electoral arena that is volatile, divided on values as well as economic issues, and deeply in flux.

13

LESSONS FROM CENTRAL EUROPE'S DISSIDENTS

Lisa A. Baglione

Democracy in Europe is facing a crisis that is unrivaled since the interwar period. Like 90 years ago, no part of the continent is immune to the challenge. In seeking ways forward, an excellent though perhaps forgotten source is the wisdom of the communist dissidents of Eastern and Central Europe. Many of these activists were inspired by the Final Act of the Conference on Security and Cooperation in Europe, signed in the summer of 1975. After two years of negotiations, this agreement committed states on both sides of the East–West divide to take steps to enhance security, improve economic ties, and promote human rights.

When the Helsinki Accords (as they have come to be called) were signed, many critics of détente insisted the Soviets had once again hoodwinked naïve Western leaders. The naysayers claimed that Helsinki allowed the Soviets and their satellites to make empty promises about upholding political and civil rights while achieving valuable strategic goals. Neither the accords' opponents nor the communist governments expected, however, that brave and principled people within these states would use this international agreement, as well as state laws, to pressure their governments to abide by the promises made in that third Helsinki "basket" and that their efforts would help bring about communism's collapse (Thomas 2001).

For more than a decade, activists all over Eastern and Central Europe and the Soviet Union, who pushed for Helsinki to be honored, suffered enormously. They were denounced by colleagues and even friends, prevented from doing the work they loved, arrested, and subjected to various forms of abuse. Still, communist officials could not stamp out the relevance of legal promises and dissidents' commitments to holding the regimes to account.

Lessons from Prague

The story of the Helsinki Watch groups, as many were called, and particularly Charter 77, the one that emerged in Czechoslovakia in the year of its name, may seem outdated today. Contemporary autocrats and populists appear to have found ways to both depoliticize the majority of citizens and allow most to exercise the civil rights that individuals deem important. A close reading of the "Declaration from Charter 77", issued upon the group's founding, shows that these activists were keenly aware of how repressive regimes promise and bestow rights, contingent upon the acquiescence of individuals to the state's power. The document emphasizes how legally enshrined rights are routinely subverted because power is centralized and informal networks and relationships are more politically important than formal, legal ones. With this theme, the authors of the charter tipped their hats to some of the great problems that challenge democracies in Europe and elsewhere today.

The rule of law has broken down or is eroding. In some places, like Hungary and Poland, the attack was direct and swift. In others, the decay has occurred almost imperceptibly until violations mounted to reveal serious concerns. In still others, such as the United Kingdom, officials were motivated to give individuals a greater say without recognizing the potential that popular power might violate liberal democracy's prohibitions against concentrating authority and weakening the rule of law.

While Charter 77 has many important passages, the most apt for this discussion is the following:

> One instrument for the curtailment or in many cases complete elimination of many civic rights is the system by which all national institutions and organizations are in effect subject to political directives from the machinery of the ruling party and to decisions made by powerful individuals. The constitution of the republic, its laws and legal norms do not regulate the form or content, the issuing or application of such decisions; they are often only given out verbally, unknown to the public at large and beyond its powers to check; their originators are responsible to no one but themselves and their own hierarchy; yet they have a decisive impact on [virtually all elements of political, economic, and social life].

The two essential points here are instructive for today: first, leaders can commandeer state machinery to negate civil rights, especially when informal channels prevail; and second, the concentration of power makes such abuse possible. Thus, activists were clearly calling for a robust rule of law and a state, autonomous from governing officials, in which powers were balanced to prevent usurpations.

Forgetting and remembering

With the euphoria of 1989, however, many dismissed or forgot these essential insights. They instead interpreted communism's failure as an indictment of state institutions and a victory for liberalism as competition, seeing markets and elections as panaceas for curing economic and political woes. At that "end-of-history" moment, most trusted that the enshrinement of civil rights in constitutions would be enough, not perceiving the dangers of reconcentrating economic and political authority. Why would these protections be insufficient, since the peoples of Eastern and Central Europe sought to "return to Europe", and they repeatedly stated they wanted democracy? Moreover, with the privatization of state industries, the influx of capital, advice, and investment from friendly democratic neighbors, and incentives in the form of potential NATO and EU memberships motivating the newly freed states to stay on track with reforms, the consensus was that the countries of Eastern and Central Europe would be able to consolidate democracy and capitalism relatively quickly, with no turning back.

This enthusiasm for markets and for reducing the power of states pervaded much of Europe and the world in communism's aftermath. The results have been increasing gaps between the rich and poor, as well as the rise of corruption in all but a few places. Ironically, in the post-Soviet world in particular, these pro-market policies have served to recreate that coupling of economic and political power that previously gave ruling parties enormous control over populations.

What has resulted farther west, particularly in Hungary and Poland, is a return to the undemocratic control of leaders and their political networks over their polities. In each case, major constitutional changes that weakened alternative institutions were achieved without great popular support. In Hungary, a slim popular vote majority translated into a parliamentary supermajority which then rewrote the constitution and undertook steps to undo alternative power centers and the rule of law. Poland's leaders, too, went after the judges, pitted citizens against each other (rural versus urban, religious versus secular), and benefited from the fear of external "others" in their efforts. Perhaps because of their past experiences, these anti-democrats in Hungary and Poland knew to attack the courts to eliminate legal recourse for abuses. The takeover or neutralization of other institutions, like the independent media, helped the new authoritarians create the desired "panorama".

That term, "panorama" was one that Vaclav Havel, a Charter 77 founder, used in his famous discussion of the way that power works in what he called post-totalitarian societies. Havel (1985–6) noted that the state seeks to provide an overarching view of conformity, approval, and acquiescence so that most individuals will neither draw "disloyal" conclusions from daily observations nor act on them. Individuals would think: everyone else is satisfied, the regime is apparently doing a fine job, I must be wrong.

Modern uses for past wisdom

Of course, the situations in European countries today are neither as bleak nor as uniform as 40 years ago in Eastern and Central Europe. In the East, some citizens and civil society organizations are resisting, although the panorama, institutional changes, and concentration of power make their tasks difficult. The EU is trying to be an ally, but it was not created to monitor its members' democratic behavior. The breakdown of institutions has also affected many established democracies, although not yet to the same extent or in the same ways.

Still, states and institutions have been weakened, sometimes in misguided efforts to bring power closer to individuals. But power to the people does not mean that rights will be preserved and that institutions will be able to effectively thwart illiberal leaders' attempts to undermine alternative power centers. The people can often be charmed by demagogues and become the supporters of rights revocations and usurpations of authority. Moreover, new media makes the creation of the desired panorama easier today; individuals, through their feeds, eagerly consume, create, and spread anti-democratic propaganda.

Thus, the wisdom of the Eastern and Central European dissidents of two generations ago echoes throughout Europe. Preserving the rule of law, dividing power, having an autonomous state and vibrant civil society, and holding leaders accountable are essential for well-functioning democracies. Let contemporary democrats return to these analyses in the hopes of preserving and strengthening the liberal political systems around the continent.

14

FEDERALISM, BORDERS, AND CITIZENSHIP
Willem Maas

Most people studying Europe in 1970, when the CES was founded, would be amazed at the progress of European integration since then. Of course, the Schuman Declaration was 20 years old in 1970, and the ECSC had been supplemented by the European Atomic Energy Community (Euratom) and the much broader EEC. But these Communities included only the original six member states (France, West Germany, Italy, and the Benelux), with the first enlargement still three years in the future, and Community institutions were generally quite hesitant to take any actions not supported by the member states. True, the European Court of Justice had promulgated the principles of the supremacy of Community law, and of its direct effect. Even so, the number and importance of instances where member states were obliged to change their policies remained quite restricted.

Federal aspirations

Perhaps the quality of the change at work was more important than the quantity. Former Commission president Walter Hallstein observed in 1969 that individual Europeans were being affected by the Community's legal system "more strongly and more directly with every day that passes". He went on to point out that Europeans were "subject in varying degrees to two legal systems – as a citizen of one of the Community's member-states to [the] national legal system, and as a member of the Community to the Community's legal system". This was a new experience for many Europeans, but it was "not a new experience for citizens of countries with federal constitutions" (Maas 2007: 21).

Raising the idea of federalism suggests that some people might be less surprised at the progress of European integration. Federalists like Altiero Spinelli and Ursula Hirschmann had proposed as early as 1943 a European "continental" citizenship alongside national citizenship. In the aftermath of World War

II most European political leaders supported creating a common European legal status for individual citizens. Thus Winston Churchill in 1948 called for "a European group which could give a sense of enlarged patriotism and common citizenship" and hoped "to see a Europe where men of every country will think as much of being a European as of belonging to their native land" (Maas 2017). Hendrik Brugmans, co-founder and first president of the Union of European Federalists, later rector of the College of Europe, saw the need to "organize a European political consciousness, in which alone federal democracy can work. This European public opinion will not be the sum of individual national public opinions, it will be something *sui generis*, an occurrence quite new in history, the discovery of common citizenship of Europeans as such" (Maas 2017: 88).

From free movement to European citizenship

The ECSC's free movement provisions had been expanded by the Treaty of Rome, which also strengthened the principle of non-discrimination on the basis of nationality; within the scope of Community law, citizens of the member states should be treated equally. In 1961 Commissioner Lionello Levi Sandri character- ized the free movement of workers as "the first aspect of a European citizenship", and Hallstein called it one of "the most spectacular points in the programme which is to lead to the integration of Europe", suggesting it would "point to the beginning of a common European 'citizenship'". In this way, Hallstein echoed Levi Sandri's assertion that free movement of workers "represents something more important and more exacting than the free movement of a factor of pro- duction. It represents rather an incipient form – still embryonic and imperfect – of European citizenship" (Maas 2007: 21).

The European citizenship seen as incipient in the 1960s has developed signif- icantly since then. At the 1972 Council meeting, Belgian Prime Minister Gaston Eyskens called for "practical steps to encourage the movement of youngsters within the Community and allow them to make full use ... of the diplomas they have gained, regardless of where they have studied in the Community". Italian Prime Minister Giulio Andreotti advocated establishing "a European citizen- ship, which would be in addition to the citizenship which the inhabitants of our countries now possess. It should permit the citizens of the Community coun- tries, after a stay of a certain length in one of our countries, to exercise some political rights, such as that of participating in communal elections" (Maas 2007: 31).

Commission President Sicco Mansholt urged going even further. He sug- gested adding "obvious content to the fact of belonging to the EC. This Com- munity, which has achieved the opening of frontiers for trade in industrial and agricultural goods, must now open the frontiers which still keep its citizens apart from one another." Mansholt also argued that "checks at the Community's internal frontiers should be done away with, and nationals of member states progressively integrated into the social, administrative and political fabric of their host countries, with the aim of gradually conferring upon them 'European civic rights'" (Maas 2007: 31). The Community's first enlargement, to the UK, Ireland, and Denmark in 1973, postponed agreement on a common European citizenship, but the process gained new strength in the 1980s, particularly with enlargement to Spain and Portugal.

The 1985 White Paper on Completing the Internal Market devoted a section to free movement under the subtitle "a new initiative in favour of Community citizens", arguing that it was "crucial that the obstacles which still exist within the Community to free movement for the self-employed and employees be removed by 1992". Citing the preliminary findings of the People's Europe report, it continued that "measures to ensure the free movement of individuals must not be restricted to the workforce only".

On the same day that the White Paper appeared, representatives of France, West Germany, Belgium, Luxembourg, and the Netherlands signed an agreement in the Luxembourg town of Schengen to eliminate border controls. The Belgian secretary of state for European affairs said that the agreement's ultimate goal was "to abolish completely the physical borders between our countries", while Luxembourg's minister of foreign affairs called it "a major step forward on the road toward European unity", directly benefiting signatory state citizens and "moving them a step closer to what is sometimes referred to as 'European citizenship'" (Maas 2007: 37). Eliminating checks at internal borders was thus tied to the development of a European citizenship.

Then and now

Europe in 2020 continues along the same path sketched out in the 1950s and developed incrementally since then: creating European citizens through free movement, education, and changing the meaning of borders. This continuing development of a common European citizenship is remarkable given the substantial enlargements from six to now 28 member states – with a possible Brexit counterbalanced by probable new enlargements in the western Balkans and possibly beyond. Robert Schuman long ago wrote that European integration should not seek to eliminate ethnic and political borders, to correct history, or to invent a rationalized and managed geography: "what we want is to take away from borders their rigidity and what I call their intransigent hostility" (Maas 2007: 61).

The search for closer coordination and common guidelines concerning citizenship flows from functional needs inevitably generated by superimposing a new supranational political community over existing national ones, resulting in shared governance within the framework of member state autonomy. Though welfare states and social systems in Europe remain national and jurisprudence safeguards the ability of member states to exclude individuals despite shared EU citizenship, legal judgements emphasize that member state competence concerning citizenship must be exercised in accordance with the treaties and that member state decisions about naturalization and denaturalization are amenable to judicial review carried out in the light of EU law (Maas 2016).

A truly federal United States of Europe remains elusive; it may indeed be undesirable given the differences and particularities present on the European continent. But the rise of EU citizenship over decades of European integration means that the EU now increasingly resembles a federal state in terms of internal free movement. Social scientists have generally accepted as an unexplored assumption that national identities are relatively fixed. As Max Weber long ago pointed out, however, differences in national sentiment are both significant and fluid: the "idea of the nation" is empirically "entirely ambiguous" and the intensity of feelings of solidarity is variable. Successive EU-wide opinion surveys show increasing numbers of Europeans identifying with Europe, while the freedom to travel, study, work, and live anywhere in Europe tops surveys asking what the EU means to individual Europeans. The continuing growth of a common European citizenship, coupled with the progressive elimination of border controls within the common European territory, are perhaps the most significant achievements of European integration to date.

15

HISTORY LESSONS FROM THE SINGLE MARKET AND MAASTRICHT YEARS?

George Ross

Analysts and observers of social and political change sometimes have difficulty separating enthusiasms from science. This has been particularly the case in the brief history of European integration. The high hopes of the initial common market years gave way to numerous worries in the 1970s. This moment was followed by renascent European energy, led by Commission activism, around the single market and Maastricht treaty. Many observers then concluded that Europe's growing pains had given way to forwards movement, a judgement that deeply marked scholarly thinking. By the mid-1990s, however, it seemed that this might not be the case. As time went on, it became clearer that what had been greeted as a golden age was really a moment of transition toward significant changes in the EU's constitution that brought their own problems. This essay briefly discusses the golden age and the less golden transition that followed.

From Eurosclerosis to Euro-optimism

By the late 1970s, many observers had written off the EC as a noble but stagnating experiment. Europe's postwar boom had ended in high inflation, low growth, and high unemployment, leading member states to protect their national interests in EC decision-making and erect non-tariff barriers threatening the common market. The European Monetary System (EMS), designed to align currencies and avoid competitive devaluations, had instead revealed the Deutschmark's power and spawned member state discontent. The early 1980s then brought "Eurosclerosis", with the British blocking EC decision-making to win reductions in their budgetary contribution and France's "Mitterrand experiment" crashing and burning.

France's new-found desire for different EC directions and Helmut Kohl's ascension to the German chancellorship renewed Franco-German collaboration, however. The 1984 Fontainebleau European Council reduced the UK's budget-ary contribution and brought the British back into the fold, agreed on enlarging to Spain and Portugal, and led to the appointment of Jacques Delors as president of the Commission.

Having been a Euro-parliamentarian and Mitterrand's minister of the econ-omy after 1981, Delors had in-depth knowledge of the challenges. A progressive Catholic "social liberal," he was familiar with the EC's many unenacted reform plans, aware of the changes underway in the global economy, in touch with pro-gressive business interests, and, above all, convinced that the EC had to renew itself. In his initial speech to the European Parliament in January 1985, Delors proposed a new initiative to build a single market: a "space without borders."

After getting an initial go-ahead from member states, Delors' Commission composed a White Paper charting completion of the internal market to ensure free movement of goods, persons, services, and capital by 1992. The plan's immediate author, Arthur Cockfield, was a British European commissioner whom Delors counted on to bring the UK and others to accept market opening via national deregulation and subsequent European-level reregulation. Together Cockfield and Delors generated a dense technical document listing more than 300 market-opening measures and a multiyear schedule for adopting them.

At the spring 1985 Milan European Council, national leaders approved the White Paper and called an intergovernmental conference to discuss changes to the Rome Treaty to implement it. This led to the 1986 SEA, strengthening European-level foreign policy collaboration, instituting qualified majority vot-ing for most of the 1992 program, and empowering the European Parliament by a "cooperation procedure" that allowed it to propose amendments and approve accession and association agreements. Because national health and safety rules could be barriers in the single market, these would also be harmonized, an important step toward European competence in social policy. Finally, there was vague reference to a future European "monetary capacity". The SEA, which helped bring forwards movement in European integration, was accepted by member states because it addressed large problems they all faced.

The SEA made European-level policy-making easier, particularly for the Commission, which did not hesitate to push forwards bold new proposals. After shepherding the final stage of enlargement to Spain and Portugal, the Commission then undertook a successful struggle for the "Delors1 Package" to address three outstanding problems, the size, content, and procedures for EC budgets (introducing the multiyear "financial perspectives" system), an overhaul of "cohesion policies" giving the Commission new powers and doubling fund-ing for regional development, and initial reforms of the Common Agricultural Policy. Soon thereafter, the Commission introduced a Social Charter to jump-start "social Europe."

The centrality of the single market allowed the Commission to frame such policy proposals as "flanking" measures to undergird the new market's functioning. New policy dynamism also increased the Commission's powers and brought greater parliamentary involvement. Commission activism, leadership, and popular policies, plus support from business and other groups, also increased the Delors team's political resources for reinvestment in additional proposals. Many scholars asserted that European integration had been relaunched on "neofunctionalist" paths, led by the Commission, and that this would continue well into the future.

Member states catching their breath

Member states and global changes dampened such neofunctionalist hopes, however. Throughout the Delors years, the French and others had focused on the "monetary capacity" reference in the SEA in the hope of changing the EMS and reducing German monetary power, arguing that the EMU was necessary to the single market to squeeze down inflation and promote monetary stability. Germany resisted, however, a first sign that not all member states would march happily to the Commission's tune.

Delors pushed ahead nonetheless, proposing a high-level committee – chaired by him – to explore what kind of EMU was needed and how to create it. The member states approved this, and the committee was formed around member state central bankers plus a few experts. Delors, who knew central bankers well, hoped that his insistent committee leadership would persuade them to accept specific EMU proposals and make their governments more favorable. The basic shape of EMU was sketched by this committee, with even the Bank of England cooperating. The next step was convening an intergovernmental conference to incorporate EMU into the EC treaties. Here Germany initially refused until the fall of the Berlin Wall, German unification in 1990, and the diplomatic complications of the Cold War's end changed its mind. In the meantime, a parallel intergovernmental conference on "political union" was called to discuss greater EC foreign and security policy roles, the implications of Schengen and the free movement of people, increasing the powers of the European Parliament, and a number of smaller issues.

The Delors Commission tried to play a central role in both intergovernmental conferences, as it had for the SEA, but fell far short, with significant consequences. At Maastricht in 1991 the member states confirmed EMU, with the UK opting out and with ordoliberal restrictions pushed by Germany that included constraining membership and convergence criteria. The Commission also sought a central role in foreign and security policy, but these matters were instead set up within a new intergovernmental "pillar". To consider the legal and other consequences of the free movement of people, member states also agreed on a second such pillar on Justice and Home Affairs. The European Parliament won new co-decision powers, but Maastricht demonstrated that member states were determined to shape institutional changes in ways that would leave them in control of the new EU.

Clearer indications that the Commission's golden age was waning came soon thereafter. While EMU was still in preparation, and in response to the EMS crisis of 1992–3, the Commission sought to "bring the member states together again" (Delors' words) around a new White Paper on *Growth, Competitiveness, Employment*. This "Third Way"-ish document analyzed the implications of globalization for the EU and then advocated supply-side active labor market policies shaped from Brussels, educational systems modified with more emphasis on training and apprenticeship programs, greater labor market flexibility to enhance worker employability, and increased investment in new technologies and "European Networks". To jump-start the EU economy and implement these proposals, the White Paper also called for new European-level borrowing.

Member states did not approve the White Paper program, mainly because its proposals for Euro-level borrowing were rejected by Germany and others. A defeated Delors Commission then quietly lived out its last year, following which member states set out to appoint more pliable Commission presidents. Behind this was member state fatigue from the "1992" years, and matters that divided them, beginning with responses to the collapse of Yugoslavia, the crisis in the EMS, and complicated national exercises to prepare for EMU and the euro. As important, they were clear that the sequels of 1989, including enlarging the EU to Central and Eastern Europe, would necessitate major institutional reforms of the Union, and that the Commission would play only a marginal role in designing them.

The golden age in perspective?

The Delors years were less a reawakening of European integration than an extraordinary moment when a gifted Commission leader, supported for a time by key member states, led Europe onto new territory by proposing solutions to problems that member states themselves knew they could not resolve. After a few good years, however, Delors' leadership and the prominence of his Commission declined, in part because member states, threatened by Delors and his Commission, regrouped. The extraordinary situation following 1989 exposed new issues that member states, reluctant to encourage the Commission again, resolved to confront intergovernmentally. It would take time, however, particularly for those convinced that the Delors years of Commission-led integration were a new normal, to recognize that a changed configuration among EU institutions had instead occurred.

The "federalizing" EU Commission continues to propose and enforce EU legislation, but its ambitions have been dramatically reduced. Member states wanted this outcome, and, in response, recent Commission leaders have removed much remaining "neofunctionalist" zeal from their institution. The European Parliament has gained authority over time but has not yet succeeded at building deeper linkages between the EU and its national citizens that the EU deeply needs. Most importantly, member states, primarily through the European Council, are now the EU's key planners and decision-makers.

This institutional rearrangement has not been completely felicitous, however. Recent enlargements, divergences in member state preferences and power, and new international challenges have consecrated the European Council as the EU's chief strategist and decision maker of last resort. As seen in the eurozone and migration-asylum crises, responses to populist and anti-democratic challenges, the urgent need for energy, defense, external border controls, and new foreign policies, and new needs to complete a single market because of changes in economic structures, mean the enlarged roles of member state have been severely tested. Recent years have thus seen controversial positions imposed by some member states on others, weak decisions that have often come too late to resolve difficult issues, or non-decisions.

Rather than progressing toward ever-greater union, the EU has evolved into a unique new power-sharing order that combines a federalizing executive Commission that formally proposes laws and enforces transnational rules that is most often subordinate to a confederal European Council that sets EU strategy and responds to the EU's recent, often very large, crisis situations, and a Council of Ministers that co-decides Commission-proposed legislation with the European Parliament. Most importantly, citizen loyalties and identities remain primarily national, implying that member states will have very different positions, priorities, and preferences.

The EU's present institutional construct is thus problematic. We should know that national power-sharing federations all have their conflicts and problems even when their citizenries have common histories, values, and traditions. The EU does not yet have citizens in this sense, however. For it, conflict resolution and problem solving is more difficult, particularly because its key problem solvers are beholden democratically to specific national citizenries. Europe is today experiencing economic, social, and political transitions that would be difficult to navigate in the best of institutional circumstances. Alas, these circumstances may not be the best.

16

THE EXTRAORDINARY, TAKEN-FOR-GRANTED ACHIEVEMENT OF EUROPE'S SINGLE MARKET

Craig Parsons

The past decade has not seen much celebration of the EU's achievements. EU headlines have been captured by crises in eurozone debt and austerity, in-fighting over migration, Eastern European proto-despotism, and the demagogic circus of Brexit. Even the core EU project to erase barriers to exchange and mobility – the famous "single market" – is perceived as faltering. "In parts it is incomplete and in others actively going backwards", complained *The Economist* in September 2019. In their view it falls well short of its aspirations to "a single economic zone much like America, with nothing to impede the free movement of goods, services, people and capital".

Some good news for Europe, however, is that this gloomy narrative is disconnected from certain aspects of reality on the ground. That is not to say that the headlines get it all wrong, of course. Europe's crises have been severe. Moreover, North–South economic divergences, contestation around free circulation of people, democratic struggles in Eastern Europe, and English nationalism are not going away soon. Also true is that the single market is incomplete in many areas and hitting obstacles in others (without mentioning other gaps in EU economic governance). The crucial correction, though, concerns a clear-eyed assessment of what the EU has done relative to what it concretely set out to do. On its core ambitions it has achieved far more than even most experts seem to recognize.

The concrete goal to which Europeans committed in the 1950s was to change their laws, regulations, and administrative processes to encourage free movement and exchange across national jurisdictions. In the 1980s they reconfirmed and deepened that commitment. Over time they also gradually extended border-opening goals across an increasingly large and diverse group of member states. What today's main narrative overlooks – and even *The Economist*, usually well-informed, gets wrong – is that the EU's single market has gone well past the United States in removing interstate barriers. It has also done so across far more diverse and powerful states than the US government ever faced.

This is a truly extraordinary achievement. Characterizing it accurately alters our sense of the EU's present and future. The EU attracts so many challenges today mainly because its core project has gone so far, not because it is weak and incomplete. That even well-informed people overlook this achievement – taking much of the single market for granted – is further testament to its robustness for the future.

Single markets compared

Making the claim that Europe's single market has surpassed America's in significant ways may seem to require a complex regulatory comparison that would far exceed the capacities of a short chapter. Actually, the comparison is so unambiguous for huge chunks of these economies – notably goods, services, and government purchasing of goods and services in public procurement – that brief treatment of these areas makes the point. A longer discussion could make similar points about labor markets but would need to acknowledge a more mixed situation in markets for capital, in many parts of which there are still more interstate regulatory impediments in Europe than in the United States.

For a start, consider legal standards. From the 1970s to the 1990s, Europe consolidated the most stringent requirements ever devised for cross-border openness in goods and services. In goods, the European Court of Justice (in the Dassonville decision) interpreted the EU's founding treaties as banning "[a]ll trading rules enacted by member states which are capable of hindering, directly or indirectly, actually or potentially, intra-Community trade". In services, the Gebhard decision found that national rules may not even "make less attractive" cross-border services provision unless they are necessary for imperatives of policy, security, health or the environment; non-discriminatory to out-of-state providers; and suitable and proportional to obtain their objective.

American states are allowed far more leeway to impede exchange and mobility. Their constitutional Commerce Clause was unambiguously intended to remove such impediments, but the Supreme Court has interpreted it to ban only "purposeful discrimination" – a far narrower standard than in the EU, allowing for all sorts of rules with discriminatory effects. In other jurisprudence the court has carved out other huge exceptions to the Commerce Clause, like confirming states' rights to reject other states' professional licensing or authorizing outright protectionism in public procurement.

These principles are borne out today in all sorts of American interstate impediments that the EU is worked hard to reduce. For practically all goods, the EU has either harmonized standards or "mutual recognition." The US has federal standards in many areas – food safety, chemicals, toys, medical devices

– but these are floors that states can freely exceed. For example, California sets higher standards for 800 chemicals. In many areas of goods, no nationwide standards exist at all. Elevator manufacturers must meet different state (or even city) standards – a problem solved by the EU's 1995 Lifts Directive.

In services, it is fair to describe the EU as a space with strong default principles of openness to which exceptions remain, while the US is a space with strong default principles of separate jurisdictions with some exceptional areas of openness. *The Economist* is certainly right to note important exceptions and incomplete enforcement in Europe's interstate services provision, but its legislation basically puts the onus on receiving countries to justify any remaining restrictions on out-of-state service providers. A large body of legislative and administrative action ensures that this principle touches ground in most areas. Harmonization or mutual recognition of professional qualifications aims for easy movement for lawyers, architects, plumbers, hairdressers, and most other sectors. The EU also invented a legal category of "temporary provision of services" that generally allows up to two years of cross-border practice with minimal constraints. All states must administer "Single Points of Contact" websites where providers can fulfill all remaining requirements.

In the United States, meanwhile, there are some important areas where federal legislation trumps state differences and barriers – telecommunications, most transport, parts of finance – but otherwise service providers must generally meet each state's requirements. There are no federal rules on professional qualifications (except for pilots, air traffic controllers, and radio operators), and very little mutual recognition of qualifications among the states. Sometimes states strike bilateral recognition deals in some areas, and private associations often promote certain training, licensing, and exams, but the prevailing rule is that professionals hold licenses for each state where they practice. The notion of temporary provision of services does not exist. Operating in a state generally means meeting its requirements, full stop. Often these requirements are near-identical, since US states are not very different compared to European countries, but even near-identical qualifications from a neighboring state are typically useless.

The EU–US contrast is especially striking when public agencies procure goods and services. Though unmentioned in the EEC treaty, non-discrimination in public purchasing was legislated in the 1970s and upgraded to a central theme of the "single market 1992" program. Gradual steps strengthened these rules over time, most recently with the 2019 requirement that most state contracts be tendered through the EU's own "e-procurement" system. Meanwhile the vast majority of US states maintain in-state preferences for all public contracts. These state laws include outright bans: Pennsylvanian agencies can only buy Pennsylvanian coal, Oregonian agencies can only purchase in-state printing services. This difference has been a running issue in transatlantic trade negotia-tions. The EU wants open procurement markets at all levels, but the US federal government has no authority to open up subnational contracting.

But most striking of all, given these EU steps well beyond its supposed American model, is how broadly mainstream European elites and public opin-ion agree on a need for further single market steps. Even single market cham-pions acknowledge it as unexciting; as Jacques Delors once said: "You cannot fall in love with the single market." Still, remarks about the project's unfinished nature are pervasive in European discourse, and large public majorities are sym-pathetic to its main lines however the question is posed. Over a thousand peo-ple are employed in Brussels specifically to keep it moving forwards. A powerful court stands ready to arbitrate systematically in favor of more openness. Despite the past decade of crises and Euroskeptical challenges – including direct back-lash against single market openness, especially labor mobility – a flow of single market-enhancing legislation has moved through the EU machinery. Though the vote for Brexit was itself substantially driven by a backlash against cross-border mobility, it has provided an unlooked-for boost for the single market, nudging continental politicians to rally together in more explicit defense of its core prin-ciples than ever before. The question going forwards is how deeply, broadly, and quickly the EU will further chip away at interstate barriers, not whether or not that will happen.

Limits to single market benefits?

If a more realistic comparison of Europe's single market to America's helps to celebrate its achievement, it also hints at limits to what the core European pro-ject can accomplish. This comparison implies that trade and mobility on both continents are less responsive to regulatory frameworks than many people assume. After all, despite Europe's barrier-eliminating efforts and the United States' indifference to similar obstacles, interstate trade counts for roughly twice as much of the American economy as the European one. By some measures American interstate mobility may be 20 times as high as Europe's.

We should not be shocked by this observation. Americans share a language, a national identity forged in wars, and a distinct culture of mobility per se. Europeans speak different languages, fought wars against each other, and move relatively little even inside their countries. We do, however, need to recognize its implications for the likely results of "completing the single market". Such steps are most often justified in economic terms, but they may not achieve the macroeconomic gains of stabilizing and growth-enhancing cross-border flows that Americans enjoy even with shambolic interstate regulation. They will surely have some economic pay-off – and the eurozone's unbalanced economic governance needs all the equilibrating flows it can foster – but a modest one. Thus, the best arguments for such steps, and the key terrain on which Europeans must debate the trade-offs of single market openness against other legitimate concerns, relate more to its direct political benefits of mobility, social integration, and international cooperation than to diffuse economic gains. Constructing an open, fair, well-governed single market remains a worthy task for Europe in its own right.

17

ECONOMIC AND MONETARY UNION: A LIVE ISSUE AFTER 50 YEARS

Dermot Hodson and Alison Johnston

The CES shares its golden anniversary with the Werner Report, a major milestone on the road to EMU. Although it was not the first high-level study on this subject, the Werner Report was the first to be taken up by member states, which set 1980 as a target date for the irrevocable fixing of exchange rates by current and aspiring members of the EC. This commitment was dropped amid the economic turmoil that followed the demise of the Bretton Woods System and the first oil shock. But the Werner Report's vision of what is needed to make EMU work has endured, more so, in some respects, than the Delors Report, which formed the blueprint for the euro's eventual launch in 1999.

Asymmetry

The Delors Report envisaged an asymmetric EMU. Monetary policy was placed under the control of a single decision-making body while economic policy remained in the hands of member states. The report implicitly rejected the link between EMU and political union, concluding that a Community with a single currency could "continue to consist of individual nations with differing economic, social, cultural and political characteristics ... and autonomy in economic decision-making" (Committee for the Study of Economic and Monetary Union 1989: 17).

No mention was made in the Delors Report of a fiscal transfer mechanism. Preoccupied with the harmful effects of national economic policies on monetary policy and the Community's economic situation more generally, it instead proposed that macroeconomic policy be subject to binding procedures and rules. So was born the excessive deficit procedure (and later the Stability and Growth Pact), with its threat of financial penalties and fines against member states that posted excessive budget deficits and unsustainable public debt. A coordinated rather than a centralized approach to banking supervision was also proposed.

The Werner Report imagined a more symmetrical EMU in which monetary policy was delegated to a Community organ modeled on the United States Federal Reserve, while economic policy was subject to the control of a supranational Centre of Decision for Economic Policy. It saw political union not only as essential for the sustainability of EMU but an inevitable consequence of it. The report trod more carefully on the question of fiscal transfers, although it acknowledged that the Community budget would increase in importance in the final stage of EMU and that regional and structural policies, as well as social partner concertation, could no longer remain national. It was bolder on financial market issues, calling for "regulations governing the activities of credit institutions and institutional investors" and the harmonization of the "structures and statutes of credit institutions" to suit a unified market (Werner 1970: 21).

The Werner Report's greatest oversight was its proclamation that once the union was complete, "only the global balance of payments of the Community vis-à-vis the outside world is of any importance", and that "equilibrium in the community would be realized at this stage in the same way as within a nation's frontiers" (Werner 1970: 10). Unlike those of the Werner Report, the authors of the Delors Report had a decade's worth of hindsight to observe how the EMU's predecessor, the EMS, operated. Indeed, the Delors Report broke with the Werner Report's rosy prediction on imbalances between member states – which many scholars now attribute as the cause of the euro crisis itself – highlighting that under the EMS, external imbalances between member states had become "markedly greater", and that divergences in wage levels and prices would generate "serious economic tensions" (Committee for the Study of Economic and Monetary Union 1989: 20). Yet, ironically, while the Delors Report was more cognizant of the divergence problems within member states on EMU's horizon, it was the Werner Report that offered a more structurally robust way of managing them.

Shortcomings

The euro crisis – Europe's biggest economic challenge of the last half-century – exposed significant shortcomings in the Delors Report's design for EMU. Although all eurozone member states entered the prior global financial crisis seemingly in compliance with the Stability and Growth Pact, the fact of compliance provided a false sense of security. Greece had hidden the true scale of government borrowing. Ireland and Spain had balanced their budgets while failing to address other macroeconomic imbalances, most noticeably in housing markets. Low interest rates and a lack of financial oversight was a recipe for excessive risk taking by financial institutions and governments alike.

Moreover, the EU's lack of attention to intra-euro wage dynamics led to some member states experiencing a persistent loss of competitiveness during the EMU's first decade, while others witnessed a continuous improvement. Although the Delors Report was alive to the problem of macroeconomic imbalances, it sowed the seeds for them by stipulating that wage negotiations should continue to be determined at the national level. Competitiveness, the report erroneously assumed, would be resolved through wage flexibility and labor mobility, adjustment mechanisms that operate imperfectly in Europe.

When these shortcomings came to light in quick succession, the eurozone found itself facing a sovereign debt crisis that threatened to tear the single currency asunder. The emphasis in the Delors Report on autonomy in economic decision-making proved costly. The eurozone lacked ready-made instruments to provide financial assistance to member states facing fiscal and financial crises. Protracted negotiations over filling this gap worsened the sovereign debt crisis in Greece and other member states. So too did the harsh conditions attached to these loans and the reluctance of other member states to engage in a coordinated fiscal stimulus or a rebalancing of wages.

Back to Werner

While member states improvised their way through this crisis, they also put in place a set of reforms that moved EMU closer to the Werner Report (Van Middelaar 2019). The most significant reform was the European banking union, which gave the European Central Bank (ECB) significant new powers of supervision over financial institutions and new instruments for dealing with distressed banks. The result stopped short of the unified capital market that the Werner Report had dreamed of, most noticeably through member states' reluctance about agreeing on a common system of deposit insurance. But it went well beyond the minimalist vision of EMU in the Delors Report.

The euro crisis broke the taboo over creating a eurozone budget, but member states remain more divided than ever about the most appropriate size and functions of such an instrument. The desire expressed by political leaders in many of the southern member states for a stabilization instrument that can cushion the impact of economic shocks chimes with the Werner Report, but that desire lacks support from northern member states, which remain reluctant to put taxpayers' money on the line.

This lack of solidarity in the aftermath of the crisis also prevented the realization of another of Werner's proposals in the area of wage policy: the establishment of a transnational space in which the Commission and social partners would study and discuss income trends across member states (Werner 1970: 18). The ill-fated Doorn Group, created on the eve of the euro's launch, had the potential to reduce sharp competitiveness divergences through cross-border coordination of collective bargaining actors across major sectoral unions. But effective coordination never materialized, and, given probable objections from Germany among others, it is unlikely to happen anytime soon.

Challenges

As the EU, and the CES, look to the next half-century, EMU remains a live issue. Reforms undertaken since 2010 leave the eurozone better prepared for future fiscal and financial crisis but they embody Delors' asymmetric vision in important respects. EU policy-makers monitor macroeconomic imbalances more closely, but they have limited sway over member states' economic policy choices and their cross-border consequences. Financial institutions are more stringently supervised but the risk that a financial crisis might spillover into a sovereign debt crisis remains all too real. Politically, the euro has become a lightning rod for popular discontent with the EU. Although support for the single currency has slowly recovered after the euro crisis, trust in the ECB remains worryingly low and populist politicians in France and Italy have flirted with the idea of exiting the euro. For these reasons, EMU remains economically and politically vulnerable, and the Werner Report, for all its limitations, remains more salient than ever.

18

PUTTING DEPRIVED URBAN NEIGHBORHOODS BACK AT THE CORE OF EU URBAN POLICY

Sonia De Gregorio Hurtado

Urban poverty began to lose relevance as a policy problem at the EU level in the early 2000s. By the end of that decade, however, the impact of the global financial and economic crisis brought urban exclusion back to the fore. The importance of the issue remains undiminished. After years of post-crisis "austerity", Europe's economies appear to be recovering. Even in wealthier countries and regions, however, urban poverty is still high.

The Seventh Report of Economic, Social and Territorial Cohesion of the EU (European Commission 2017a: xv) shows that the risk of poverty or social exclusion remains higher than before the crisis in cities, towns, and suburbs in those countries that were members of the EU before May 2004 (the EU-15). In 2014 there were 34 million people in the EU at risk of poverty or social exclusion living in cities, and 24.2 million people living in towns, and suburbs (Eurostat 2019). Most of these people are concentrated in deprived neighborhoods. These are areas that should become specific policy objectives of the urban dimension of Cohesion Policy in the post-2020 period.

There are other powerful reasons to place the focus for EU Cohesion Policy on deprived neighborhoods. Long-term developments related to demographic trends, technological innovation, climate change, and social interaction will have a stronger negative impact on the inhabitants of deprived urban areas. At the same time, the EU adopted Agenda 2030 for Sustainable Development of the United Nations and its 17 Sustainable Development Goals (SDGs) in 2015. SDG number 1 is *no poverty*.

This short chapter proposes a critical review of the experience developed by the EEC and, from 1993, the EU in addressing the problems of deprived neighborhoods from the early 1990s to the present. That temporal perspective is useful in revealing the changing definition of the "urban problem" and the evolution of policy priorities over time. A longitudinal analysis also helps to underscore the lessons learned through the development of a specific policy for tackling deprived neighborhoods over the past two decades. That experience can be the starting point for the creation of a new specific instrument in EU Cohesion Policy to face the problems of vulnerable urban areas after 2020.

Urban areas have long posed a challenge

Many European economies underwent profound structural changes in the 1960s, 1970s, and 1980s that had a powerfully negative effect on urban areas. Some neighborhoods proved particularly vulnerable. These places experienced a reinforcing combination of low-quality urban space, environmental decline, high unemployment rates, increasing social inequality, social stigmatization, poor urban facilities and public services, crime and insecurity, and lack of economic opportunities. The result was a vicious poverty cycle that threatened the advancement of social equality and economic integration in European cities.

Urban governments could not deal with these problems acting alone. As a result, international, European, and national actors began to get involved. In the framework of the EEC, the European Commission became aware of the increasing relevance of the urban issue. The Commission published a Green Paper on the Urban Environment to make the case for targeting urban decline specifically, and it launched a new policy initiative in 1989 under the name of Urban Pilot Projects.

The policy initiatives that took place during the second half of the 1980s were the basis for the development of a transformative policy during the 1990s. In 1994 the Commission launched its Urban Community Initiative (URBAN), as an instrument for urban regeneration. It was particularly designed to face the problems of deprived neighborhoods through an area-based approach. In that sense, URBAN is the most explicit and specific urban tool launched and developed by the Commission so far.

In the definition of URBAN, the Commission was heavily influenced by experience in the United Kingdom, and particularly by City Challenge, a program for urban regeneration launched by the British government in 1989. URBAN was also aligned with the outcomes of the 1992 Rio Summit of United Nations regarding sustainable urban development. That summit introduced two important methodological elements to regenerate deprived neighborhoods: the integrated approach to tackling urban challenges across a range of different policy dimensions and the participation of the local community during the whole process of urban regeneration.

From URBAN to the Urban Acquis

URBAN contributed importantly to the formalization of what we call today the "urban policy of the EU", a dimension of EU policy funded by the Cohesion Policy, and particularly through the European Regional Development Fund and the European Social Fund. The URBAN method demonstrated that the integrated, participative, and area-based approach is a necessary condition to understand and address the complex and specific processes that reproduce urban decline in vulnerable neighborhoods. Because of this, the URBAN method has been replicated by different member state governments, regional authorities, and city administrations to act in deprived areas.

The experience achieved through the implementation of 188 URBAN programs in 15 member states during the Cohesion Policy's 1994–9 and 2000–6 programming periods yielded considerable insight on the benefits and limitations of the URBAN method for urban regeneration, something that has contributed importantly to the construction of the EU's so-called Urban Acquis. The Urban Acquis refers to "the construction of a common European methodology of intervention in urban areas" (Atkinson & Rossignolo 2008).

This Urban Acquis builds on the lessons derived from the URBAN method to integrate a range of proposals made by the Commission and other actors in other policy documents on urban matters. The Urban Acquis has provided conceptual guidance and shared principles for sustainable urban development in the EU during the last decades, significantly influencing the definition of EU urban policy over time and, of course, the urban policies of the member states. In the context of this work, it is relevant to point out that the documents integrated in the Urban Acquis, such as the Leipzig Charter, are completely aligned with URBAN, adopting as main objectives the necessity of developing specific and transformative projects to foster an integrated approach to regenerating deprived neighborhoods.

Urban mainstreaming

The framework developed during the 1990s underwent a significant transformation during the 2000s. In the 2007–13 programming period of the Cohesion Policy, URBAN disappeared as the Commission shifted its attention to what it called "urban mainstreaming". This mainstreaming was an approach aimed at integrating the guiding principles of URBAN in the action agreed among the Commission, the member states, and the regions (through the so-called Operational Programs). The goal was to reinforce the urban dimension of EU policy.

As an approach, this urban mainstreaming was voluntary for the member states. They did not have economic or policy incentives to adopt it. The result was that the Commission's vision was not implemented by most of the member state governments and the urban issue lost visibility. This took place in a period in which the Cohesion Policy underwent a comprehensive reform and was transformed into an investment policy that focused on several EU priority topics. The Cohesion Policy program package for 2014–20 reflected this shift in priorities. As a result, that package focused on a limited number of policy objectives through the so-called Smart Specialization approach. This is a vision that considers that each region can make the most of its Cohesion Policy expenditure if it first identifies its core strengths. When applied to urban policy, however, Smart Specialization has led policy attention at all levels to focus far from vulnerable and deprived urban areas.

Of course, the urban issue did not disappear entirely. The Cohesion Policy program for 2014–20 was the first to run alongside a requirement that member state governments ring-fence 5 per cent of their European Regional Development Fund expenditure for Integrated Sustainable Urban Development. In that sense, the allocation of funding to foster urban action has increased significantly when compared to previous Cohesion Policy programming periods.

The point to note is that this increase in funding has taken place during a broad reconceptualization of EU urban policy. The new policy concept shows an important change both in direction and in priority. For example, the Cohesion Policy framework now specifies priority topics that make it hard to adapt an integrated approach or to address the complex mix of interrelated problems that characterize vulnerable urban areas. These priority topics also constrain the ability of municipal authorities to develop strategies that address their own specific needs and problems, particularly when important local issues do not fall completely within the objectives set out in the Cohesion Policy framework.

Most important, perhaps, the Cohesion Policy framework does not identify vulnerable neighborhoods for explicit policy attention. Member state governments can address the needs of those neighborhoods voluntarily, but they have to do so within the context of a policy framework that creates few if any incentives to regenerate deprived neighborhoods through integrated and area-based strategies. Indeed, it could be said that the policy and administrative conditions set by the current Cohesion Policy framework makes it almost impossible for municipal authorities (and especially for the medium and small ones) to implement the regeneration programs inspired by URBAN.

Time to act

The current Cohesion Policy program will finish at the end of 2020. When it does, that policy program will not have contributed to overcoming one of the main EU challenges at present: urban poverty and the increasing social polarization in cities. That is an important opportunity missed. Now is the time to restore urban poverty to the core of EU Cohesion Policy. That policy framework was specifically created to achieve the social and economic integration of the EU at the local and regional level. Such integration is particularly important in a period in which urban areas continue to face poverty and social exclusion resulting from the recent economic crisis, and in which international actors are warning about the threat of a new potential economic recession in Europe.

The first step will be to reconsider the "urban problem" in the framework of the Cohesion Policy. Such reconsideration will make it possible to set the priorities for urban policy in the post-2020 period. Now is the time to reflect on the action undertaken during the 1990s and 2000s. That experience provides important lessons on what worked and what methodological aspects of the URBAN method need to be reviewed. This can lead to an "update" of the Urban Acquis, a framework that can provide again guidance to EU cities and other actors in their path toward sustainable futures. Such an update needs to focus more attention on the challenge of regenerating deprived areas through integrated policies that take local considerations into account. These vulnerable neighborhoods are crucial for the future of European urban areas and their citizens.

19

THE POLITICAL INTEGRATION OF THE MIDDLE CLASS

Paul Marx

If we ask a political economist, "what is the biggest issue confronting Europe today?" the likely answer we will get is: "where should I start!?" Indeed, there is no shortage of candidates: the macroeconomic divergence of the EU's member states, the conflicts about EMU, the powder keg of immigration policy, the growing concentration of wealth and political power, the wave of populist mobilization after the Great Recession, and, on the horizon, technological changes with unforeseeable implications for the structure of European economies. One could add the (real or self-imposed) limitations in fiscal capacities of many welfare states to deal with future challenges (an ability that I would nominate, without expecting much disagreement, as a "significant achievement from Europe's past").

Many of these problems can be linked to the question of what happens to Europe's middle classes – as workers, consumers, and citizens. This does not mean that we should stop being interested in, concerned about, and solidaristic with Europe's "precariat" or "outsiders". But in terms of sheer numbers, it should be clear that Europe's societies will look very different if they fail at the political integration of its middle classes. Much research suggests that this political integration is inextricably tied to labor market experiences and consumption opportunities. In the light of growing economic inequalities and their social repercussions, it is this link that begins to appear precarious to many contemporary observers.

Admittedly, the fate of the middle class has not only to do with economic facts and measurable insecurities but also with psychology. To appreciate the problem, we have to move from an individualistic to a relational perspective. Economists still sometimes pretend that people care about money per se. Empirically and theoretically, it is more plausible to assume that people are primarily motivated to feel included in groups and to get as high a status in these group as possible (Marx 2019a, 2019b). In capitalist societies, money is an important material and symbolic resource to acquire status. A wealth of evidence in psychology, sociology, and biology shows that humans are incredibly sensitive to even subtle social cues signaling inclusion or exclusion. Successful social situations trigger the release of hormones that make us feel proud, happy, elated. Failing to reach the standards of our groups is an equally visceral experience that usually feels pretty terrible. The experience of failure takes the form of some mix of anxiety, guilt, anger, and shame. The physiological correlate is, for instance, an elevated cortisol level. The behavioral correlates can be devastating.

Relationships matter

While this obsession with social status might have had survival advantages in humanity's distant past, it can be stressful in contemporary capitalist societies. The reason is, as has been emphasized already by authors such as Thorsten Veblen, Max Weber, and Pierre Bourdieu, that such societies tend to moralize economic success and failure (contemporary examples are the works of Luc Boltanksi and Eve Chiapello, Michèle Lamont, or Richard Sennett). Economic differences are translated through countless subtle mechanisms into a symbolic order that represents and legitimizes them. Consumption and lifestyle choices are not simply benign expressions of identities; they are symbolic acts to fulfill the twin desire for inclusion and distinction.

The practical consequence for many European middle-class citizens is that, for all their apparent prosperity, they find themselves in an endless succession of micro-status competitions. Viewed through this lens, we inhabit a world of elaborate symbolic boundaries that inform us about our social standing. And the sites for status struggle seem to encroach upon ever more realms of life. They range from classical conspicuous consumption, over leisure activities and tastes that allow projecting a refined, creative self, to the investment into children's cultural capital. Although it must often appear to an outside observer as the "narcissism of small differences", the prospect of moving to the wrong side of these boundaries can be horrifying. Sometimes economic inequality also translates into actual boundaries if it leads to unaffordable housing and residential segregation.

The rising importance of status competition

This short digression into social theory is necessary to appreciate the challenge European societies are facing. It highlights how important for well-being – but also how precarious and contested – status claims are. Status competition is certainly an old phenomenon, but a number of observations suggests that it has intensified in the past decades.

First, postindustrial societies have developed an ethos that glorifies work in creative occupations and denigrates many traditional jobs. This amounts to denying a large group of people a source of status that is at least partly independent of money. This creativity ethos also structures the status worthiness of consumption and leisure activities so that the same people lose out culturally in several realms.

Second, growing income inequality has raised the stakes in status comparisons. If the upper middle class and the rich race away, it is easy to feel relatively deprived compared to a standard that is increasingly hard to reach. If the lower middle class inhabits a totally different life world, the prospect of joining their ranks becomes terrifying. This forces middle-class citizens to care deeply and constantly about whether they have the right amount of "Veblen goods"; only that the finish line in the race for distinction or emulation is a moving target. Inequality then provides incentives for households to increase labor supply on the intensive and extensive margin as well as to whip their offspring into a successful future. Income inequality therefore tends to be exhausting and to harbor a great potential for frustration.

Third, the internet has aggravated the ferocity of status struggles. This should be intuitive for anybody who occasionally visits social network sites, but there is also hard evidence for how these platforms make people unhappy through unfavorable comparisons. The equivalent for academics is browsing colleagues' publication lists. The catch is, of course, that you always find a profile (or publication list) with which you compare unfavorably.

The precarious middle

What follows from this line of argument is the admittedly stylized picture of an anomic middle-class family, entangled in simultaneous upward and downward status competition, willing to intensify labor as much as is necessary to succeed in it, or to rely on credit cards if even that is not enough. Maybe this characterization pushes things a bit, but if this stylized picture resembles only a fraction of the European middle class, we have reason to be concerned. Because what would happen if European societies enter a situation in which the status order is markedly shaken up?

Take for instance the much-discussed scenario that digital technologies will crowd out a significant number of decent jobs. "Redundant" workers would probably not find much comfort in the argument that these technologies might create, as labor economists insist, jobs for other workers. Even lagging moderately behind in income growth can feel like a defeat in the status struggles the middle class has to internalize. Nothing guarantees, moreover, that the income effects of the digital transformation will remain moderate.

As mentioned above, the subjective experience of frustrated status claims is grounded in negative emotions. Particularly if people accept the neoliberal ethic of self-responsibility, such an experience can lead to self-denigration and shame. It seems difficult to avoid these feelings entirely if one is embedded in a societal ideology that glorifies economic success and attributes it to merit. From a viewpoint of individual well-being that is problematic, because negative self-conscious emotions are painful and often lead to destructive behavior. But such emotions can also turn into a societal problem.

There is much to say about the emotional dynamics that come with status relegation. For now, it is enough to highlight that, with the rise of populism, virtually all European countries have political templates and organizations in place whose core principle is turning other negative emotions into anger. Populists' versatile rhetoric offers, as it were, a coping mechanism for self-denigration by collectivizing the problem and by projecting blame outward (Marx 2019b). Being angry is more pleasant than accepting responsibility. It is not surprising then that populist rhetoric becomes appealing for people exposed to status concerns.

Anger is not necessarily bad. It can be politically productive. It is possible that people recognize their status relegation as systemic and illegitimate, and that they unite in a progressive left project. This is not what history and current trends should lead us to expect. Much suggests that the negative emotions resulting from status threat are easily exploited by political projects that rely on scapegoating and aggression against out-groups. Here lies a major challenge for Europe about which much has been written. If anger politics continues to grow and to spread cynicism, it can reach a point where it turns into a threat for democratic institutions. It is also difficult to see how productive solutions to foreseeable ecological and economic crises can be found on the European level if the standard operating procedure in domestic politics is agitating against Athens, Berlin, Brussels, Paris, or some sort of "caste".

An open future – to make

To sum up: status-seeking is part of the human condition. Growing inequality and its ideological underpinnings have arguably let status competition escalate. This makes unequal societies particularly vulnerable to shocks upsetting the status order. Status relegation causes intense negative emotions which, in turn, provide the raw material for political mobilization strategies that could turn out to be quite destructive for European democracies.

Of course, many parts of the argument lie in contingencies and conjectures, and the future is open. If we accept the above scenario for the moment, is there anything to be done to make European societies less vulnerable? I would like to end with some thoughts in this direction, although few of them take the form of concrete, let alone feasible suggestions.

To begin with, the key insight of the relational status perspective is that society as a whole would be better off if all of its members had a status dimension on which they excel. That becomes a thorny issue if status claims are based on ethnicity or gender, but there might be some denigrated cultural practice that could get a bit more "breathing space" in societal discourses without sacrificing egalitarian values.

Next, money is such an important status resource that we cannot be allowed to distribute it as unequally as we do today. European societies have, to varying extents, let inequality escalate; now they should do everything to reverse the trend. This should include substantial taxation of the income and wealth of the richest citizens, which would also allow the sufficient funding of welfare states to buffer the effects of upcoming economic crises. We could look more confidently toward the future if we could trust on the social and macroeconomic policies that have proven so useful in the past instead of worrying about debt brakes, bond spreads, or lenders' conditionality.

Welfare states can also help to keep status warfare at bay. If the state provides, for instance, decent education and public housing, it prevents these existential aspects of life from turning into positional Veblen goods. At least some of the important status arenas would be shut down.

A few additional thoughts also merit consideration. First, whether we like it or not, jobs will remain the core status resource in the foreseeable future. If labor demand is insufficient, states have to find ways to create jobs. Second, not all criticism of the EU is cynical and irrational. To the contrary, it could do much to avoid being the target of anger. Particularly inside the EMU, the EU has to find a way to overcome the current construction, which has contributed to a highly divisive economic divergence of its members. Finally, Europe should regulate the aggressive business models of (mostly American) internet platforms heavily. There are many serious issues, from taxation and data protection to the manipulation of elections. In analogy to the tobacco industry, care should also be taken to prevent deliberate design elements that foster compulsive usage.

20

THE LEFTOVERS: VULNERABLE POPULATIONS IN THE GLOBAL, POSTINDUSTRIAL AGE

Cathie Jo Martin

Crises of society, economy, and democracy are rocking the foundations of Europe. As Nathan Gardels writes in the *Washington Post* (21 September 2018): "Across Western democracies, the social cohesion that once sustained political consensus has severely eroded." Social cohesion requires interdependent individuals to perceive societal well-being as crucial to peace and prosperity, and to cooperate for shared social goals (Council of Europe 2008: 7). Yet marginal groups are suffering in the contemporary political, economic, and social climate, and outsiders are increasingly vocal about their discontent. Right-oriented protest groups often concentrate their free-floating rage on border-crossing flows of refugees and workers. Yellow-vested protesters and neofascist memes more broadly signal malaise with state authority and with societies that forget the leftovers.

Economic malaise certainly contributes to the crisis of social cohesion. Postindustrial change, a jobless recovery from the financial and euro crises, and rising inequality threaten economic well-being, and citizens at the margins receive little from mainstream society. Child poverty rates are on the rise in two-thirds of OECD countries. Young people who are not in employment, education, or training constituted 14 per cent of 15–29 year olds within the OECD in 2016.

The crisis of social cohesion also reflects the deficit of democracy within the EU and receding agreement on the mission of the EU. Despite ardent efforts to construct a supranational Europe with symbols and narratives, a collective European social identity seems out of reach, as few consider the EU to be a whole that is larger than the sum of its parts. Mass voters fear that EU elite technocrats have little interest in respecting national political and cultural traditions. EU collective action is grounded in political or legal logic, rather than in cultural norms of cooperation. This democratic deficit contributes to a legitimation crisis of both national and supranational political authorities.

Varieties of society in a global context

Countries have historically built on diverse models to reconcile growth and social solidarity. These models make different assumptions about the importance of marginal groups to national growth projects and to the health of the polity. The social democratic model found in the Nordic countries posits that each individual should contribute to building a strong society and economy. Therefore, even the most marginal groups require social investments in skills, and the neglect of these groups weakens the social fabric. The model reconciles economic growth with social solidarity, and the state is central to the national project. The liberal model found in the Anglo countries espouses vastly different conceptions of the individual's role in society, the legitimacy of the state, the role of markets, and the inclusion of marginal groups. This model has a less developed view of society, seeks to protect the individual from the excesses of the state, leaves much to markets, and sees marginal groups as playing no particular positive role in broader social well-being. Exclusion of marginal groups is bad for the individuals (and the deserving poor should be protected), but this exclusion has little bearing on the rest of us.

National cultural conceptions of society, government, and vulnerable groups have deep historical roots and shed light on divergent policy paths. One may observe significant differences in countries' cultural depictions appearing in literature dating back to at least 1700. To study these cross-national differences, I derive lists of fiction written between 1700 and 1920 (about 500–600 for each country), obtain full-text files of these works, construct snippets of text around themes (such as education, poverty, and labor), and use natural language processing techniques to identify words and topics associated with these themes (Martin 2018; Martin *et al.* 2019).

One may observe a contrast between British and Danish literary depictions of education dating back to the eighteenth century. Danish literary narratives espouse education as a means for strengthening society and for ensuring that each citizen contributes to societal goals. Conversely, Britain develops public education for the middle classes to further individual self-growth, and eighteenth-century fiction writers say little about the societal benefits of educating the working class. Instead, many feared that mass education could prompt social instability (Martin 2018). The data I have collected demonstrate that large corpora of Danish and Swedish literature (in countries with strong states and collective social identities) have significantly more references to labor in snippets of text surrounding education words than the large corpus of British texts. Second, British authors are more likely to associate education with individualism than Danish and Swedish authors. Third, Danish and Swedish corpora contain significantly more references to government in education snippets than

British and French texts. These comparative findings suggest that investing in society has long been a central aim of education in Denmark and Sweden but not in Britain; therefore, it is not surprising that the Nordic welfare and education systems retain a focus on social investment today.

In like fashion, Dennie Nijhuis, Erik Olsson, and I demonstrate that literary depictions of labor going back centuries are associated with high levels of cooperation words in Denmark, the Netherlands, and Sweden; this sheds light on why these coordinated countries – with vastly different industrial structures – developed such similar institutions for industrial relations (Martin *et al.* 2019). In comparison, class conflict has long been a central cultural tenet of labor relations in liberal Britain. References to cooperation in snippets of text surrounding labor words are significantly higher in the coordinated countries than in Britain (Martin *et al.* 2019). Cultural memes show how rampant individualism amplifies class resentments in Britain from the Luddites to Brexit.

Neoliberalism and societal bonds

Neoliberalism – the reigning political philosophy of the past four decades – exacerbates the pressures on social solidarity and status anxieties of the postindustrial economy. Pressures for convergence on the neoliberal model exacerbate the negative impacts of structural changes and pose problems for the economic, political, and social well-being of contemporary Europe. Countries with stronger cultural and institutional traditions of coordination have sustained higher levels of social solidarity; however, even these countries struggle to sustain solidarity against liberalizing trends. Neoliberalim challenges the tried and true prescriptions of the social democratic formula, even though the Nordic model has historically been highly successful. The Nordic countries more successfully reconciled growth and equity historically, and the Nordic model provides a better alternative for coping with the postindustrial age.

The economic, political, and social chaos associated with contemporary neoliberalism reminds one of past failures to reconcile growth and solidarity in liberal countries; and indeed, contemporary neoliberalism shares many cultural assumptions (about individual, society, social classes, and state) with the liberal model of the past. The Anglo countries constitute ground zero of neoliberalism, because individualism is deeply woven into the cultural fabric. The logic of neoliberalism – rewarding winners and neglecting losers – holds the seeds of its own destruction. Neoliberalism shifts the goals of government from building society to helping the entrepreneurial individual and espouses equality of opportunity as a means for those who strive to thrive. Yet, equality of opportunity rewards winners and conveys the sense that inequality is fair. Meritocracy justifies blaming the victim, because losers are held responsible for factors often beyond their control. Neoliberalism saps the strength of society as well as assaulting solidarity, because it deprives society of economic contributions by the group of workers at the bottom. Populist parties on the right flourish, in part, because non-elites feel both excluded from economic gains and blamed by the meritocracy.

Neoliberalism has also taken its toll on collective social identities across Europe because the pressure to conform to a single model denies the sharp contrasts – rooted in deep cultural symbols – in the varieties of national collective identities. EU policy-makers who wish to build a shared EU political identity must reckon with vastly different conceptions across countries of the individual's role in society, the legitimacy of the state, the role of markets, the inclusion of marginal groups, and the causes of social problems. European technocrats prescribe ideal policy solutions and encourage national governments to utilize their own methods to implement these best practices. Yet citizens in countries with different perceptions of society hesitate to accept political and social solutions at odds with national traditions; moreover, diverse cultural expectations contribute to the uneven implementation of best practices. Varying degrees of social solidarity among European countries make it difficult to construct a social Europe.

A way forward

Solidarism, peace, and prosperity demand a turn away from neoliberal individualism and a recognition of the yearning for social collectivism. Economic policies must halt the expansion of the precariat; these should be couched in terms of how poverty detracts from society and what everyone can contribute to social well-being. Commitment to a strong society drives social investments. Attaining a European collective social identity requires cultural work.

PART III

THE CHANGING FACE OF EUROPE

21

NATIVISM ACROSS THE ATLANTIC: THE END OF EXCEPTIONALISMS?

Jan Willem Duyvendak

Ever since Alexis de Tocqueville famously claimed America and Americans to be "exceptional", comparisons between the United States and Europe have privileged differences over similarities. We have seen this in many scholarly fields, but the emphasis on differences is particularly noticeable in the field of migration studies. While immigration and diversity are burning issues on both sides of the Atlantic, the framing of the debate in the United States – at least until recently, and in contrast to many European countries – did not focus on the failure of ethnic and racial minorities to integrate into the native majority. Blacks in the United States are of course not postcolonial immigrants, but the descendants of slaves with histories in the country going back centuries. Many authors thus consider blacks in the United States as natives, as African-Americans.

But what about the rise of political nativism in the United States today? "The rapid growth of Mexican immigration and most especially undocumented immigration since the early 1990s has led to a growth in nativist rhetoric and punitive laws targeting both legal and illegal immigrants and even their children" (Waters 2014: 153). Is the new American nativism comparable to developments in Europe? How did nativism emerge in a country where immigration is so central to national identity, where nobody (except Native Americans) can claim proprietary rights based on historical rootedness?

Myths and ideologies

A common claim is that nativism as an ideology is more likely to flourish in Europe because of how countries construct and teach their national histories. Scholars here suggest that migration plays a limited role in the "origin myths" and "national identities" of European countries; while the history of immigration is mobilized as a core feature of American identity, European national myths hold that there are "true" Europeans who are geographically and historically rooted in the land. Alba and Foner (2015) suggest that it is much more challenging for European societies to include newcomers in the national "we". North Americans, looking at West European anxieties about immigration – especially the cleavages between the European secular/Christian mainstream and Muslim immigrants and their children – often see confirmation of this idea. In a similar vein, recent scholarship notes that nativism as an ideology to limit further immigration is more heatedly contested in North America. The United States – the ultimate immigration country – cannot experience (a return of) nativism such as that seen in many European nations.

But when we dig deeper into the debate on where nativism most easily takes root, we see surprising similarities between the United States and parts of Europe (this line of reasoning draws distinctions between the countries of Europe). Some claim that the rise of nativism remains improbable in both France and the United States, given their laws on citizenship. In both countries, citizenship is based on the principle of *jus soli*: that anybody born on national territory has automatic access to citizenship. This principle is often claimed to serve as a bulwark against nativism, as children of immigrants are as French or American as children of parents born in the country. In contrast, the ground is fertile for nativism in countries with a *jus sanguinis* tradition, such as Germany, and countries that combine *jus sanguinis* and *jus soli*, such as the Netherlands.

Law and identity

As Rogers Brubaker argued in *Citizenship and Nationhood in France and Germany*, the legal differences between France and Germany are consequential, not only because they determine who gets access to citizenship, but because of the national self-understandings that these laws give rise to. In much of the literature, France is the embodiment of a country that wishes to be inclusive – to its minorities as well as to immigrants. But this universalism comes at a price: all aspiring French (wo)men must assimilate into a cultural unity, embracing French values and speaking the French language. "The rhetoric of inclusion is not disembodied or free-floating. It is grounded in a distinctive national self-understanding, in the sense of the grandeur of France, the assimilatory virtues of French territory and institutions, and the universal appeal and validity of French language and civilization" (Brubaker 1992: 111).

As many scholars have argued, the alleged universalism of the French state is also a particular form of group identity. Although mobilizing around "particular" identities is frowned upon as non-republican, the pronounced cultural content of French-ness suggests that the clash is not between "universalism" and "particularism" but between different cultural identities. Can cultural homogeneity and national groupthink be the outgrowth of universalist republicanism? Do the seeds of nativism lie within republicanism as such? While the origins of French and German national self-understanding may differ, don't the nativist consequences look very much alike?

Does this again imply a gulf of experience between Europe and the United States? Is there once again an American exceptionalism when it comes to nativism? We should not be too hasty in drawing this conclusion. John Higham's seminal *Strangers in the Land: Patterns of American Nativism, 1860–1925* convincingly showed us that nativism is not alien to American political culture. Although many see in Trump's rise to power a new wave of nativism, the phenomenon as such dates to the country's founding. Being a "country of immigrants" does not mean that all men and women equally belong. White propertied Protestant men saw themselves as the core of the new nation, and for a long time thereafter. Immigrants perceived to be close to this core group enjoyed easier access to the country than those perceived to be "different". Polish, Italian, Irish, and Jewish immigrants suffered exclusion because of language, religion, and suspicions of maintaining "foreign" loyalties. Such discrimination lessened over the decades as these groups started to be considered white, which at the time was not self-evident at all. Passing the color line made them American, relativizing their other differences.

There has thus long been a hierarchy between those who "own" the country, those who truly belong, and those who are, in one way or another, "foreign" and "not like us". As in France, American policies encourage assimilation. But in the United States, belonging to the nation is more compatible with maintaining other collective loyalties and identities. Hyphenated identities – Asian-American, Latino-American, African-American – emphasize the American-ness of various minority groups while giving space for diversity within American unity. This respect for group identities – dismissed by French politicians as multiculturalism or "communitarism" – should not be misunderstood: the United States seeks to assimilate newcomers, but this does not require them to give up all other group identities and loyalties. Whereas in France the push toward a homogeneous cultural unity privileges a "native" group to define what Frenchness is, in the United States it is the flipside of heterogeneity, of hyphenated identities that produces American nativism: hyphenated Americans are American to a lesser degree than those who don't need such hyphens.

More similar than exceptional

The rise of nativism in both France and the United States may seem surprising given the access to citizenship on the *jus soli* principle. This political openness, however, comes with cultural closure: the openness is only possible because of the assimilatory powers of state institutions. The alleged universalism of both France and the United States is in fact a very particular form of "group identity" that allows for nativist discourse to flourish – as in other European countries with different citizenship traditions.

For empirical reasons, then, I hope that, in the next 50 years, we focus more on similarities than exceptionalisms across the Atlantic. Similar empirical developments on the two continents require new concepts and theories. Rather than looking for explanations at the level of nations – while assuming or exaggerating differences between them – we need to explain why developments have been so similar, even in contexts that some of us are used to seeing as very different.

22

GOVERNING MIGRATION: POLITICAL CONTESTATION AND POLICY FORMATION

Jennifer Elrick and Oliver Schmidtke

Over the past decades, Europe has turned into a "continent of immigration" that is increasingly shaped by cross-border mobility and a growing ethno-cultural diversity of its population. The end of the Cold War divide in 1989, the completion of the single European market, and the accelerating speed of globalization have been the main driving forces behind this development. Clearly there is variation in this trend across Europe, but in general terms, Europe now shares some of the experiences of larger and sustained levels of immigration that are characteristic of immigrant settler states such as the United States or Canada. With the gradual, yet momentous, sociopolitical transformation of European societies through migration, the governance of cross-border movement, settlement, and cultural diversity poses some fundamental political and policy challenges.

The politicization of "them" and "us"

The most obvious of these challenges arises at the interface between political contestation and identity politics. Migration has become a highly contested and emotionally charged issue that has transformed competitive party politics in Western democracy. In particular, nationalist-populist actors have made migration and the protection of national borders the central theme around which their political mobilization revolves. Anti-migrant rhetoric and the scapegoating of migrants have become the cornerstone of right-wing populist ideologies across Europe. The resurgence of exclusionary nationalism and anti-immigrant forces has the potential of developing into a veritable threat to the viability of liberal democracies in general and the rights of minorities in particular. The politics of migration is likely to continue dominate electoral agendas and public debates on citizenship, identity, belonging, and community. In this respect, the politicization of migration is critically tied to a wider public debate about the transformation of traditional collective identities that historically have been shaped by legacies of colonialism and images of ethno-cultural homogeneity.

It is a short step from identity politics to the racialized exclusion of migrants. The xenophobia, scapegoating, and populist backlash linked to the refugee crisis, ongoing refugee movements, and demographic change has a strong racialized and racializing element, particularly when it comes to characterizing Muslims as fundamentally incapable of becoming full members of European societies. This racialization (of Muslims and others) has long generated social inequalities in the labor market, education, housing, and social mobility, among immigrants and their descendants alike. In countries like the UK, France, Belgium, the Netherlands, Spain, and Portugal, there will have to be a reckoning with colonial histories, including the legacy of these and other countries in perpetuating economic, political, and climate inequalities for centuries around the world that are now partly responsible for generating the cross-border movements that become racialized and perpetuate patterns of social exclusion toward immigrants and native-born.

The "refugee crisis" has raised the temperature of the debate. The irregular influx of hundreds of thousands of refugees into Europe, especially in late 2015, has demonstrated that cross-border mobility and the protection of borders speak to the very core of the sovereign prerogative of the nation state and are highly contested when it comes to transferring authority to the supranational level. The "refugee crisis" has posed a serious challenge to the EU's ability to coordinate policy, share settlement responsibilities, and foster cross-border solidarity. The limits of the EU Dublin Regulation for handling asylum claims in a coordinated manner has underlined the severe political challenges involved in moving toward a common approach to governing migration and refugees.

The legacy of the dramatic events of 2015–16 is likely to shape the future development of Europe in two ways. First, the EU is likely to intensify the securitization of its external borders (most prominently through Frontex and collaboration with states such as Turkey and Libya) and enact measures against irregular migration that collide with the EU's fundamental commitment to human rights. Second, the failure of the EU to address the ongoing challenge of refugee movements will effectively lead its member states to (re)assert their own powers to regulate border crossings. This could call into question cross-border mobility as one of the EU's fundamental freedoms and the likelihood of a broader pan-European approach to governing migration. One critical dimension of the politics of migration is the link between anti-immigrant populism/nationalism and the proliferation of Euroskeptic or anti-EU positions.

Migration as a structural challenge

Global forced displacement is a long-term challenge. Given the rising number of forcefully displaced people around the globe (and the mounting effects of climate change induced migration), responding to global migration patterns and the governance of borders will pose a fundamental political and ethical test to the EU's commitment to human rights and political right to asylum. The tension between the protection of human rights and the securitization of the EU's external border will shape political debates and policy-making over the coming years and decades.

Migration and demographic change are also deeply intertwined issues. Given the continent's aging population and resulting challenges to the labor force and social security systems, European countries will experience socioeconomic pressures to consider continuing, if not expanding, immigration programs directed at meeting labor market needs. In turn, states will need to develop measures for facilitating migrants' societal integration and equitable inclusion into the labor market or educational system. They will also need to manage growing cultural and religious diversity in European societies effectively, in order to promote inclusivity.

Policy-making will have to adjust to new social realities. It is worth noting that there is a tension between the simultaneous push for closure toward refugees and desire for openness toward high-skilled immigrants, as though the people in world mapped neatly onto these parsimonious state categories. This tension is likely to pose some considerable policy challenges: the way that states in Europe and elsewhere "see" individuals who cross borders, in terms of voluntary "economic" immigrants (and their family members) or involuntary "political" refugees will need to evolve. The driving forces for cross-border movement are set to become more complex, as the evolving debate on climate refugees shows. At the same time, measures for accommodating refugees and immigrants have long been converging around structural integration initiatives both in education and the labor market. In light of the political, economic, ethical, and demographic issues already highlighted here, states would do well to find new ways of thinking about, talking about, and managing newcomers who will, more often than not, become long-term members of their societies.

The complexity of migration governance

Migration management takes place across Europe's multilevel governance system and is an important, evolving field of public policy-making in Europe. Due to this arrangement, it will matter in the future how policy evolves across different levels of government. While nation states are still fully in control of admissions and settlement policies pertaining to non-EU citizens, subnational levels of government (e.g. cities) are often responsible for social integration and diversity management. The transfer of policy authority from municipalities to regions and the European level constitutes an emerging issue for the research and policy community. Another critical development is the proliferation of non-governmental actors in the governance of borders and migration, including civil society organizations, the courts, cross-border networks, and private business. That trend is likely to become more pronounced in the future.

Governing migration is a multigenerational project as well, which creates important opportunities for students. Migration and cultural diversity are – considering their politically contested nature and growing governance relevance – intellectually fascinating research areas for students in a variety of disciplinary and cross-disciplinary fields. The increasing role of migration in shaping European societies will open new opportunities for transatlantic comparisons and joint research projects in addition to new opportunities for policy-oriented research and professional involvement.

23

CAN EUROPE RECOVER FROM ITS LATEST WAVE OF US-VERSUS-THEM POLITICS?

Karen Umansky, Alberto Spektorowski, and Joel Busher

Europe today faces a succession of major challenges. Some of the most daunting of these relate to climate change and its attendant ecological, societal, and economic impacts; continued and rapid globalization that easily outstrips the pace of change within political and legal institutions; growing pressure on welfare systems in countries characterized by aging populations and aggressive tax avoidance by elites and major corporations; the economic, security, and legal implications of increased automation and artificial intelligence; rising economic inequality; and the growing geopolitical influence of regimes that show scant concern for the protection of human rights.

Selecting which among these challenges will be the most significant is almost certainly an impossible task, not least because of the complex feedback loops already evident between a number of these issues. What we can say is that for Europe to respond to these issues effectively, and without major damage to its social and political fabric or harm to its citizens, European societies must also address two further challenges.

Lack of trust

First, is Europe able to rebuild trust in its public institutions? While there are important national and subnational variations, trust in key political institutions is worryingly low across much of Europe. In a 2018 YouGov poll, across the EU only 42 per cent of those polled said they trusted the EU, and just 34 per cent said that they trusted their national government. Such low levels of trust undermine the effective functioning of governments and other public institutions and hinder public participation in formal political processes. It also favors the politics of polarization and conflict, creating discursive opportunities for political entrepreneurs to claim foul play whenever events don't work out quite as they hoped, or promised – a tactic deployed frequently, although certainly not uniquely, by a number of leading Euroskeptic voices and parties around Europe.

Perhaps more worrying still, distrust of public institutions corrodes the hegemonic position of democracy itself. While support for overtly authoritarian forms of government remains low across Europe, public satisfaction with democracy in some countries is astonishingly low. In a 2018 poll, some 43 per cent of Germans described themselves as dissatisfied with the way that democracy is working in their country, and in another poll some 40 per cent expressed support for "more authoritarian social structures". In Britain, 55 per cent described themselves as dissatisfied with the way that democracy is working in their country. In Spain this number was 81 per cent, and in Greece 84 per cent.

Turning inward

Second, can European societies successfully halt their apparent slide toward the resurgence of exclusionary nationalism? Again, we must recognize important national and subnational variation, as well as an important and growing resistance to such politics. Yet today exclusionary nationalism is again very much a part of European politics and the everyday lives of European citizens, whether in the form of aggressive "country X first" rhetoric and foreign policy, the strong electoral showings of radical right parties, or the all-too-pervasive practices of discrimination and dehumanization on the grounds of people's race, ethnicity, religion, or nationality.

There are signs that European societies are turning inwards, and that, as ever, minority communities are finding themselves the focal point for projected fears and antipathies. In the same 2018 YouGov poll described above, immigration was cited as the top issue of concern in 21 of the EU's 28 countries: in the remaining seven, it was terrorism. In another recent poll, across ten European countries, 48 per cent of respondents self-identified as having an "unfavorable view" of Roma, 43 per cent an unfavorable view of Muslims, and 16 per cent an unfavorable view of Jews. And while it is difficult to identify clear medium-term Europe-wide trends in hate crime, a range of social and political events, including terrorist attacks, high-profile legal rulings, elections, and referenda, have generated spikes in hate crime.

Can Europe address these challenges?

So far, the jury is very much out. One of the principle reasons for this is that these challenges are not simply accidents of history which, now identified, can be addressed. Rather, both the low levels of trust in public institutions and the diffusion of exclusionary nationalism are, to some degree at least, the product of active strategies, by non-marginal actors, to undermine current political and social systems. There are people in positions of considerable influence who not only benefit from the decline of trust in public institutions and the resurgence of exclusionary nationalism, but are actively trying to promote it.

To take the currently low levels of trust in public institutions: part of the reason for this is of course that these institutions have struggled to meet the demands placed upon them by rapidly changing societies and economies. We can think for example of their apparent failings, or at least limitations, when it came to preventing or managing the economic and social effects of the 2008 financial crisis; of the repeated inability to form or sustain national governments in countries such as Italy and Spain; or in Britain today, the present government's travails as it seeks to "deliver Brexit".

Dramatic changes in how we communicate and access information have also served to curb trust in public institutions, with the growing importance of social media lending itself not just to the rapid dissemination of information, but also to the polemicization of news, the construction of "information bubbles", a deepening distrust of established news media, and attendant opportunities for radical groups to reach and engage new audiences.

Yet, the corrosion of trust in public institutions is also the product of deliberate political strategies. One of the defining characteristics of populist, anti-establishment strategies, particularly, but not exclusively, among radical right actors, has been the adoption of discourses that foment distrust in key public institutions, whether in the form of claims about "fake news", questioning the impartiality of the judiciary, or indeed tarring them as "enemies of the people".

Similarly, if we take the apparent resurgence of exclusionary nationalism, a worrying picture emerges. Such politics are far from new, of course. But today it would not be credible to argue that prejudice and discrimination are primarily the preserve of "extremist" fringe movements or reactionary masses. Rather, politicians and other members of "mainstream" elites are also adopting these strategies of power, albeit usually while taking care to maintain plausible deniability.

For example, when, in 2015, a bloody and protracted civil war in Syria produced a substantial rise in refugees entering Europe, more than half of the 45 countries in Europe responded with an increase in government harassment or use of force against religious groups, with 27 reported as deploying widespread government harassment or intimidation of religious groups. In the run up to the UK's referendum on EU membership, claims about the possible entry of Turkey into the EU worked on anti-Muslim sentiment; and Boris Johnson himself, just over a year before becoming prime minister, was accused of playing dog-whistle politics when, albeit in the context of a piece criticizing a Danish ban on face coverings, he made comments likening women in burqas to letter boxes and bank robbers – comments that appear to have resulted in a surge in anti-Muslim attacks in Britain.

Reasons for optimism

So where does this leave us? Was Carl Schmitt right? Was liberal democracy always doomed to be replaced by yet another quest for enemies and the politics of conflict? We would say "no", albeit tentatively. This is because, alongside these causes for concern, there are also reasons for optimism. First, while populist actors and strategies have been central to the diffusion of this latest wave of us-versus-them politics, the success of these strategies has also been a function of the limitations and failures of political systems: populism can, after all, be considered something of a barometer of democratic societies, alerting the political system about its own malfunctioning. There is evidence that, today, significant parts of the political and societal elites are at least alert to this challenge, with questions about how to enhance transparency and accountability, and about the desirable parameters of the role of the state, now firmly back on the agenda and a focus of public and political discourse.

Second, while changes in the way that we communicate have undoubtedly created opportunities for proponents of us-versus-them politics, these are not the only forms of politics making use of such technologies. There is reason to believe that, with appropriate governance, these technologies can, and will, also be used to foster greater public understanding of and engagement with public institutions, and as a vehicle for constructive critical engagement that seeks to hold these institutions to account, rather than seeking simply to undermine them. As the recent climate strikes have shown, such technologies can also facilitate the blossoming of broad-based and transnational movements that articulate an inclusive vision of transformative and democratic change.

Third, and finally, it is likely that those who seek to sell simple and divisive solutions to complex questions about how we organize our societies and our lives will sooner or later be found out. The key question, however, is whether we can ensure that, when this happens, liberal democracy, and not a turn to even more exclusionary forms of politics, is the most appealing option available.

24

FEARING MUSLIMS AS THE OTHER

John R. Bowen

Europe is at its most noble when it strives for respect for all within its borders. The very persistence of the EU shows that such respect can be achieved among states, which is no mean feat given the ghastly past century. The massive migration of Muslims tests whether such respect can be achieved across perceived civilizational divides. Here the jury is out.

After all, Muslims are Europe's "perfect enemy". They evoke the historical schemas of Saladin and Charles Martel, ready to be weaponized when useful. And they are suspected as deep-down radicals, who at the right moment will show their true colors. The problem is not that there are no dangers, but that commentators treat Muslims as essentially the same, as defined by putatively fixed characteristics of their religion.

Of course, Muslims are not the only targets of what the philosopher Charles Taylor has called "block thinking". Treating Jews, Roma, Irish, and so forth as "races", defined by an immutable essence, has long been the basis for everyday discrimination and mass murder. But today Muslims are the main collective target for everyday character assassination. It has become usual for journalists and politicians to slip from using "radical" to "Islamist" to "militant" when writing of those Muslims deemed not to be playing the state's precise integration game. They do not adapt, and we can never be sure precisely what they think. And there are more specific claims of otherness. One regards children.

Fearing birth

Since the carnage of the world wars, repeopling the nation has been a matter of national urgency across Europe. If not enough citizens could be grown quickly enough, then workers would be imported as economic placeholders. But when many of these "workers" came to be seen as "Muslims", they also became a threat, and not a solution, to the peopling problem.

Critics claim a visceral demographic threat, that "they" will soon replace "us", and thereby accomplish by stealth the conquest of Europe first attempted over a millennium ago. The attacks also have both a general and a nation-specific component, corresponding as they do to the particular historical narratives of citizenship in France, Germany, Britain, and so forth.

The most proximate source for these fears is a manifesto published in 2013 by the writer Renaud Camus called: "No to Changing the People and the Civilization". Quickly picked up across the far right and center right, its pro(white)natal call was turned against the movement for "marriage for all". Pseudo-demographics is its bread and butter. The viral "Muslim Demographics" video on YouTube tells viewers that France has 1.8 children per family but "Muslims, 8.1 children per family" and that "in just 39 years, France will be an Islamic Republic".

France does not even collect demographic data by religion, but demographers estimate that Muslim women born in European countries are doing precisely what was expected: having far fewer children, quickly approaching the birth rates for non-Muslim natives. In 2017, looking at changing rates of birth and immigration, the Pew Research Forum projected that the percentage of Muslims in Europe would grow from 6 per cent in 2010 to 8 per cent in 2030, and under a scenario of medium immigration, to 11 per cent by 2050; far from the scary Muslim Conquest scenario (Pew Research Center 2017).

Fearing halal

Halal has become another trope for the stealth Muslim invasion of Europe. As with demographics, the halal fear has its broad form and its country specifics. The broad form is that we are forced to eat halal. The particular has to do with ideas of place and identity, from the role of religion in public space to the nature of home and neighborhood.

In Britain, against the background of "mad cow disease", fear of halal is mainly fear of Muslims sneaking unwanted foods into the regular supply chain. In France, however, anything religious (and not part of background Catholicism) is suspected of violating the boundaries of public and private, and of shared and particular. Although restaurants and food shops are not precisely public space, they have come in for official abuse when they stock only halal foods. In an early instance from 2010, eight Quick fast-food restaurants in Roubaix, near Lille, went all-halal. Seven parliamentary deputies quickly denounced Quick for "imposing halal ... contrary to the laïcité of French society" and thereby taking a "step toward the balkanization and ghettoization of our society". Catering to religious needs means destroying the social fabric.

In the Netherlands, by contrast, producing halal products designed to be "typically Dutch" was celebrated as a laudable effort to integrate immigrants into

Dutch society. But when animal rights groups objected that some animals were killed for halal marketing without stunning, supermarkets responded by saying they would market only to Islamic communities. Unlike in France, a logic of demarcating communities was fine, and would allow trumpeting Dutch moral superiority, placating the coalition partner Party for the Animals, and avoiding accusations of religious discrimination.

Fearing normalization

Here is the kicker: people also fear it when Muslims create schools, houses of worship, or other institutions that signal their desire to adapt to how Europeans do things. A true hermeneutics of suspicion encourages you to read such efforts as trying to disguise ill intentions with outward conformity.

Take schools. Across Europe, Muslims have created Islamic schools according to the national models. In France, that has meant limiting religious instruction to one hour per week, teaching the national curriculum, and accepting non-Muslim pupils. In return, they can ask to receive the same generous state subsidies as do Catholic schools that choose to follow those same rules. British faith schools are free to devise their own curricula, but in order to successfully compete for pupils they must show good results in the national exams. Dutch rules and attitudes toward coexistence, often still known by the term "pillarization", are the most favorable toward the creation of Islamic schools, where the main formal impediment has been acquisition of the Dutch language.

And yet, fear generates a need for control and a substratum of suspicion, even when things go well. For example, Muslim private-school pupils in the Netherlands perform better on academic subjects and with respect to measures of civic values than do public school pupils of similar class backgrounds. In 2018, three of the ten top-ranking primary schools in the Netherlands were Islamic. (Most teachers at these schools are non-Muslim.) With some work you can find these data, but media coverage focuses nearly exclusively on some problematic statements by teachers at one particular Amsterdam Islamic school. Even attentive readers would infer that Islamic schools are a threat.

France's first Islamic *lycée* was among the highest-ranking schools in the country soon after it received state accreditation. But the first attempt to create an Islamic school was met with non-stop state harassment. The difference? In state-centric-and-saturated France, the earlier school leadership heretically insisted on remaining outside the state's designated Islamic partner umbrella, the French Council of the Muslim Religion, whereas the later school conformed to the Napoleonic model. In France, independent means uncontrolled, suspect.

The place for Europe

These fears are not analytically captured by the blanket charge of "Islamophobia" so often leveled at European societies. The attacks target Muslims, but in ways that are specific to the political fault lines in each country. Prejudice takes on national characteristics, and even Muslim conformity elicits suspicions regarding plots and true intentions. These "adaptations" of fears to local fault lines make it difficult to surmount barriers to acceptance country by country. To regain its internal nobility, the European project must, on a broad scale, unite around tolerance, recognizing the costs to the continent of moral weakness and disrespect.

25

THE CHALLENGE OF EUROPE'S NATIONS
Gregory Baldi

By most accounts Europe has had a difficult twenty-first century. Those who were of academic age in the 1990s can remember a vision of Europe marked by confidence in the future. The end of the Cold War, the reunification of Germany, and the relaunch of European integration offered the promise of unity and harmony in the new century that had eluded the continent in the previous one. Instead of history reaching its end, as some predicted, the past two decades have borne witness to a Europe locked in seemingly perpetual crisis. Observers tasked with selecting a single "biggest" issue facing the continent have a long list from which to choose: the slowing of economic growth, sovereign debt default, immigration, refugees, Russia and Ukraine, the fragmentation of national electoral politics and the rise of populism, a decaying transatlantic relationship, and Brexit, not to mention longer-term challenges such as climate and demographic change, could all qualify.

The biggest issue facing Europe today, however, is not economic, institutional, strategic, or environmental, but lies in the differences among Europeans regarding the purpose and meaning of the nation and the nature of their identification with the national community. Conceptions of the nation serve as the lenses through which leaders and publics interpret their interests, understand problems, and conceive of solutions. These "national" differences exist both within and across countries in Europe, straining politics and constraining policy at the domestic level and thwarting cooperation and joint decision-making at the European level. The net effect is government at both levels that frequently fails to address many of its most pressing problems and finds itself locked in a cycle in which perceived political incapacity feeds public discontent, which itself leads to a hardening of the different perspectives.

Varying visions of the nation in Europe are not new, but what has changed in the past few decades are conditions both within and outside the nation. The acceleration of interconnectedness brought forth by economic interdependence and free movement across borders, and the adoption of neoliberal economic policies, which tend to create winners and losers and lessen social protections, have dramatically elevated the salience of national differences and the challenge they pose for Europe.

Nationalism, open and closed

Nationalism has its origins in early modern Europe, when the spread of the written vernacular, shifting views of religion, and emerging compacts between populations and their rulers led to a new vision for communities that until that time had a limited view of "the people" as a source of legitimate power. As the nationalism scholar Liah Greenfeld (1999: 37) has observed, this new idea of the nation consisted of two principles: popular sovereignty and fundamental equality in the community. Combined with its structural political partner, the modern state, and its formal membership unit, the citizen, the nation state would become the most successful form of political organization in the world, overtaking its premodern dynastic, imperial, and feudal rivals. Regimes across the globe have, with few exceptions, assumed the national mantle and made the promotion of national identities and culture a priority.

Within Europe, nationalist expression has shaped a vast spectrum of modern politics, serving as a foundation for democracy, the welfare state, and civil rights, on one side, and as an inspiration for expansionary warfare and genocidal campaigns of mass murder, on the other. Motivated by the diverse scope of national expressions, scholars have long attempted to classify and compare different understandings of the nation, particularly within its European birthplace, constructing a range of oppositional national conceptions, including political versus cultural, civic versus ethnic, Western versus Eastern, collective versus individualistic, and liberal versus illiberal.

The nationalisms that divide Europe today reflect many features of these existing conceptions. Yet the most salient differences among contemporary European national visions can be seen in the degree to which they are open to accepting voluntary constraints on the nation's sovereignty outside of state borders. For more open nationalists, membership in the EU and other regional or international bodies, as well participation in the global economy, is viewed as entirely compatible with traditional nationhood. The nation, in this perspective, is just one provider of economic wealth and security, and measures such as the transfer of increased regulatory and fiscal powers to EU institutions are viewed as sovereignty investments rather than as irredeemable expenditures. Open nationalists are less likely to view immigrants as a challenge to national cohesion and more likely to adopt a multicultural vision of the nation, which de-emphasizes cultural assimilation as a prerequisite for national membership, and a multinational vision of the state, calling for the establishment of regional parliaments or assemblies and minority linguistic and cultural rights.

Among current European leaders, the open nationalist vision is promoted by figures such as French President Emanuel Macron and Austrian President Alexander Van der Bellen, both of whom have spoken of the need for a culturally diverse nationalism (or, in the case of Macron, "patriotism") both within their countries and in Europe more generally. Open nationalism is prominent among Europe's greens, liberals, and factions of social democratic parties, but aspects of it can also be seen among Christian democrats such as German Chancellor Angela Merkel, who, despite her stated opposition to multiculturalism and at great political cost, took the dramatic step of retaining an open border with Austria during the mass movement of refugees in Europe in 2015, allowing tens of thousands of Afghan and Syrian war refugees to enter Germany.

For closed nationalists, by contrast, sovereignty is viewed in zero-sum terms: it can be gained or lost but cannot be shared or pooled. The role of regional or global organizations, according to this view, should be to guarantee rather than assume a nation's sovereign authority. The nation itself is considered the main source of income and employment for the population, and immigration, even in cases of clear labor shortages and business demand, is largely viewed with suspicion. Cultural homogeneity and the uniformity of identity are generally promoted over economic orthodoxy.

Populist-style leaders such as Hungary's Viktor Orbán, who regularly criticizes the EU, and justifies curbs on immigration and refugee settlement with reference to the incompatibility of non-Christians with the culture and identity of Europe's nations, and former Polish Prime Minister Jarosław Kaczyński, who has called for the rejection of multiculturalism in favor of a uniform Polish identity rooted in Catholic traditionalism, are among the most vocal and politically successful proponents of the closed nationalist perspective. Yet the vision is becoming increasingly articulated by West European leaders as well. In Italy, former Deputy Prime Minister Matteo Salvini has put the reclaiming of Italian sovereignty at the center of his party's political program, closing ports to ships carrying African migrants, threating to expel Roma communities, and pursuing protectionist economic policies while in office. Regaining national autonomy and curbing free movement also comprised the cornerstone of the Brexit referendum campaign led by the UK Independence Party and the pro-Brexit faction of the British Conservatives.

Competition and conflict

The competing visions of the nation can be seen across key European policy debates. While open nationalists have supported fiscal solidarity in Europe, with some even advocating measures such as pooled-risk eurobonds, closed nationalists have favored policies promoting fiscal autarky. Whereas open nationalists have adopted a largely humanitarian vision of refugees, calling for the protection of those fleeing conflicts to be the first priority of governments, closed nationalists view refugees through the lens of security and cultural infiltration, showing reluctance to participate in European migrant settlement schemes and, in some instances, constructing physical barriers to deny them entry. Open nationalists see immigration as a solution to the problems of declining population and demographic imbalance, while closed nationalists seek to increase national fertility levels through a combination of financial incentives and cultural appeals. On climate change, open nationalists seek regional solidarity and international solutions; closed nationalists frequently reject the science of climate change or view it as the problem of larger states responsible for the bulk of emissions.

The conflict between open and closed nationalists has arguably overtaken the left–right social class divide that characterized European politics in the twentieth century. But unlike that divide, which could be addressed – though not eliminated – through policies of wealth redistribution and social mobility, the problem of competing national visions may not prove so tractable to interventionist solutions. Europe may well find the challenge of nations to endure deep into the twenty-first century.

26

CAN EUROPEAN STATES BE "COUNTRIES OF MIGRATION"?

Justin Gest

One of the most controversial things that can be said about European countries is that they are "countries of migration." Certainly, all countries today include some number of foreigners, but the term puts European states – historically deriving their national identities from soil, sacrifice, and traceable lines of heritage – into the same category as the settler states, like Australia or the United States, that they colonized and populated. And yet, Switzerland features among the world's highest shares of the foreign-born, France and Sweden have among the world's highest naturalization rates, and free movement is a cornerstone of the EU itself. This fundamental irony is now at the center of debates over the European future (Boucher & Gest 2018).

National states versus settler states

The tension arises from within the national state. On the one hand, how can the nations of Europe be reinstated when they never truly existed outside the imaginary? On the other hand, acknowledging that European states were never so homogenous, how can globalism be reconciled within the enduring power of nationalism? These are questions that also face the very settler states from which European leaders like to distinguish themselves. However, European governments negotiating transformative demographic change lack the organic advantages that come with having been "settled" as colonies and populated with immigrants.

Settler states crafted civic – rather than ethnocentric – identities that are more open to evolution (Gest 2016). Settler states embrace multicultural policies that recognize the value of diversity. Settler states cite previous generations of immigrants to endow confidence in their capacity to absorb future generations. In short, settler states acknowledge that they are "countries of migration", which emboldens their citizens to understand immigration as a norm but also to see themselves to some extent in new generations of arrivals. Indeed, Americans treat the assimilation of immigrants with evangelical zeal, as if conversion brings some civic redemption.

Of course, these supposed advantages are mere constructs, institutionalized by settler state governments; they are not off limits to European leaders today. They are not pursued by Europeans simply because of the backlash they fear such moves may generate.

In response to demographic change and multiculturalism, backlash by people who feel threatened or displaced by foreigners translates nativist anxiety into discriminatory regimes, proxy debates, and other grasps for social control. For control is at the core of all nativism under circumstances of swift demographic change.

Control

Nativists seek to control the demographic distribution, the means of violence, the national culture, and, if nothing else, the historical narrative. This search for control explains why, when confronted by the arrival and integration of the "other", the incumbent constituency turns to the past. Nostalgia exudes a sense of predictability, but also allows the storyteller to reframe the significance of past events and attributes.

In new comparative research in countries subject to transformative demographic change, I have found nativist backlash focuses on three arenas: policy, politics, and society.

First, backlash to demographic change focuses on immigration policy because immigration (before fertility rate disparities) was, in all cases, the core driver of the demographic change in the first place. Governments recruit those immigrants deemed to be of desirable origins to reinforce their dominance and oppose the naturalization of others.

Second, where immigration policy cannot turn back the demographic clock, in election-based systems nativists turn to the electoral institutions that determine how and where power is distributed. Naturalization may determine who has the right to vote and be counted. However, governments can also amend voting rights, revise census rules, and alter constituency districts (gerrymander) to mitigate the political impact of demographic change.

Third, backlash can simply take place to reassure native communities of their social status. These are the politics of symbolism, in which the rhetoric of solidarity binds the endangered constituency, in which political actions may change one life but comfort hundreds of thousands.

These efforts to assert control are all loose attempts to define the nation in the face of disorienting change. And they are unable to address the differential fertility rates driving much of demographic change, the Maastricht Treaty enshrining free movement as a cornerstone of Europe, or the ethnocentric understandings of national identity. They are merely anchors for ships tossed in the tempest of crisscrossing global currents.

- "Take back control", exhorted the Leave campaign during Britain's 2016 Brexit referendum.
- *"Au nom du people"* – in the name of the people – proclaimed Marine Le Pen's far-right National Rally party in France.
- *"Wir sind das volk!"* – we are the people – declared Germany's far-right Alternative für Deutschland.

However, these ubiquitous slogans raise the questions: Which people? Who had or has control? Who are "we"? Such questions always go unanswered, for it is far easier for such movements to define the "other" than to define the nation purportedly entitled to power. "We may not know who we are, but we know who we are not", today's populists seem to be shouting in their backlash to immigration, Muslims, and the emergence of an increasingly globalized culture.

The future of us

Defining who "we" are has grown challenging because it necessarily entails exclusion in many countries heretofore concerned with the preservation of a liberal order and constitutions protecting individual rights. Hardliners ignore the ways that social boundaries have blurred over the course of generations of global mobility, intermarriage, and statecraft; they also resist the global diffusion of ideas, identities, and norms that have weakened territorial links between blood, soil, and self. Being a "country of migration" merely acknowledges the never-ending nature of nation building. Indeed, even those states with very little migration have evolved in light of other forces beyond their control. They are all works in progress.

Outstanding questions abound: How do parties and leaders resist short-term political calculations and appeal to a broadened understanding of the nation? What are the rights of a majority constituency to protect their numerical advantage and the enduring character of the nation they have historically governed? Can the politics of heritage coexist in a liberalizing world?

Whether they acknowledge their status as countries of migration, how governments and thought leaders address these questions will define the social future of Europe, its capacity to sustain power-sharing institutions, and its capacity to govern. On the right, parties have acted swiftly to embrace more muscular nationalism for short-term electoral gains, but long-term complications for social solidarity and immigrant assimilation. On the left, the rise of a strident migrant rights and racial equality movement has alienated many native-born Europeans. To nativists, this movement's aggressive pursuit of legal protections and recognition suggested a sense of entitlement and general insubordination. More problematically, the left's weakening of Keynesian social democracy suggested that the promotion of immigrant and racial justice was mutually exclusive with the economic justice historically sought by unions and working-class people. This general embrace of globalization and neoliberal economics has made the principal disputes between left and right fall along cultural lines.

In these cultural debates, the post-1991 left has struggled to make both its newest members (urbanites and upwardly mobile immigrants) and oldest members (native-born working-class people) feel welcome, represented, and respected. To the extent that the left attempted to craft broader national identities, its liberal values were so broad and vague that they lacked any meaning or distinction. Strong, effective identities require a mix of exclusivity *and* inclusivity; a tall order.

Heritage politics

For now, a simple test can illuminate whether the actions of states, organizations, and individuals are oriented toward a future of coexistence or conflict: Are they reinforcing the social boundaries among themselves or somehow transcending them? Ultimately, the answer to this question lies in the notion of "heritage".

This notion of heritage does not have to be about race, ethnicity, or religion at all. It should be about elements that cross such social boundaries. First, heritage is about continuity, a sense of connection to the past, a legacy, and – in some cases – a genealogy. All people desire a sense of "groundedness", rooted in blood, soil, or a long-term struggle. Second, heritage is about submission to greater powers: the power of time, institutions, and nature that equally constrain us as human beings and reveal our quest for causes bigger than ourselves. Heritage is sacrifice. Third, heritage is about evolution. It is a living, breathing phenomenon that endures only because it evolves to retain its relevance by adapting to new environments. Heritage is not preserved as much as it survives. Heritage is ritual.

Understanding heritage in these ways lends it to alternative expressions. For example, heritage can refer to the way that social boundaries have always been used to divide the weak and populous to achieve narrow ends. This division must be resisted, and lessons must be learned. In a more positive sense, however, heritage can be about recognizing one's place in a lineage of people who have made sacrifices and endured adversity for a shared mission or cause. The metamorphosis of that cause and its backers secure its endurance. Finally, heritage can be expressed by an equal reverence for guardians of the past and the vanguard of the future. These two groups should know each other and be able to see themselves in the eyes of their counterparts.

Social differences between people participating in a unifying heritage is not a source of insecurity; it is a source of strength. Europeans must ask themselves what they have inherited and how it can bring them together.

27

BATTLING OVER EUROPE'S IDENTITY: RIGHT-WING POLITICS, RELIGION, AND AN UNCERTAIN FUTURE

Fabio Capano

The European project is built on the concepts of freedom, rule of law, and social justice. Over the course of almost 70 years, this project has transformed a continent that was shattered by World War II into one of peace, stability, and economic prosperity. Too often, however, the success of a shared economy has been seen as the key to European integration. On the contrary, economic progress has proven insufficient in the fostering of political unity and social cohesion across an increasingly heterogeneous continent. Indeed, using economic growth as a barometer of European success is misleading. Economic factors on their own fail to account for the values, customs, and understandings of identity within each participating country. It also fails to reveal how tightly these considerations are bound to a sense of belonging within local and national communities. Among many factors, national identity and religion play a key role in shaping people's sense of belonging and loyalty toward their community. Indeed, the interplay between national identity and religion may represent one of the greatest challenges to the European project.

Instrumental faith

The challenge arises from efforts to construct exclusive identities for political mobilization. A wide network of political actors, agents, and parties use religious symbols to advance a specific political and anti-European agenda. Matteo Salvini, the leader of Italy's Northern League and former minister of the interior, is a case in point. His speeches often reference the cross and the rosary in an attempt to reassert the country's Catholic identity and legitimize his extreme approach to the refugee crisis in the Mediterranean.

Both Christian faith and Greek-Roman traditions have played important roles in the shaping of Europe's historical trajectory. Nevertheless, the separation of church and state remain key to the past, present, and future of European democracies. In criticizing Salvini's use of religious symbols, Antonio Spadaro, a priest who is also a close advisor to Pope Francis, made it clear that, "the cross is a sign of protest against sin, violence, injustice and death. It is NEVER a sign of identity" (Giuffrida 2018). In this statement, Spadaro warned against the peril that the use of religion for political purposes poses to modern societies.

More often than not, Spadaro's warning goes unheeded. Salvini's rhetorical use of religion to mobilize the public against mass immigration is anything but unique. On the contrary, it is representative of the increasing popularity of an exclusionary notion of citizenship that politicians can use to rally segments of the European public around a homogenous idea of national identity. Salvini is among other right-wing leaders such as Marine Le Pen and Viktor Orbán who have also attempted to relaunch the idea of national identity as being exclusively white and Christian at a time when European integration continues to be threatened across the continent.

This idea of a white and Christian Europe has fostered a fortress mentality that is not only antithetical to the reality of European demography but also to Europe as a unique and sole entity anchored to the more progressive concept of constitutional patriotism advocated by, *inter alia*, Jürgen Habermas. This is why the instrumental use of religion to promote a xenophobic political agenda only furthers a "clash of civilizations" worldview and threatens the idea of Europe as a union of states that embraces democracy and relinquishes economic and political sovereignty in exchange for prosperity and peace.

From this perspective, the increasing strength of nationalism within European public discourse and its use of Christianity as the foundation of national identity has also shaped restrictive state legislation in areas such as immigration and citizenship. Heated domestic debates on these topics have criticized the EU and have accused it of interfering in domestic affairs. As expected by right-wing parties, such arguments have further exacerbated public resentment and have advanced their anti-European agenda. While these debates have certainly strained social coexistence in the EU, they have also highlighted the importance and lasting influence of religious symbolism within the national public sphere.

Fundamental values

The spectacular growth of migration across the Mediterranean has added fuel to right-wing political groups. With a solution to those problems that push people away from their own countries and toward Europe nowhere in sight, right-wing politicians have been able to exploit people's fears of an alleged "invasion" and appeal to its implicit threat to Europe's Christian heritage. In this way, migration gives added emphasis to divisive narratives that have long centered on the defense of a Christian and nationally constructed identity in contrast to the idea of a diverse, multicultural, and multiethnic Europe. In turn, not only have right-wing political parties, leaders, and movements fomented hatred and intolerance, but they have also launched a single spearheaded attack on the fundamental values underpinning the European project.

European scholars and policy-makers have long debated the spiritual and cultural dimension of Europe. In doing so, they have promoted the idea of a broader European cultural space with the goal of preventing any potential conflict that would arise from the complicated coexistence of multiple national cultures and religious faiths. Indeed, the complex interplay between these two key dimensions accompanied the drafting of the European Constitution, which ultimately reasserted religious freedom as one of its key elements. The document also confirmed the autonomy of religious communities and the cooperation between church and state. In a secular fashion, it also avoided explicit references to the Judeo-Christian heritage that shaped the historical trajectory of the European continent, a potentially divisive element for a continent striving to make diversity, pluralism, and peaceful coexistence its greatest strengths.

From this standpoint, using religion to mobilize divided nations against a "common enemy" whose language, culture, and faith do not mirror the newly projected model of exclusionary citizenship is cause for great concern. Such appeals to religion-as-identity endanger the idea of Europe as a secular, pluralist, and inclusive space. Most important, the right-wing emphasis on Christianity as a defining trait of national identity is not only fomenting hostility and resentment against foreigners and minorities but also encroaching on the importance of a shared Christian heritage as a unifying element of European identity. It is a short step from exclusive Christianity to conflict within the faith.

Identities as complements

This entanglement of religious and national identity fundamentally threatens the European project at its core as it fails to acknowledge the complementary rather than mutually exclusive nature of each nation's unique religious heritage as well as its historically constructed identity. Thus, a vibrant public debate that reproposes the centrality of overlapping secular and religious values such as brotherhood, compassion, solidarity, and peace would be more beneficial, both for the European project and for politics within the member states.

A public debate on the complementarity of contrasting religious identities would provide the public with an opportunity to get better insight into the disruptive aftermath of the antagonistic rhetoric on the right, which only aims to foment mutual distrust and fear within European borders. Above all, an innovative and progressive political agenda devoid of sectarian, religious, and nationalist claims would allow the European public to rediscover transnational similarities that, anchored in democratic and secular values, could help to mitigate the disruptive effects of a right-wing political rhetoric that attempts to turn religion into a building block for nationally rooted and exclusionary identities.

28

BOSNIA AND HERZEGOVINA BETWEEN EU ACCESSION, UNHEALED TRAUMA, AND MIGRANT CRISIS

Alma Jeftić

The war in Bosnia and Herzegovina, which began shortly after the breakup of Yugoslavia, influenced the intergroup relations of the former republics and led to the formation of several different (and difficult) collective memories of past conflicts (and the time before the conflict). Although the war ended more than 25 years ago, it has had unprecedented consequences for the citizens of Bosnia and Herzegovina, and has led to a change in population structure and relationships among people within the country. Currently divided into two entities and one district, and burdened by a heavy bureaucratic apparatus and debt, Bosnia and Herzegovina is struggling with the accelerating "brain drain" of its young citizens to EU countries and the influx of refugees and migrants from the Middle East who, unable to cross the border to Croatia, remain "detained" within Bosnia and Herzegovina. In this chapter I will try to briefly present the major problems that Bosnia and Herzegovina has been going through since the end of the 1992–5 war while focusing mostly on intergroup relations, unhealed trauma, and how these interact with high brain drain, corruption, EU accession, and current migrant crisis.

Movements

There are different reasons why people leave the country, but unemployment, low salaries, threatening political rhetoric, high levels of corruption, poor forecasts for the future, and accession to the EU could be considered the most common. As Samir Huseinović (2019) reported, an estimated 30,000 citizens have left Bosnia and Herzegovina since the beginning of 2019, and a further 178,000 citizens have left the country in the last five years. Those who leave are working-age people who want to provide a better life for their families, away from the divisions and still-present nationalism.

While the youth of Bosnia and Herzegovina is leaving the country, there has been an influx of refugees and migrants from the Middle East – particularly in the last two years. Those immigrants do not intend to stay in Bosnia, but they are unable to cross the border with Croatia and continue their journey. Therefore, they are doomed to spend time moving between Bosnia and Serbia, often illegally, in a vain attempt to gain access to one of the countries of the EU. Meanwhile, Bosnia, as one of the poorest countries in Europe, is unable to provide sufficient housing or to support adequate living conditions for an increasing number of immigrants. On top of that, the financial assistance provided by the EU has proved insufficient either because it is inadequate or because it is inadequately used.

The social reception of these immigrants is not positive either. The people of Bosnia and Herzegovina have gone through a terrible four-year war during which a large number of residents had to flee to other European countries (and beyond). This experience has not made the people sympathetic to others in need. Attitudes toward migrants and refugees currently in the country are not based on empathy and prosocial discourse (at least according to what was stated in the media and reported by the NGOs that have been providing assistance). Instead, many of the people of Bosnia and Herzegovina have become exclusionary and resentful. In July 2019, an announcement was made of a bus company whose driver in the Tuzla–Sarajevo route (which is approximately a four-hour ride) had reserved front seats exclusively for white people, meaning locals. Migrants and refugees had to sit in the back. This is how twenty-first century apartheid emerged in a small, poor country that continues to struggle to fulfill the tasks necessary to become a full member of the EU. The enormous state bureaucracy fails to act with a necessary sense of urgency. This sluggishness explains why Bosnia and Herzegovina returns to the start of negotiations every year. In the meantime, citizens struggle with the familiar leave or stay dilemma and with different options (and opinions) to overcome the migrant crisis.

Scars

The traces of war trauma are still alive and visible, both in everyday discourse and political rhetoric. Recent empirical research on collective memories for different and difficult war events conducted among citizens of Sarajevo and East Sarajevo (two cities very close to each other geographically, but far apart politically), revealed that one of the most frequently reported words is *čemer*. When translated into English, *čemer* corresponds to the combination of several emotions and feelings: sadness, sorrow, bitterness, despondency, and grief. The word *čemer* can be used to describe one special condition when a person becomes too overwhelmed by certain negative feelings and emotions, and consequently becomes bitter inside and is slowly destroyed. *Čemer* is the word most used by citizens of Sarajevo and East Sarajevo when asked to give a first association with the 1992–5 war (Jeftić 2019).

Resentment and bitterness lead to difficult intergroup relations and an inability to cope with the past. Faced with several different narratives about the 1992–5 war but also weary of day-to-day problems, including low wages, a poor health care system, divided teaching curricula, and corruption, the citizens of Bosnia and Herzegovina are having a difficult time coping with the emerging migrant crisis. The truth is that no country is having an easy time with immigrants, and no country can hold on to all of its talented young people either. Brain drain and different types of migration happen everywhere. Yet, as a postwar country that has also experienced the breakup of Yugoslavia, Bosnia and Herzegovina seems trapped between that old, Yugoslav era and a way of life and a new era in which most people (especially the young) do not see a bright future. Divisions in memories, education, and politics have led to divisions of needs and expectations for and from the future, which is an important but often neglected fact.

Reconciliation

What do people need? The people need to move beyond religious and ethnic differences if they are to reconcile themselves with one another and with their past. Nurit Shnabel and Arie Nadler (2008: 116) developed a needs-based model of reconciliation that is predicated on the idea that following an episode in which one side has been victimized by another, both the victim and the perpetrator are deprived of certain unique psychological resources. Hence both sides have the right to meet their needs, and such a process leads to reconciliation. Although it sounds simplistic, this model, when applied to the current situation in Bosnia and Herzegovina, is a perfectly reasonable approach to analyzing the current situation and giving a response to an unanswered question from public discourse: why are the people not getting what they need?

The answer is that leading political parties have that special need to group people. Moving beyond religious and ethnic differences contradicts that political agenda. It is therefore no surprise that refugees and migrants are mistreated and that a new apartheid has emerged in Bosnia and Herzegovina. Unhealed post-conflict society does not have the strength to cope with population fluctuations. It also does not have the strength to do what is necessary to join the EU.

The EU seems to be eager to help Bosnia and Herzegovina make progress in the accession talks. The EU has some ambivalence toward the country, but it remains broadly supportive of its membership prospects. Nevertheless, Bosnia lacks the political unity and visionary leadership to respond to such assistance. Meanwhile, the unhealed traumas, brain drain, and migrant crisis take their toll on the country's citizens. If current trends continue unabated, there will be no one but retired people left in Bosnia and Herzegovina to enjoy the consequences of the EU accession (if it ever happens).

The lesson from Bosnia is that we should focus more attention on the psychological needs of the country's citizens and possibility for their recovery. Bosnia and Herzegovina cannot cope successfully with challenges related to corruption or migration without reconciliation happening first. Bosnia certainly cannot undertake all those reforms necessary to join the EU. By placing too much emphasis on the country's membership perspective, we neglect the country's real state of affairs. The scars of war run deep, the young people are leaving, and those who stay behind are reacting badly to new immigrants. Only lasting reconciliation can lay the foundations for Bosnia and Herzegovina to aspire to EU membership.

29

SOCIAL MOVEMENTS AS A SOLUTION TO EUROPEAN APORIA?

Marcos Ancelovici and Guya Accornero

The EU is facing a critical moment in its history. The sustained growth of Euroskeptic and populist parties, the recent economic and financial crisis with its corollary of austerity, the never-ending soap opera of Brexit, the increase in terrorist attacks by Islamist radicals and far-right activists, the deaths of refugees in the Mediterranean, and the abandonment and repression of migrants in the north of Paris or in Calais, are only some of the critical issues challenging the EU. These problems are partly a consequence of EU politics and policies. They are also, in one way or another, all connected. More fundamentally, several of these problems challenge the very founding principles of the European project.

Europe's crisis of hospitality and solidarity

Traumatized by the horrors of World War II, the founders of the EU first aspired to lay the foundations for lasting peace. In this respect, their project has been incredibly successful. Europe has never enjoyed such a long period without wars (one could point out the wars that followed the collapse of the former Yugoslavia, but they were not within the borders of the EU). However, several other founding aspirations of the EU have not enjoyed such fortune. Article 1 of the EU's Charter of Fundamental Rights states that human dignity is inviolable and must be respected and protected. The following articles go on to celebrate the right to life, the protection of human integrity, and the prohibition of degrading treatments. Similarly, the digital portal of the EU asserts that "The EU protects all minorities and vulnerable groups, and stands up for the oppressed. Regardless of a person's nationality, gender, language group, culture, profession, disability or sexuality, the EU insists on equal treatment for all." Such noble principles are allegedly at the core of European values: "the EU values are common to the EU countries in a society in which inclusion, tolerance, justice, solidarity and non-discrimination prevail. These values are an integral part of our European way of life."

These declarations sound great and should give rise to humane policies. But according to the Missing Migrants Project, between 2014 and 2018 about 18,000 refugees died in the Mediterranean. Instead of trying to rescue them, contributing to making their journey safer, and welcoming them for the sake of human dignity and the respect of international human rights norms and agreements, the EU turned back the refugee boats out at sea and negotiated with neighboring Turkey to keep refugees at bay in exchange for €6 billion in financial aid. The EU also asked Libyan coastguards to patrol the Mediterranean to hunt and stop refugees before they reached the Italian coast. According to Amnesty International (De Bellis 2019):

> Through the donation of ships, the setting up of a Libyan search and rescue zone, and the construction of coordination centres, among other measures, European taxpayers' money has been used to enhance the Libyan capacity to block people attempting to flee Libya and hold them in unlawful detention. And this was done with no conditions attached, even if such cooperation results in gross human rights violations like torture.

So much for human dignity and standing up for the oppressed. Even worse, several EU countries such as France and Italy have prosecuted activists and ordinary European citizens who have tried to help refugees by giving them clothes, food, or shelter. These countries have thus de facto turned solidarity – allegedly a prevailing European value and integral part of the European way of life – into a crime with the tacit complicity of the EU. Put simply, the EU has failed miserably to stand up to its own professed ideals.

It is in such a context that activists and social movements have come to the rescue of not only refugees but also European ideals. The latter are indeed today defended and embodied principally by NGOs, such as SOS Méditerranée, Médecins Sans Frontières, Sea Watch, and Open Arms, that operate primarily off the coasts of Italy and Greece. These NGOs have mobilized several ships, such as the *Aquarius*, the *Sea Watch 3*, and more recently the *Ocean Viking*, to rescue refugees at sea before they drown. The captains of these ships have paid a heavy price for their humanitarian activism. Suffice it to think of Carola Rackete and Pia Klemp, who are facing investigations and potentially several years of imprisonment.

In addition to interventions at sea, many activists are getting involved on the ground as they witness the plight of refugees and migrants. For example, since 2015, and in response to the wave of Syrian refugees, many activist-managed shelters and infrastructures have popped up in Greece, particularly in Athens' neighborhood of Exarcheia. In France, the most well-known case is perhaps that of Cédric Herrou, who got arrested for helping more than 250 migrants and refugees cross the Franco-Italian border in the Roya Valley. Although he was eventually found not guilty, he had to defend himself for several years in court.

There are plenty of such local initiatives across Europe that inspire and feed one another and sometimes operate in a coordinated manner. They directly contribute to building transnational and international solidarity and are one of the most powerful responses to the crisis of hospitality and integrity that the EU has fostered.

Euroskepticism and Europe's crisis of representation and legitimacy

European activists and social movements have also contributed to solving Europe's crisis of representation and legitimacy. This is a crisis that both the EU and the member states have been experiencing for many years. The challenge to European representation and legitimacy has become particularly acute since the 2008 global financial crisis.

Although the EU's democratic character and functioning have been questioned from the beginning and critics have often denounced its technocratic and nontransparent decision-making process as well as its lack of genuine accountability, the EU management of the financial crisis made things worse. The neoliberal diagnosis of the crisis as resulting from the public overspending of so-called "undisciplined" countries – especially Portugal and Greece – became the justification for austerity policy packages imposed on the governments of those countries by the EU. Whether it was as a condition for financial assistance as set down in national memoranda signed with the Troika (the EU Commission, the ECB, and the IMF) or under the general fiscal rules of the EU designed to control public deficits and inflation, these austerity measures had not only economic but also social, political, and administrative implications.

In the case of Portugal, specific sections of the Troika Memorandum asked for more centralization of the country's administration. Portugal was already one of the most centralized countries in Europe and this reform undermined not only the citizens' involvement in the political decision-making process, but also the functioning and work of the central government itself in so far as the central authorities started to lack proper information from local inputs. In Greece, the EU strongly interfered with the democratic process and, in July 2015, forced left-wing Prime Minister Alexis Tsipras to ignore the large majority that had voted against the signing of a new memorandum with the Troika. In several European countries, the Troika directly undermined the legitimacy of national and supranational arrangements by ignoring the popular will and leaving very little room for maneuver, if any, to elected governments.

Such disregard for democratic accountability has directly contributed to the growth of populist parties and movements defending national sovereignty. In some instances, the rise of pro-sovereignty groups has also entailed the growth of xenophobic, anti-immigrant, and anti-refugee as well as racist claims. At the same time, the European anti-austerity social movements that have emerged in those countries directly affected by the Troika's Memoranda – Portugal, Spain, Greece, and Ireland – did not target "Europe." In contrast to the Global Justice Movement (which emerged from the "No Global" protests that started at the end of the twentieth century), mobilizations such as the Portuguese *Geração à Rasca* and *Que se Lixe a Troika* or the Spanish and Greek *Indignados* targeted their respective national governments rather than focusing their attention on large multilateral organizations. In doing so, these groups accused their political class of ignoring their responsibilities and delegating their authority to supranational entities and international markets.

These anti-austerity movements did not result in a transnational mobilization, unified against common transnational targets and by a common idea of Europe. There were a few exceptions to this tendency, such as the "Blockupy movement" in Germany. Nevertheless, pro-European discourse remained strong at the micro and meso levels among left-wing activists and organizations. In this respect, there are no major differences between traditional contentious actors – like trade unions – and new social movement organizations. They are all not so much opposed to Europe as they support the idea of another Europe and advocate for more or less radical reforms or changes depending on their affiliation.

Many activists in new social movements also stress that they moved from more Euroskeptic positions to "Eurocritic" and "Euroalternative" ones because of the growth of far-right populist parties and movements that they strongly oppose. They believe that only a united Europe can resist to the threat of the far right. Finally, because of international mobility within Europe for academic and professional purposes, many activists have transnational trajectories and this is in itself a strong reason for supporting a united Europe.

Activist Europe

These activists and movements which are often violently repressed or delegitimized by European states play a critical and invaluable role in the construction of a genuine "Europe from below". More important, these social movements go beyond a critique of the lack of representation and legitimacy of national and

European institutions. They develop and implement democratic and innovative forms of participation at the local level and translate the abstract ideals of the EU into concrete, everyday practices. If the idea of Europe stands a chance today, it is in great part thanks to them.

30

BELONGING TO BERLIN: A CASE OF BUREAUCRATIC DYSTOPIA, MINORITY AGENCY, AND SOLIDARITY

Anlam Filiz

In the 2010s, as large numbers of asylum seekers arrived in Europe, anti-migrant discourses rose throughout the continent. Within this overwhelmingly xeno-phobic atmosphere, many migrants and members of minority groups did not accept their outsider status but showed that they belong to Europe in different ways. This chapter presents an example from Berlin, Germany which illustrates how minorities in Europe show their centrality to the working of their cities and receive support from different parts of their societies (Filiz 2018). The goal is to provide an example of minority agency and solidarity contributing to the scholarship on how immigrants respond to the emerging challenges they face in Europe.

In 2015, code enforcement offices in certain neighborhoods in Berlin started to enforce a previously ignored law that forbade most shops from opening on Sundays. This law was enforced especially for *spätis* (corner shop-like businesses that are open late hours and on Sundays when most other shops are closed) in northern parts of Neukölln, a "hip" neighborhood known for sizable migrant populations. This sudden change affected many Turkish shopkeepers – where "Turkish" refers to individuals who migrated from Turkey or whose parents or grandparents came from Turkey, and not to an ethnic identity – who made up a large portion of *späti* owners and workers, especially in neighborhoods affected by this enforcement. Thus, members of the largest minority in this European capital experienced a bureaucratic dystopia that contradicted Berlin's permit-ting and diversity-friendly image. Turkish owners and workers did not simply accept this sudden change which threatened to bring an end to their operations. Instead, they responded to this bureaucratic dystopia by defining their busi-nesses as indispensable for this cosmopolitan European city.

Responding to the Sunday bans

The law entitled "Berlin Shop Opening Law" (*Berliner Ladenöffnungsgesetz*) regulates businesses' operating hours and states that shops are not allowed to open on Sundays. In response to the enforcement of this law, *späti* owners established a professional society under the name Berliner Späti e.V (Berlin Späti Organization). The group started their operations when the Sunday bans intensified in 2015 and had their official opening after the local elections in September 2016. Almost all the members were Turkish when the organization was founded.

One strategy *späti* owners used to counter the bans was to define their shops as "tourist stores", to which the law gives an exception. The variety of business models adopted by *späti* operators (for example, some are at the same time bakeries and some are internet cafes) make it possible for them to identify their stores as "tourist shops". Members of Berlin Späti Organization situate themselves as indispensable to Berlin by arguing that they produce value for the city as "tourist shops". According to *späti* owners, the fact that tourists frequent their businesses is obvious. Therefore, they find it only natural that their businesses be treated as such. Selim, for example, a *späti* owner who came to Berlin in 2011, suggested that he served tourists frequently and therefore contributed to Berlin's economy. He compared his neighborhood to boroughs that are known to be tourist areas to make his point that his shop was indeed a "tourist shop":

> Most of our customers are German, Italian, Spanish, English. This street is a tourist area. Here, there are neither Turks nor Arabs. They are not here. All [of our customers] are foreigners, tourists. They say that Ku'damm [an upscale shopping boulevard] is a tourist area, Warschauer [a street and its surrounding area in the former East Berlin famous for its nightclubs] is a tourist area. Then what is this place? There are more tourists here. [...] A beer in Warschauer costs two Euros, here [it costs] 1.50.

By stating that his customers were not Turks or Arabs, Selim disputed the claim that businesses owned by minorities were inevitably for minorities. He insisted that his shop (like many others in his neighborhood) served Germans and international customers. His emphasis on the cheaper beer he offered (compared to shops in a street known to be frequented by tourists) pointed to an emerging type of international customer: the newcomer on a tight budget who wants to experience the rebranded "hip" yet affordable Berlin. *Spätis* like Selim's appear as spaces embodying this chic identity that bring foreigners on a budget to Berlin.

Like Selim, many shopkeepers I talked to perceive their serving tourists as proof that they serve Berlin. They understand and present their shops as contributing to Berlin's economy and to its image as an affordable, convenient European city, easily enjoyed by foreigners. Hasan, a *späti* owner who came to Germany in the mid-1990s through marriage, for example, stated that tourists were some of his most valuable customers. According to Hasan, delivering tourists goods and services when other shops are closed benefits the German capital. Even though his business is not in a conventionally "touristic" neighborhood such as the ones around famous landmarks like the Brandenburg Gate, he stated that he still contributed to Berlin's tourism economy:

> Tourists come and get city maps. They buy stamps. They buy Berlin postcards. [...] When they ask us for an address, we explain it with great comfort. [...] Because small business owners on the outside [of Berlin's touristic center] need customers – because the issue is our means of existence – we say, when a guy comes here, 'he might talk about me differently elsewhere [put in a good word for me].' Because I serve him differently [in a positive way], this guy surely talks about Berlin in a good way. [...] I think Berlin benefits from this.

Many Berliners agree with owners about the significance of these shops for the city. In fact, a German copywriter started a petition against the Sunday bans in 2015. More than 38,000 people signed this petition and supported the shop owners. Political parties also got involved in this issue, especially during the local elections in 2016. For example, in its local Berlin party program, Angela Merkel's CDU (Christlich Demokratische Union Deutschlands) reserved a section to "protecting *spätis*." They stated: "*spätis* belong to Berlin like *Currywurst* and Brandenburg Gate; they are a Berlin institution" (CDU Berlin 2016: 32). Likewise, in their part program, the Greens declared, "*späti* culture" belongs to "the openness and economic diversity of Berlin" (Bündnis 90/Die Grünen 2016: 19). Whereas these statements can be perceived as politically motivated, they still present a case of solidarity. As a result of Berlin Späti Organization's efforts and this solidarity, in 2016, *späti* owners achieved the right to open their shops until 8 pm on Sundays with some restrictions on what they can sell.

Redefining who belongs

As almost a million asylum seekers arrived in Europe during the civil war in Syria, and discourses that present (especially Muslim) migrants as impossible to integrate into European society have proliferated. At the same time, this overwhelmingly xenophobic atmosphere confronts its opposite: discourses that "welcome refugees" and praise "multiculturalism". This duality stems from a struggle to define what it means to be "European". This illustration shows that minorities are active participants in this struggle to determine who belongs to Europe.

Turkish shopkeepers in Berlin successfully challenged the implementation of a previously ignored law that forbade their businesses from opening on Sundays. They did so by presenting their operations as serving Berlin's tourism economy. Thus, they asserted that they create value for the German capital. This assertion was endorsed by many Berliners and some political parties. Their example illustrates how minorities can assert a claim to be central to the life of the cities in which they live. It also shows how such claims can receive support from different parts of European society. The challenge for future research is to examine how minorities reject their marginalization and the strategies they use to respond to challenges that hinder their participation in Europe's economy and society.

PART IV

EUROPE'S FUTURE

31

QUO VADIS EUROPA?

Juan Díez Medrano

Huge reductions in transportation and communication costs in the post-World War II era have increased the economic advantages and facilitated the formation of large markets. This benefits large and populous countries like the United States, China, India, and Brazil, and provides incentives to small countries to cooperate in creating large trade areas. The EU has been most successful in meeting this challenge. Its complex and unique multigovernance structure provides a common and encompassing bundle of market institutions and yet respects the member states' political autonomy in sensitive policy and executive realms. Its success in promoting trade in goods, services, and capital has been such that until China's forceful entry in world markets in the early 2000s, globalization and Europeanization were virtually the same thing. The solidity of its architecture was evidenced in the 2008–14 period, as it weathered, certainly not without casualties, the Great Recession.

Consensus as the path of least resistance

European integration has proceeded largely through consensual decision-making by the EU member states (and rulings by the European Court of Justice). New members had to commit to and implement the *acquis communautaire* before joining. This consensus-based process has gradually vested competence and power in EU-level institutions in areas directly and indirectly related to market regulation and the circulation of goods, services, capital, and people.

European integration has thus followed a path of least resistance. Those competences and aspects of governance that are still left largely in the hands of the member states are to a significant extent those which neither citizens nor elites want to transfer to the supranational level (such as taxation) and those for which the citizens' or their political and economic elites' dominant preferences diverge the most and are most difficult to reconcile. For instance, whereas citizens in the EU's south tend to favor the strengthening of the EU's competence on issues pertaining to labor relations and welfare state provision, those in the EU's north oppose such strengthening; whereas citizens across the EU support the creation of a European army, the member states' political elites are still dragging their feet. European integration in areas that remain largely under state control has also become more difficult because the EU has become a very big club. In the past 40 years, it has grown from nine to 28 member states. This has propitiated a significant expansion of the range of views expressed at the European Council and made consensus decisions more difficult to reach.

Because of the strong political and emotional sensitivity of the normative and policy competences still retained by member states, and because of the EU's larger membership, it is not surprising if more integration, in scope and depth, has become slower and increasingly controversial since the approval of the Treaty on European Union in 1992. Recent soft or hard Euroskepticism in many political manifestos across Europe expresses this lack of consensus on further integration. The task of Euroskeptic voices is made all the easier by the fact that although European citizens support cooperation in most areas of governance, a large majority does not support a transfer of sovereignty to European institutions. This is partly because their primary geopolitical identification is national, not European (Díez Medrano 2020). All that Euroskeptic parties have to do in order to attract support to their cause and undermine further efforts toward integration is invoke threats to the national interest and identity, and to allege a lack of democratic legitimacy. If they are not more successful it is to some extent because the EU is still rather inconspicuous. National media and political elites devote very little time to discussing EU politics and policies. Criticism of the EU also lacks traction because most citizens are oblivious to the extent to which sovereignty is shared or has been transferred to the EU level.

The sensitive character of competences that remain largely national (like education), coupled with the negotiating complexities associated with an EU comprising 28 member states, also explain increasing reliance on the Open Method of Coordination as a vehicle for integration. This, of course, adds bureaucracy and bureaucratic costs, which cancel some of the benefits of integration in the areas concerned and become the target of public criticism.

Prospects for change

Based on this discussion, it might be reasonable to expect no significant changes toward further integration or to the EU's governing institutions in the coming decades. Fifty years, however, is a long time and unanticipated events or transformations could impact on the member states' preferences, as well as on those of national and transnational stakeholders, which would then make change possible. For example, political and military tension in Eastern Europe, uncertainty about the United States' level of military engagement in Europe, large economies of scale in the defense industry, and the growing absolute and relative costs of maintaining Europe's welfare states, may eventually persuade EU political elites to agree to a merging of national armies into a single European army. As mentioned above, public opinion surveys consistently show that they would find unanimous agreement on the creation of a common army in the population.

The EU states' preferences could also converge because of ongoing changes taking place at the societal level. This would facilitate further integration. I am part of a group of researchers that has been examining these changes over the last decade. Our research has shown that highly educated and multilingual Europeans, mobile Europeans (mainly those who move abroad permanently), and binational couples formed by Europeans, for instance, are more prone to develop European identifications than are other groups in the population (Fligstein 2008). It is conceivable that the next 50 years will witness significant increases in the proportion of university graduates and of people able to speak more than one European language, in the propensity to travel, study, and live abroad, and in the propensity to marry or cohabit with other Europeans.

It is unlikely, however, that these changes will be of such magnitude as to challenge the primacy of national identifications, mainly because the main container in which individuals grow up and spend most of their lives is still the national state, with its national and local curricula, its media, and its national politicians and political groups. At the same time, Europe is aging rapidly, because of longer life expectancy and a low rate of fertility. The younger, more cosmopolitan cohorts are relatively small in size, which means that for a long time, general orientations to Europe will be shaped by the views of generations whose outlook is largely national. Finally, large regional economic inequalities (such as North–South or East–West) will still stand in the way of a convergence of national preferences in areas like welfare state provision. Therefore, in the most optimistic scenario, it will take at least several generations for social changes to produce something similar to a European society, where preferences over Europe's institutional structure vary along variables other than nationality.

While significant movement toward more integration in coming decades is unlikely and only conditional on unforeseeable economic or political changes, the opposite evolution toward a more fragmented Europe is also unlikely, or if so, only temporary. The reduction in transportation and communications costs that has propitiated globalization is not reversible. Globalization spans more than 250 years and has only been interrupted once, in the 1930s and 1940s, and just for a few years.

This increase in the size of markets has been simultaneous to the creation of empires, first, and then, in the post-World War II era, of two-level and other multilateral systems of governance (Gancia *et al.* 2018). A significant process of disintegration would thus be bought at an enormous economic cost, especially now that China has become a world economic power and has yet to develop its internal market. Disintegration may happen, but the economic consequences would be so dire that it would not last long. Of course, this does not preclude some devolution in areas that are only tangential to the single market and the circulation of goods, services, capital, and people. Historically, national states have also experienced periodic decentralization and recentralization processes. The basic EU architecture – that is, the one that was put in place in 1993 – is unlikely to unravel.

A sense of perspective

Disintegration could also happen if member states decide to leave the EU, as the United Kingdom did in June 2016. The United Kingdom, however, is in the unique situation of being able to be part of and even lead an alternative two-level governance system, whether the Commonwealth or the European Free Trade Association. It remains to be seen whether any such arrangements would pay off. The United Kingdom would purchase sovereignty at the price of the uncertainties and costs resulting from a less than perfect market (non-tariff barriers, uneven compliance with market rules in different countries, more judicial uncertainty for firms investing in other countries that are part of the alternative free trade area) and the inefficiencies resulting from obstacles to the international mobility of workers. It is doubtful that the experiment would succeed, even in the unlikely scenario where a few other EU members would defect and join the UK-led market. At best, the new trade area would gradually come to resemble the EU.

Social scientists like revolutionary change and in today's highly competitive world they often cannot resist the temptation to turn minor changes into major crises. This is because revolutions and crises make their work more socially relevant. The EU, like national states, certainly confronts big challenges. A sober and theoretically based analysis of the large macrosociological and economic processes that underlie not so much its contingent creation but certainly its adequacy to the current world and its evolution over the years, suggests, however, that it is here to stay and that, in the absence of major and unpredictable external shocks, it will not change significantly in the next few decades.

32

EXIT, VOICE, OR LOYALTY? THE COLLAPSE OF NATIONAL ELITE CONSENSUS ON EUROPE'S FUTURE

Matthias Matthijs

It is not easy to be a Europhile these days. During the early 2000s, all EU member states agreed to set up a European Convention tasked with drafting an EU Constitutional Treaty. That bold idea drew direct inspiration from the 1787 Philadelphia Convention in America. Back then, the EU was widely touted as the next superpower. The books that were written about the EU back then had ringing titles like *The European Dream* and *The United States of Europe*. Almost two decades later, it is hard to find anyone taking those ideas seriously. Instead, the EU finds itself in a period of deep introspection, still coming to terms with the fallout of its perfect storm. Multiple overlapping crises – over the euro, immigration, Russian bellicosity, democratic backsliding, Brexit, and how to deal with Donald Trump's America – have made for dire predictions. The books being published and sold these days have titles like *The End of Europe* and *The Strange Death of Europe*.

Much of the current pessimism is unwarranted, even though the EU's problems are real. While the end is not nigh for Europe, it is undeniable that Euroskepticism is on the rise, and not just on the political fringes. Over the past decade, what the EU does and how it affects citizens' everyday lives has become fiercely politicized across the political spectrum. Euroskepticism has made significant inroads into traditional Christian and social democratic parties. With the exception of Germany, where both centrist *Volksparteien*, the Social Democratic Party of Germany (SPD) and the Christian Democratic Union (CDU) remain firmly wedded to the European project in its current form, most other EU member states have seen Euroskepticism creep into their political mainstream. Many center-left parties question the EU's orthodox approach to economic policy and excessive focus on market openness and free competition. Center-right parties are deeply uncomfortable with the EU's more progressive stance on questions of migration and identity.

Longstanding patterns of political party competition in much of Europe have been upended by new and old populist movements on both left and right, while centrist forces have struggled to stay in power. The multiple crises of European integration have transformed the reigning elite consensus over EU affairs into skepticism or outright opposition. Remarkably so, the big four – Germany, France, Italy, and the UK – today have fundamentally different and largely incompatible views of how the EU should develop. At the same time, many EU officials and observers continue to take comfort in Jean Monnet's famous dictum that "Europe will be forged in crises, and will be the sum of the solutions adopted in those crises". But as Craig Parsons and I have previously argued, while it is a reassuring narrative during hard times, it is not actually borne out by the historical evidence (Parsons & Matthijs 2015). In the past, the European project has almost always moved forwards when national elites came together around a positive vision for future institutional steps toward closer integration. A crisis by itself is not enough.

National responses to Europe's cage

With the benefit of hindsight, the period of the mid-1980s to the mid-1990s was a time of unusual economic polity consensus among Europe's elites, based on neoliberal and ordoliberal principles. Both the SEA and the Treaty of Maastricht signified a radical break with the American-led postwar consensus of "embedded liberalism", the idea that sovereign nation states would gradually steer their economies in a broadly liberalizing direction but would maintain economic policy discretion to respond to domestic challenges. While the transition from "embedded" liberalism to a more "disembedded" neoliberalism was happening everywhere, the EU's member states went one step further by pouring that consensus – on open and competitive markets, free movement, balanced budgets, and independent central banks – into supranational treaties with strict rules that could only be changed by unanimity. In effect, the EU moved from the "rescue" to the "caging" of the nation state.

While a detailed analysis of Europe's multiple crises over the past decade is beyond the scope of this chapter – and has been done exhaustively in other venues – what has been striking is the radically different elite responses they have elicited in the EU's "big four" over the past few years (Matthijs & Blyth 2018). A well-known framework to make sense of the reactions in the UK, France, Italy, and Germany is to borrow Albert O. Hirschman's *Exit, Voice, and Loyalty*.

While Germany's elite seems comfortable with the institutional status quo, the respective political and economic establishments in the other three member states seem anything but. From Angela Merkel to her putative successor as leader of the CDU, Annegret Kramp-Karrenbauer, to Olaf Scholz of the SPD and the leadership of the Greens, or even Christian Lindner of the Free Democratic Party, the best way to describe their stance toward European integration is one of "loyalty" to the current system. Indeed, many of them still want to tighten the rules even further. In many ways, German elites feel vindicated by the past 15 years of relative growth and prosperity in their country, and see it as proof that other member states should enact similar structural reforms as then SPD Chancellor Gerhard Schröder instituted in the early 2000s.

While the desire of the UK to "exit" Europe's "cage" has been overdetermined in both the long run and the short term, the UK's future relationship with the EU remains very much in doubt. The Brexit campaign was fraught and based on deliberate perversions of the truth about the EU's power. Despite the agony of two years of Article 50 negotiations, the majority of Britain's elite has accepted that the UK's relationship with the EU can be an arm's length one at best. Many believe that their country will temperamentally be better off being "out" of the EU with lots of "opt ins" rather than being "in" the EU with lots of "opt-outs." Boris Johnson and Michael Gove want to return to the neoliberal heyday when Margaret Thatcher was in charge; Jeremy Corbyn also yearns for more domestic control of the national economy, but for him in order to protect workers from foreign competition and to create UK industrial champions through state aid. It is hard to imagine the current generation of UK leaders fully embracing a rules-based and disembedded EU.

Macron's vision of Europe's future – *l'Europe Qui Protège* – is embraced by much of the EU establishment in Brussels and Frankfurt. It points toward a lot more powers for the EU's supranational institutions, but also toward more discretion at the EU level, and some more national flexibility within the existing rules. Macron's view, traditionally shared by France's postwar political elite, comes closest to a "socially embedded" Europe with significantly more EU-wide solidarity. In essence, it comes down to more "voice" for France in Europe, and would need Germany to quite drastically change its current loyalty to the institutional status quo. But it is without a doubt a forward-looking vision that believes in Europe increasingly playing the same role and providing similar protections to those national governments currently provide for their citizens. He is however a lonely voice for "more" Europe in the current political climate that points toward "less" Europe and a widely shared national yearning to "take back control."

Finally, Matteo Salvini's view of Europe – *l'Europa delle Nazione* – is more backward looking. It imagines a return to the European Communities of the 1960s, that is, an "embedded liberal" world where national governments hold all important policy levers and have maximum discretion over economic policy, including fiscal, monetary, labor market, and immigration policies. Salvini points toward a lot more "voice" for national member states in deciding important matters of domestic and foreign policy. It is harder to make sense of the views of the Five Star Movement, as it hints at more solidarity and more national discretion at the same time. However, the tensions between Italy and the EU have been building up well before the coming to power of the 2018 populist coalition, which ended up lasting just over a year. It is worth pointing out that Matteo Renzi, the former prime minister and leader of the center-left Partito Democratico, used to rail against the constraints of the Stability and Growth Pact and did not think Europe's banking union was set up in the national interest of Italy (or its banks) at all.

Transforming Europe's cage

During the early 1950s and again during the early 1990s, when the EU made great leaps forwards in economic and political integration, progress in EU institution building was made possible by a striking degree of elite consensus among the national establishments of key member states on where the EC, and then the EU, should go. What is deeply problematic about the current moment is that the views of Merkel, Johnson, Macron, and Salvini are not only far apart but also mutually incompatible. This does not bode well for the process of European integration in the near term.

So, where does the EU go from here? The good news is that there is no need for a breakup or to start over from scratch. While both the euro and the single market still lack the supranational institutions to make them work for everyone, and their overall macroeconomic fragility remains a challenge, Europe's leaders and EU officials would do well to revisit Alan Milward's basic premise that Europe was not meant to cage its nation states but to rescue them. Rather than offering "more Europe" as the answer to all of its problems, asking "what kind of Europe" its people want is a much better starting point. More voice – both at the national and at the supranational level – would be a good starting point.

In order to do so, the EU will need to move away from the primacy of its disembedded technocratic economics and back toward the primacy of its still mostly nationally embedded democratic politics. In the process, European integration has taken away so many policy levers from its national governments that many citizens have started to wonder what they are still there for. Democratic legitimacy, for better or worse, remains with Europe's nation states. There are no technocratic solutions to Europe's political problems no matter how hard one tries to find them. As the late historian Tony Judt observed back in 1996, while there is nothing "inherently superior about national institutions over others, we should recognize the reality of nations and states, and note the risk that, when neglected, they become an electoral resource of virulent nationalists" (Judt 1996: 129–30).

Europe's leaders need a new grand political bargain that extols a basic division of labor between Brussels and national capitals. The EU needs to recast its common market and its common currency that allows its nation states to breathe through enough economic policy discretion. Europe's states thereby need to be set free from their current EU cage. Occasionally breaking the rules of both the single market and the single currency will allow national elites to deal with specific national problems and to respond to their voters' legitimate concerns by giving their electorates a genuine democratic choice in policy. It is a *politically* much better solution to let "the people" choose what national trade-offs they are willing to make, rather than having EU technocrats in Brussels and Frankfurt make that choice for them, which could well be optimal in economic terms.

At the same time, the EU will need more solidarity at the supranational level, starting with a common safety asset (or "eurobond"), common deposit insurance, and an EU-wide industrial and climate policy. And given that we live in a much less benign international multipolar system, the EU will also need to ramp up its tools of economic statecraft. This begins with a geopolitical role for its single currency and a more robust strategic use of its trading powers to achieve its joint foreign policy objectives. Finally, there can be no debate as to the EU's enduring commitment to democratic values and the rule of law.

Building European institutions that strengthen rather than weaken its member states will be key. More power at the bottom will result in more robustness to shocks at the top. More solidarity at the top will mean less disintegration from the bottom up. Let us hope tomorrow's leaders can find common ground in such a new grand bargain, and put the EU onto a more sustainable footing.

33

DIFFERENTIATED INTEGRATION THROUGH MORE INTEGRATION, DECENTRALIZATION, AND DEMOCRACY

Vivien A. Schmidt

The EU is going nowhere unless and until it successfully responds to its multiple crises – of policy, politics, and polity – in ways that enable it to ensure the best possible future for its member states and non-members alike (Fabbrini & Schmidt 2019). Europe's policy crises are in key areas such as money (how to move forwards in the eurozone), borders (what to do about refugees and migrants), security (how to develop effective security and defense cooperation), the integrity of the EU (how to manage British exit from the EU), and "rule of law" (what to do about the "democratic illiberalism" of Hungary and Poland). Europe's political crises are apparent in the increasing politicization "at the bottom", as people feeling "left behind" and fearing loss of social status or political control have voted for Euroskeptic parties; from "the bottom up", as national politics constrains EU decision-making, for example, by making it harder to reach consensus in the Council between North and South in the eurozone crisis or East and West in the refugee crisis; and "at the top", in the politicized dynamics of interaction among EU institutional actors, for example, between Council and Commission or ECB in the eurozone crisis. Finally, Europe's "polity" crises affect both national and EU levels, with European integration having eroded the national foundations of democracy as more and more decisions are removed from the national to the EU level without any appreciable improvement of democratic access at the supranational level.

How the EU responds to these crises will shape its future, for better or for worse. But the EU's governance capacity is also a victim of its multiple crises. To reinforce its governance while resolving the crises, the EU has to manage a complex balancing act in which it needs to promote at one and the same time deeper integration and greater decentralization while enhancing democracy at both EU and national levels. Although this may sound like squaring the circle, it is doable so long as EU development is envisioned through the lens of differentiated integration (Schmidt 2019). But what kind of differentiation? Rather than integration at multiple speeds or by way of a hard core, the EU would do better to conceive of its future as a "soft core" Europe made up of the overlapping participation of different clusters of member states in the EU's many policy communities beyond the single market, all with voices across communities but with votes only in those areas in which they participate.

Differentiated integration in the EU's many policy communities

Differentiated integration is generally taken to mean that EU member states – beyond belonging to the single market and being liberal democracies – need not all proceed together at the same rate to converge on the same array of policies. But rather than thinking about such differentiation in terms of a multispeed or hard core Europe, we would do better to see the EU's future organization in terms of a soft core Europe. This is a Europe made up of overlapping clusters of member states participating in the EU's many different policy communities, all administered by a single set of EU institutions, with most member states involved in most areas.

The fear with a multispeed Europe is that it will all fall apart, as member states pick and choose communities in which to opt into or out of. The problem with a hard core Europe coalesced around a deepened eurozone is that there is no guarantee that the core players (France and Germany) will be able to reach productive agreement across policy areas, in particular given how much they still diverge on the eurozone. Such a hard core might also create a deeper rift between the smaller core and the rest. And why assume that a cluster of member states that takes the lead in one policy area (the eurozone) would have the ability, let alone the will or imagination, to lead in the others (in security or migration, for example)? A soft core of multiple clusters of member states, in which any duo or trio of member states would take leadership in any given policy community, would be better.

Seeing the future of EU integration as a differentiated process of member state participation in different policy communities beyond the single market would allow for each "community" to develop further while constituting its own special system of governance. Within this soft core Europe, some policy areas still require deeper integration. In the security and defense policy crisis, for example, the failure to move toward any significant integration continues to plague the EU's Common Security and Defense Policy, and this despite the continued instability in the Middle East or the threat from Russia. In this area, deeper integration is likely to come with continued differentiation, with more cooperation and targeted investment through any of the many recently created instruments. Refugee and migrant policy also suffers from a lack of coordination and increasing fragmentation, with its failures having been grist for the mill for right-wing populists. This area requires deeper integration through EU-wide agreement on principles of treatment accompanied by more differentiated integration regarding the modalities of implementation, for example with positive incentives in place of imposed quotas.

The eurozone is different. EU governance has arguably gone both too far in deepening integration, by "governing by rules and ruling by numbers", and not far enough, by failing to institute the mutual risk-sharing instruments necessary for any fixed-currency zone to flourish. Differentiated integration here would mean democratizing and decentralizing the eurozone's elaborate architecture of economic coordination, which remains highly centralized and top down, and not particularly effective. The EU level could be made more effective as well as more democratic by treating the governing rules and numbers more as guidelines for variable yearly targets set by the ECB, with country-specific deficits and debt targets to be debated with the other member states in the Council with the Commission and the European Parliament. The European Semester could be democratized by making it more bottom up and decentralized to the benefit of national actors. This would not only work better, to the benefit of Europe's diverse national economies, but could also help counter the populist drift as mainstream political parties would again to be able to differentiate their policies, with debates on the different pathways to economic health.

None of this will work, however, if not accompanied by deeper eurozone integration through various "solidarity" mechanisms, such as significant investment funds, a serious fiscal backstop and individual deposit insurance, some form of mutualized debt, and Europe-wide unemployment insurance. If this is not forthcoming, then at least allow member states to invest in growth-enhancing areas without counting this toward the deficit or debt numbers of the European Semester. But other crisis areas also need more solidarity mechanisms, such as an intra-European "EU mobility adjustment fund" to support the costs for social services and worker training not just for countries with greater than usual EU migrant worker inflows (such as the UK) but also to recompense countries with excessive outflows of workers (like Lithuania, Romania, and Greece). Any such EU mobility adjustment fund should equally be accompanied by a European fund for refugee support.

Differentiated integration in EU institutional processes

But soft core differentiation also has certain common institutional requirements, including one set of laws overseen by the European Court of Justice and ensured by national courts, with one set of central, overarching institutions, including the Commission, Council, and European Parliament. In other words, there can be no differentiation in the EU's core commitments to the rule of law and democratic principles guaranteeing free and fair elections, independence of the judiciary, and freedom of the press. But any number of specialized institutions may be established to deepen integration in any given policy community, and is "made-to-purpose", as is the case in the eurozone.

For such differentiated integration to work effectively and legitimately, and for all member states to feel part of this soft core EU, whatever their level of involvement, they should be able to exercise voice in all areas, but vote only in those areas in which they participate. For the eurozone, this could mean envisioning that when some members, say, pledge their own resources to an EU budget, their representatives would be the only ones to vote, although everyone could discuss it. For Schengen, this could mean that current non-EU participants (like Norway and Switzerland) that are not EU members would have voice and vote. This could equally apply to their participation in the single market. For the moment, such countries experience a major loss in democratic legitimacy, since they must follow single market rules and contribute to the EU budget without the exercise of voice, let alone vote. For a Brexiting UK, this might be the best way to handle future relations.

But to make EU governance truly workable, the institutional decision-making rules also require revision. The unanimity rule for intergovernmental decision-making needs to be abandoned, replaced by "constitutional" treaties amendable by two-thirds or four-fifths majorities. At the same time, many of the current treaty-based laws should become ordinary legislation, and thereby open to amendment through political debates and compromise in the co-decision mode of EU governance. Beyond this, the European Parliament would also need to find more ways to bring national parliaments into EU-level decision-making.

Conclusion

In short, re-envisioning the future of the EU in terms of a soft-core multiclustered Europe best reflects the differentiated future of the EU, in which deeper integration goes hand in hand with greater decentralization and democracy at all levels. To extend a metaphor I have previously evoked, the future would offer neither one set menu (*prix fixe*) for the chosen few or "Europe *à la carte*", where everyone orders different dishes. It would instead involve a gourmet "menu Europe", with a shared main dish (the single market), all member states sitting around the table and engaging in the conversation, only some choosing to sit out one course or another, while others may join in for one or another course, learning the manners of the table as they too engage in the conversation.

34

REFLECTIONS ON THE DIRECTION OF THE EUROPEAN PROJECT

Mare Ushkovska

This year marks the thirtieth anniversary of the fall of the Berlin wall, the physical manifestation of the ideological divisions of the European continent and a symbol of the decades-long split between European nations. The European project, which is the term used for the idea of a united Europe, developed as a consequence of World War II and intensified after the end of the Cold War, because it was perceived that the pursuit of national self-interest by European countries has long threatened peace on the continent. With time, this vision materialized in the form of the EU, currently encompassing 28 (27 after the UK left) out of the more than 40 countries in Europe. The success of this supranational entity relies on the premise of eliminating borders between European states and invalidating the role of nationhood and sovereignty, for the benefit of consensual decision-making. Therefore, the question of national sovereignty and the degree to which individual states are willing to forego self-rule is at the heart of the debate on the future of the EU.

The preamble of the Treaty on European Union emphasizes the commitment assumed by all member states to "continue the process of creating an ever closer union among the peoples of Europe", solidifying an ideal of a European integration, the level of which remains vague. It is precisely this undefined form of the ever closer union which has been the cause of many a disagreement between member states, all of which have demonstrated a distinct understanding and preference for what the end result of the European project should be. Expressions of these preferences could be seen in the numerous opt-outs of the United Kingdom, the referenda in France and the Netherlands voting down a European Constitution, the push for a greater political union of the Western member states versus the partiality for preserving sovereign decision-making of the Eastern member states, and last but not least in the reality of Brexit. While the prospect of the United Kingdom's exit from the EU was observed with general disappointment, many among the European federalists also viewed it as an opportunity for the EU to pursue its plans for a closer political integration. Nevertheless, there remains a dissonance among the remaining EU member states on the final stage of European integration and the level of sovereignty states are willing to cede.

The roots of diversity

There are many historical, cultural, and political reasons for the difference in views and behavior of individual countries. The United Kingdom, for example, as both an island nation and former imperial power, has long perceived itself as separate from what it refers to as "the Continent". Some countries that emerged from the former communist bloc, having finally (re)gained full sovereignty in the 1990s, are now wary of propositions to simply renounce it. There is also the question of relative power between countries. Large states, which are either economic or military superpowers, have a significantly greater sway in determining strategic priorities or policy direction at a European level than smaller states. Therefore, a political union of European nations would be disproportionately influenced by the interests of large states, which accounts for the absence of fear in them from the transfer of sovereignty to a supranational European entity. Smaller states, conversely, benefit greatly from an economic European union, but significantly less so from a political one.

Hence, it is not surprising that there are different, and at times seemingly incompatible, perspectives by member states today on the ultimate shape of the EU that all should be working toward constructing. Even former German Foreign Minister Joschka Fischer stated, in a speech in 2000, that the founding members created the union without a "blueprint for the final state" (Fischer 2000). While many EU officials and state politicians now argue that the sole logical direction the EU can take is that of a full-fledged federation, the finality of the European integration process was never defined in any specific terms either in written form, or in the form of an unwritten consensus between constituent states. And even when agreement is to be found between government representatives, the debate remains unsettled among the general public. While believing in the fundamental goodness of European integration, citizens in France and the Netherlands voted against the European Constitutional Treaty in 2005, which was "a symbolic line in the sand marking the extent to which nations were willing to see the European supranational entity override nation-states" (Ushkovska 2019: 2). Later, with the eurozone crisis and the migration crisis exposing some weaknesses in the common European monetary and foreign policies, the benefits of a supranational Europe began to appear deceptive, resulting in a growing anti-EU discourse emerging in many EU states.

Europe is not the United States

Given that Europe is a constellation of nations, each with its own unique language, traditions, and history, it is unsuited for political projects that would attempt to emulate the United States of America's federal model. The United States is a country fostered on the principle of citizenship, rather than ethnicity, and founded by persons willing to embrace the same linguistic and cultural background. A project for European unity requires an altogether different, and more flexible, vision. The EU at present is a one-of-a-kind entity, more than an international organization, but far from a federation of states, or even a confederation. Putting aside the existence of European institutions, the EU is unlikely to replace or supersede nation states and national institution of member states in the foreseeable future. A clear indication of this limitation is that key decisions are still made by the European Council, where heads of states or governments vote guided by what they perceive to be in the national interest of their respective countries. The EU is, after all, a club of states. Furthermore, the federalist idea of an EU future seems less likely than other options given the growing national sentiment within many of the member states.

The scenario known as a "multispeed EU" has garnered a great deal of attention. That scenario appears to be an attempt to address the growing divide between member states on the level of political integration the EU should have. Presented in a White Paper on the future of the EU by the European Commission in 2017, it proposes "coalitions of the willing", where those member states that opt to cooperate more closely in areas such as taxation, social policy, and a common defense policy, can choose to proceed toward a greater political union. Other states that may not wish to participate in that group, would remain dedicated to supporting the single market, with the option of potentially joining the more integrated bloc later on. While the White Paper insists that this scenario would preserve the unity among all member states, it lends itself to the idea that it could create a class distinction between participating countries, where states that show skepticism toward closer political integration could become outsiders. This is what makes this scenario a controversial one and one that is presented as the last resort by the European Commission, should member states not be able to agree on a common way forwards.

Voices from some of the larger member states nevertheless openly favor the possibility of a two-tier Europe. The arguments they make in support of this scenario are twofold. First, a multispeed EU would be a truly democratic option where each state could decide for itself the level of integration it wishes to pursue, without the pressures that come along with the need for a unanimous vote. Second, a multispeed EU would put an end to the slow and ineffective work of EU institutions caused by the sometimes long and impossible negotiations between national governments on common policies. Furthermore, they add, a multispeed EU already exists. Some member states have the euro as their currency, while others do not, and some states are part of the Schengen Zone, while others are not. Therefore, an EU with differentiated integration would be more sustainable.

The unity of Europe

What becomes problematic is that this concept of multiple speeds undermines the basic idea of a united Europe. By attempting to reconcile divergent interests between countries, the EU would effectively pursue a path of setting up blocs within the bloc, leaving the EU divided internally. In addition, over time, this multispeed Europe could develop into an institutional and political arrangement where Western members create all the policies, while Eastern states look on from the margins. It is also to be expected that, once the multiple concentric circles of integration are established, the countries that move first would place conditions on those member states that wish to move up later.

Such conditions could form a set of (prohibitive) criteria according to which more integrated states would evaluate and judge the less integrated state on its suitability to join their club, not unlike the accession process currently in place for non-EU states with a candidate status. Such conditionality would place some states, who are nominally full-fledged members of the Union, in an inferior position to other member states. The situation would be reminiscent of the Europe that existed prior to the EU's 2004 enlargement to the east. As an indication of this, the European Commission's White Paper notes that "[c]itizens' rights derived from EU law [will] start to vary depending on whether or not they live in a country that has chosen to do more" (European Commission 2017b: 20).

The implications for Europe are worth underscoring. A multispeed scenario may be the most probable option for the future of the European project. However, embracing a multispeed EU as the most optimal and realistic way forwards essentially means accepting the fact that Europe cannot be united in absolute terms. Embracing multispeed Europe also means that there are substantial differences between member states which cannot be overlooked. Once we consider those European countries that are yet not admitted to the EU, or that do not wish to join the EU, it is necessary to acknowledge that a united Europe may only remain a theoretical ideal, rather than a political reality.

35

THE EU'S RULE-OF-LAW CRISIS AND THE PROBLEM OF DIAGONALITY

Csongor István Nagy

The EU's ongoing rule-of-law crisis, entailed by constitutional backsliding in some of its member states, and the fierce debate as to whether and how EU institutions should intervene, have grown into one of the core issues of the European project. Nowadays, it is generally accepted that the rule-of-law predicament undermines the European integration and, sooner or later, a solution needs to be found. But how can there be a rule-of-law crisis in the EU? Rule of law and human rights (hereafter collectively: rule of law) are said to be the fundamental values of Europe (Article 2 of the Treaty on European Union) and the EU has its own detailed bill of rights (EU Charter of Fundamental Rights).

The problem is that EU law has no doctrine of "diagonality". This term refers to the application of EU rule of law against member states, as opposed to "straight application", which refers to the application of EU law requirements against EU institutions, as well as the application of national constitutional requirements against member states. EU law contains a comprehensive set of rule-of-law requirements, which have a full application against EU institutions ("straight application") but only a very limited one against member states. EU rule of law applies to member states when they implement EU law ("paradigm of scope"), however, notwithstanding its substantial spillover effects, this diagonality is false, as here member states act as the agents of the EU ("apparent diagonal application"), contrary to cases, where EU rule of law is applied to member states acting in their own field of operation ("genuine diagonal application").

The dead end of the European rule-of-law debate

The ongoing rule-of-law crisis in Europe brought to the fore a fundamental contradiction of the EU's legal and institutional architecture. On the one hand, rule of law and human rights are (at least on the level of declaration) at the cornerstones of the EU: they are clearly recognized by the founding treaties, serve as non-negotiable preconditions for accession, and ensure that the various European mechanisms based on mutual trust and recognition are operational and effective. On the other hand, EU law has no doctrine of diagonality and appears to have very limited power when encountering recalcitrant member states who are contemptuous of the EU's fundamental values. Unfortunately, if these values are outrageously defied in the member states, that may demolish the EU both as a community based on common values (principled reason) and as a mechanism based on mutual trust and recognition (practical reason).

The fierce scholarly and political debate as to whether and how EU institutions should intervene underscored the fact that EU law has failed to develop a solid doctrine of diagonality. While the ongoing rule-of-law crisis has stimulated various proposals on how to enforce rule of law on member states as well as within them, we still do not have an answer to fundamental questions about why such a doctrine is needed, if it is needed, and what the justification for a diagonal application of EU law on the member states would be. Notably, the diagonal application of EU rule of law is not simply a vertical question of top-down legal authority. While the straight application is based on the consideration that no public authority may exist without rule-of-law limits, this rationale is not valid in an EU–member state relation where member states conferred sovereign powers on the EU and not the other way around. The answer to the question is deeply rooted in the EU's self-identity and conception of purpose. This leaves EU law in a very difficult situation where the EU is expected to eat its cake (protect EU rule of law) and have it too (preserve national constitutional identities).

EU rule of law's application against member states is, for the most part, linked to the scope of EU law ("paradigm of scope") and the debate on human rights in member states has centered around how to define this scope. Nonetheless, the general perception is that the spillover effects of this apparent diagonality are insufficient to address the problem that arises when member states flout the EU's fundamental principles. The paradigm of scope seems to be flawed: on the one hand, it does not provide protection in genuine domestic matters; on the other hand, it tempts EU institutions to overreach by seeking to apply EU rule-of-law principles without taking into account national constitutional identities.

Multilevel constitutional architectures and comparative federalism

Fortunately, comparative federalism provides an array of experiences, solutions, and techniques, which can assist the European legal community in addressing the diagonal rule-of-law problem. The most straightforward approach as to the diagonality of human rights is found in federal systems like those in Austria, Belgium, Germany, and Switzerland. Some federations use various methods to give room to regional "constitutional identities". For example, the Canadian Charter of Rights and Freedoms does not distinguish between straight and diagonal application and applies equally to the federal government and the provinces. However, neither the depoliticization, nor the uniformization of Canadian human rights is as determinate as it may appear at first glance. Federalism is factored into the charter and its case law at various points, and the provinces (as well as the federal government) are given the right to opt out from the charter's central provisions unilaterally.

Australian constitutional law relies on "constitutional silence" to create more space for diversity. The Australian constitution does not list an explicit bill of rights but instead sets out a handful of fundamental rights, some of which limit only the federal government (or commonwealth), and some of which also apply to state governments. Nonetheless, the Australian constitution fails to build up a comprehensive system of human rights protection. In practice, Australia has normally given legislative (political) answers to the eventual human-rights-focused tensions between the federal and the territorial political communities. For instance, contrary to the US and Europe, state sodomy laws were quashed through legislation and not by judicial intervention. In the Toonen case, after a successful complaint submitted to the United Nations Human Rights Committee against Tasmania's anti-gay laws, the Commonwealth of Australia passed the Human Rights (Sexual Conduct) Act 1994 (Cth), which was designed to override the pertinent provisions of Tasmania's criminal law.

The current EU architecture parallels the first century of US constitutional history: although today, because of the incorporation doctrine, most fundamental rights held to be valid against the US federal government can also be invoked against state governments, the first century of US constitutional law was more similar to the current EU approach in terms of offering only loose controls on state governments. Although the US Supreme Court sporadically established constitutional limits on state governments that may be regarded as human rights in nature, the arsenal of human rights protection as enshrined in the federal bill of rights did not apply at the state level until the adoption of the Fourteenth Amendment after the Civil War. For a century, states were limited only by their own constitutions. The American Civil War proved that certain common core values have to be respected throughout the Union, if the Union is to hold together, and there are certain practices that violate the Union's "most basic notions of morality and justice".

A doctrine of diagonality

Against this background, the paradigm of "scope" that prevails in EU law today should be replaced with the paradigm of "core standards". EU law needs a "Copernican turn". The paradigm of "scope" holds the scope of EU law stationary at the center of the EU "rule-of-law" universe. A paradigm of "core standards" would instead place member state action at the center of the analysis and would aim to ascertain whether that is reconcilable with the EU's core values. This way, instead of stretching (and at times overstretching) the scope of EU law, European jurisprudence could apply diagonally to the extent necessary to preserve the core values of the EU.

This core standards paradigm would not imply that all EU rule-of-law requirements having a straight application are also applicable against member states (e.g. not all rights listed in the EU Charter of Fundamental Rights have a warrant to be applied diagonally). On the contrary, the courts should give due deference to member states and their constitutional identities wherever possible. A diagonal application of EU law is not meant to create an exhaustive rule-of-law protection scheme, but to protect the EU's rule-of-law identity, built up of the common core of European constitutionalism, and to make European mechanisms based on mutual trust, cooperation, and recognition operational and effective.

The proposition is that the straight and the diagonal applications have different rationales, which inform the way they should work. The choice between the two modes of application is determined by two considerations: the protection of the EU's rule-of-law identity as a cornerstone of the integration and the respect for national constitutional identities. EU law should set up a non-exhaustive but comprehensive diagonal system based on the "core standards" paradigm, which, as a result, would be selective and respect member states' margin of appreciation. While this approach may appear to be overly complicated in comparison to a more comprehensive application of EU protections on the member states, it is far from unprecedented and it is capable of both preserving the core values underpinning the EU and respecting the constitutional identities of the member states.

36

MORE UNION, MORE STATES
Josep M. Colomer

The EU has achieved a great union of the private economy, but little union of the public sector. The paradox is that European public finances are so scant that the EU has to intervene, control, and eventually bail out the public finances of its member states, a process that many regard as undemocratic. The EU is too interventionist because it is too weak. The alternative is for the Union to bolster public resources for large-scale initiatives, stop controlling and interfering in domestic policy-making, and return more fiscal autonomy to the member states.

We need to discontinue the idea of a "fiscal union" between member states and, instead, provide the European Commission with more fiscal resources. The fiscal autonomy of each of the levels of government, both the member states and the Union, as well as the local and regional governments, is the best formula for efficient public management and democratic accountability.

Comparing Europe and America

Some inspiration can be taken from the process of building the first modern union of states in a great continental area and inspired by democratic principles: the United States of America. The lengthy process of building the American Union, which was gradual, conflictive, and asymmetric, might be reminiscent of the process currently under way in the EU. It took close to 125 years from the initial undertaking to form the Union, the ratification of the US Constitution toward the end of the eighteenth century, to the point that the United States achieved solid federal institutions. From this standpoint, the EU, which has lasted to date around half this time, has made greater progress in many fields than the United States had halfway through its construction process. However, the EU's principal hurdle lies in its public finance sector.

At the very start of its existence, the US federal government was extremely weak, as weak as the EU is now in terms of financial resources. The majority of its expenditure, including that on the wars against the British, came from the individual states, which had proclaimed their sovereignty before accepting the US Constitution. After the wars, the US Treasury decided to "mutualize" the states' huge debt: in other words, the Treasury decided to create a federal debt able to absorb those of the individual states. It began to bolster its strength at the states' expense, exchanging debt payments for power. The federal government was also strengthened with the creation of a permanent federal income tax to fund the Civil War effort.

Nevertheless, the main federal institutions responsible for security and finances, the Federal Bureau of Investigations, and the Federal Reserve, were not created until the 1910s. The federal government only secured control over more than half of total public expenditure as late as 1940, some 150 years after its creation, due to the sudden expansion of the public sector in response to the Great Depression. It has been only since then that the US government has had enough financial clout to develop wide-ranging federal programs in the fields of defense, infrastructure, research and development, and social security. Unlike the EU, the US federal government has been able to implement broad-based stimuli against recessions, most recently since 2009.

The other side of the coin has been that, alongside this process of bolstering federal resources, the United States ceased providing financial aid to insolvent states or cities as early as 1840. Thousands of local governments have gone bankrupt, especially during the Civil War, the Great Depression, and most recently the Great Recession: California, Illinois, and Detroit, to name but a few. State or local government debt is never mutualized, and states and cities can file for bankruptcy without federal bailouts or rescues. Against this backdrop of federal retraction from underwriting state finances, almost every individual state has adopted financial responsibility criteria, including balanced budget amendments in their constitutions.

After this long-term evolution, fiscal relations in the United States are now the opposite of those between the EU and its member states. The US federal government is financially stronger than the state governments, in contrast with the weakness of the EU compared with its member states. At the same time, and despite some appearances to the contrary, Washington regulates the states much less than Brussels does the member states. As the US federal government has far more resources than the institutions in Brussels, it is much more capable of developing its own large-scale policies and does not need to get involved in the shaping of public policies in individual states.

The low degree of federal interference and the autonomy of the individual states allows for a significant legislative disparity between the states of the American Union, especially with regard to contract, property, and family and criminal law, including on issues such as taxation, abortion, gun ownership, or the death penalty. American state governments are also more responsible for some of their own decisions – particularly with regard to their financial viability – than the member states of the EU.

More EU power, more member state autonomy

During the recent Great Recession in Europe, some government leaders decried the risk of "moral hazard". The suspicion was that some European states had embarked upon careless financial ventures because their leaders thought that, if they went bankrupt, they could always blame the EU and demand a bailout using money from other member states. However, the EU has not created its own debt capable of mutualizing the public debts of its member states. That is why the EU had to impose the supervision, regulation, and control of member state finances.

From 2010 on, the eurozone member states were energetically prodded to adopt a balanced budget mandate in their domestic legislation, preferably at a constitutional level. Since 2013, the European Commission has monitored the budgets of the member states more closely. Initially, the focus was on the magnitudes of deficits and forecast debts, but gradually more attention was paid to specific expenditures, taxes, and other incomes, a decision that proved highly controversial.

In the case of Greece, for example, a Memorandum of Understanding with the European Commission committed the Greek government to implementing fixed policies on taxes, pensions, healthcare, bank regulation, the labor market, energy, administration, the fight against corruption, and many other issues, "for many years". In many countries, EU directives are the foundation for the majority of the Parliament's agenda on the annual budget and many economic and social policies.

The EU needs to confirm that it has learned a lesson from the handling of the Great Recession: it should avoid any more large-scale bailouts of member state governments in crisis. The IMF's reluctance to get involved in the bailouts of other European countries gave an indication of the turn events would take. Financial insolvency within the Union may be the only option for governments in crisis in the future. This would mean that the institutions in Brussels would have more confidence in themselves. It would also mean that the member states would have gained more respect in terms of their real powers.

The EU should be able to spend more than its current budget of 1 per cent of the gross European product. These days, about two-thirds of the EU budget are allocated to agricultural subsidies and regional funds, and so little remains for other policies capable of directly stimulating growth and employment. Although the Union may rely heavily to the ECB, the European Stability Mechanism, and the European Investment Bank, the total amount of resources available to it is barely twice the strict EU budget.

Once again, in comparison, the US federal government spends more than 20 per cent of the country's gross domestic product (GDP). However, excluding defense and social security, it has discretionary power over only around 3 per cent of GDP. This figure could provide a provisional target for the EU. Such a target would allow Brussels to broaden the scope of some Europe-wide public policies, especially with regard to infrastructure, energy, the digital economy, and research and development, which can be crucial in promoting sustained growth. The recent proposal to create European-level taxes on large corporations and transnational technology platforms, which now escape state-based taxation and regulation, may also go in the right direction.

Money for freedom

The EU's financial strength is the price to be paid by the member states for cutting back on the EU's excessive interventionism and restoring a good chunk of their lost autonomy. The states would be able to develop their own policies on issues in which they decide to be different, including civil law and social welfare. The states would also be responsible for their own finances and able to comply with their own laws and constitutions requiring balanced budgets, without having to be overseen by the EU. They would be free to go bankrupt and not expect to be bailed out by the EU at the expense of other member states' taxpayers. At the same time, a better financed and less regulatory EU would be a more effective and more accountable one.

37

THE EU'S CHALLENGE WITH SIZE, SOVEREIGNTY, AND MUTUAL BENEFIT

Ludmila Bogdan and Twamanguluka N. Nambili

John Bruton once said, "the European Union is the world's most successful invention for advancing peace", and some may argue a great symbol for effective globalization and collaboration. While Europe is vast beyond the EU, rarely do we view the continent without considering the EU. Nevertheless, with many looming issues and concerns, one wonders: How successful is it really? Will it grow to encompass the rest of Europe? Is it really the savior for all of Europe? And if there are pressing issues, what are the steps to be taken, in order to keep the EU alive throughout the next decades? The number of EU skeptics continue to increase, while the EU supporters decrease. In the light of Brexit, many increasingly wonder if the EU will exist by 2050.

There is no doubt that Europe will continue to transform and flourish over the next decades, and that would be due in large part to the EU's reach and influence. We are pro-EU optimists who want to see Europe and the EU to flourish in the next decades and believe the EU will remain in existence by 2050, but we predict that it will go through, and needs to go through, serious changes and reforms with regards to gender equality, union size, member state sovereignty, and domestic policies, as well as the way member states work together.

More women, fewer new member states

In the wake of a gender awareness era, we predict that the EU will promote women in key decision-making positions, in politics and the economy, to appeal to the masses. With the current EU gender pay gap of 16 per cent (European Commission 2019), this promotion of women is a much needed rebranding that will significantly advance the performance and quality of work in the EU region. Women also outnumber men in all of Europe (Smirnova & Cai 2015). This raises the question of how the EU hopes to appeal more to the people and current member states' citizens, if not providing equal treatment to men and women. Amending the current discrepancy would be a great strategic move that inspires young generations to support the EU even amid difficult times. This move would also set a great example for member states and the rest Europe, bringing about a new era of gender equality transformation on the continent.

Equally important, we envision the size of the Union being more restricted, by halting plans for expansion, as a means of enhancing the Union's longevity. This, of course, may not bode well for the other European non-member states that want to join in the future. If not counting the six with limited recognition, Europe has 50 countries, and, after Great Britain's departure, 27 of those make up the EU. That said, the grim reality remains that decision-making in the EU has significantly slowed down during its expansion. The logic is simple: more members, more interests, more differences, and more difficulties reaching a common ground, as seen with Greece and the refugee "crisis".

Lately, the EU has focused on expanding its membership rather than focusing on providing quality services for existing member states. In the future, that balance will tip the other way. Solving such a problem would be instrumental, should the Union wish to retain its existing members as well as contribute to meaningful development in Europe. We believe that it is highly probable that the rest of the European non-member states will still benefit from the EU through special trade agreements and development consultations from the EU – benefits such as those currently enjoyed by countries such as Norway and Iceland, which are part of the European Free Trade Association but not the EU. This therefore gives those non-member states an opportunity to reform, develop, and keep up with their EU counterparts.

Sovereignty, migration, and mutual benefit

Additionally, we predict that the EU will re-evaluate its current policies with regards to national sovereignty and domestic policies of member states. This re-evaluation is necessary if the EU hopes to remain in existence by 2050. Current policies are too restrictive and give rise to significant conflict in the domestic politics of the member states. Meanwhile, Britain has set an example that the Union can be left. Other strong economies may follow suit if the EU does not re-evaluate its policies in efforts to give member states significant autonomy over their domestic and foreign policies. To be effective, the EU should remain an organization that promotes unity and development across the European continent, and not develop policies that makes it operate akin to a single government.

Allowing member states to retain their significant sovereignty on topics of immigration and employment is pivotal. Current EU policies make it easy for EU citizens to migrate to any member state and find a job, as well as have full access to public funds and benefits. Naturally, the overwhelming number of people who migrate are those from poorly performing member states. Such flows can put tremendous stress on the member state that receives immigrants, especially since EU policies prevent member states from limiting such immigration. Migration across Europe will continue to grow as a result of globalization, however. Allowing countries to have sovereignty over their immigration policies would lower the amount of people migrating between member states for employment or public benefits.

Finally, we predict that the EU will remain because membership collaboration and unity helps member states fight battles that they might otherwise lose on their own. We see this unity spreading beyond member states to non-member states, by means of collaboration and trade agreements. As it stands, many countries are highly dependent on the Union as a safety net, particularly underperforming states. This dependency will hinder many member states from leaving the Union as work is better completed when you have allies.

While having allies can be helpful, the EU needs to understand that membership in the Union needs to be mutually beneficial. The EU should and will learn from Brexit, to consider the interests of all member states. When a member is losing more than it's gaining from the Union, then it will have little desire to stay. Currently the union is set up where all member states absorb the mishaps of other member states, and more often it is the bigger economies that gain little in return. Having allies certainly helps, but an ally relationship needs to be mutually beneficial to be sustainable.

The EU and the future of Europe

The EU is one of the most successful institutions promoting stability, collaboration, development, globalization, and security in Europe. However, we see the EU being reformed with regards to gender equality, union size, member state sovereignty, and domestic policies. Such reform is necessary in order for the EU to be sustainable and successful until 2050 and beyond. Reform of the EU will not only foster more effective cooperation but also strengthen the EU for decades to come in ways that will benefit all of Europe.

38

BREXIT: THE GOLDEN CHALICE OF EUROPEAN DEMOS FORMATION?

Erin O'Leary

In all its chaos, divisiveness, and uncertainty, Brexit has not only raised considerable constitutional questions for the UK but has also led to the EU reflecting on itself, its direction, and how it comprehends and defines its existence both internally and on the global platform. One branch of speculative discussion on what a post-Brexit EU will look like is consideration of the role that the English language will play in the EU's institutions once the EU loses the member state that houses the demos with whom that language is associated. While much of this discussion has necessarily focused on whether a different language could become the unofficial lingua franca of the EU institutions in terms of the practicalities of its day-to-day workings, the future role and use of the English language as a democratic legitimacy tool has barely been remarked upon.

As such, a simple reframing of the component parts of democratic legitimacy (well, as simple as one could hope when attempting to deconstruct and reconstruct the tenets of democratic legitimacy) by means of considering whether the removal of the English language's associated demos could allow for language as a tool to be moved from the social legitimacy forum into the realm of formal legitimacy. And if so, whether this change in the role of the English language could provide the instigating spark for the eventual creation of a European demos, forged on alternative criteria to that constructed out of ideas centered on the post-nation state. Instead, the new European demos would be conceptualized within newly constructed frameworks that are more relevant and appropriate for its post-national (and multilingual) platform.

Social and formal legitimacy

Democratic legitimacy is widely accepted to encompass two distinct component categories: one formal and one social. Formal legitimacy corresponds to legality and thus concerns the democratic institutions and processes of law making within the EU, whereas social legitimacy does not take procedures into account, but rather refers to a broad social acceptance of the system. Consideration of what "social acceptance of the system" means in the EU context has necessarily focused on consideration of how to generate a European people; a single European demos. This focus in the literature emanates from the broadly accepted position espoused by Dieter Grimm that a European public sphere cannot exist unless or until a European demos possessing a collective identity is forged that would serve as a frame for political unity.

The point to note, however, is that the entire positioning of this argument finds its basis in the post-Enlightenment preconception that a common language is vital to collective demos formation at the nation state level, and therefore features as one of the many necessary components of social legitimacy. Our entire discourse on demos formation centers around the idea that identity as a socioconstructivist construct is made up of cultural symbols such as a common language, common myths and stories, archetypes, flags, anthems, and many more (Anderson 1983; Smith 1992).

National languages have necessarily played a significant part in the construction of modern nation states, being the tool used to carry the cultural and ideological constructs of shared myths and stories. Yet, the issue with the dominance of such a perspective in the discourse is that it permits the maintenance of an outdated eighteenth-century construct which is no longer fit for purpose in a globalized world. Such post-national institutions as the EU – which is consistent with a globalized world – should not be developed within the same sociologically constructed or imagined frameworks as nation states. Hence, at this post-national EU level, there is the potential to deconstruct these eighteenth-century preconceptions and conceive of the possibility that language's use as a marker of social legitimacy is much more suited to the realm of formal legitimacy. In that sense, Brexit has arguably handed the EU an event which has triggered the possibility of this deconstruction taking place by detaching the use of the English language from its associated collective demos. English may be socially legitimate in the United Kingdom, but it is only formally legitimate in the post-Brexit EU.

Transformative English

Of course, we must not dismiss the membership of the both the Irish and Maltese nations, for whom English is a national language that is spoken as a first language in both professional and personal environments. But the peoples of these nations have other languages which are more so symbols of their national collectives, as opposed to English which is seen as a symbol of British imperial power in the national contexts. As such, Brexit may result in the weakened notion that English is inextricably tied to its native speaker culture and instead has the potential to be a truly post-national phenomenon of procedure and function. In viewing positioning English as a formal, technical tool rather than an assertion of Britishness within Europe there is the potential to instigate a truly post-national phenomenon: language can become disassociated from its nationalistic, cultural demos association and instead be asserted firmly in the purely procedural and functional forum as a tool of formal legitimacy.

English language use at EU institutional level is arguably already more of a formal, procedural feature than being "culture-specific" in any way (although there have been consistent utterings of concern that the use of English at institutional level prioritizes British concerns). Yet the various "Englishes" spoken as *lingua frankenstinas* across institutional corridors have taken on different principles of grammar, sparked new idiotic phrasings, and even generated numerous neologisms that native English speakers would never be aware of, all because of the second-language user status of its speaking population and the procedural communicative needs posed by the particular day-to-day institutional happenings of the EU.

What is important, however, is that the use of English within EU institutions should not develop in a way which connects it to the values, traditions, and norms of its users. To do so would be to fall back on post-Enlightenment nation-centric conceptions of imagined communities, something that the post-nation of the EU should give a wide berth if it ever hopes to forge a post-national European demos on novel terms and concepts that are more appropriate for its post-national existence. Brexit will denationalize the English language by rendering it independent of its people, and this denationalization is the first step in breaking the socioconstructivist, nation state-centric framework that we have come to rely on.

Making space for a new Europe

By instigating the move away from the shackles of our nation state-centric framework through the reframing of the tool of language in terms of formal legitimacy rather than social legitimacy, Brexit could potentially spark a shift in the conceptualization of the EU's "us" demos altogether. Were it to spark a truly post-national reconceptualization of what it means to be a collective, it could begin to move Europeans away from the damaging nationalistic dichotomy of "us" and "them" and toward a truly "united in diversity", novel, and post-national demos. Just as we acknowledge the uniqueness of the post-national structure that is the EU, so too must we forge alternative collective identity criteria against which the EU can begin to shape a truly novel post-national demos which is not based on the destructive and negative forces of othering's constructed and imagined symbols and concepts.

If it is possible to reframe language away from its traditional function as a marker of nation state bordered collective identity, surely this suggests that the same can be conceived of for our conception of collective identity. If language can serve a different subfunction for the forging of democratic legitimacy, then surely we are able to reformulate and reframe other elements and allow the European demos to finally be realized. This is where the beauty and the potential of Euro-English post-Brexit lies; its use at institutional level does not rely on a collective European demos to exist and adequately perform a necessary functional role. It can (and already does) play a purely practical role as a tool of the institutions without carrying the weight of a cultural collective consciousness with it. Brexit will surely and hopefully only enhance and enable this to a greater extent.

39

WHO WANTS TO LIVE FOREVER? EUROPE

Veronica Anghel

The biggest issue confronting Europe today is moving forwards with the EU project. Studies focusing on the EU as well as public discourse concentrate disproportionately on the flaws of this supranational construct, giving the impression of constant crisis. This incentivizes the counterfactual reasoning that post-World War II social and economic progress would have been possible in the absence of the EU. What is worrying about our present situation is not the increased fragmentation of views on what Europe could become but the growing acceptance (and increasing familiarity) of things as they have always been. EU integration is a simultaneous process of creation and destruction that slowly erases the sovereignty of the nation state. This rattled the old European order and is met with resistance from the nation state. And yet twenty-first-century challenges cannot be addressed with nineteenth-century institutions, meaning nation states first and foremost. An increasingly complex global environment presses to stride forwards with the remodeling of the European institutional system.

The new prominence of the EU in political discourse seems to suggest that this is a project in peril of disintegration. The argument is that building a monetary system that makes sense in Finland just as much as it would in Greece is too difficult. It is that rule of law means different things in Hungary and in the Netherlands. And it is that "Russian connections" spell gas pipelines in Germany and existential threats in Estonia. However, the need to give some kind of unifying meaning to rules and concepts was always inevitable. It is fanciful to assume that there would be no resistance from national and local interpretations to unifying European rules. "Building Europe" can only happen at the expense of national sovereignty. Much like the popular movie line from *Highlander*: in the end, there can be only one. Either the EU or the nation state will predominate. My goal here is to sketch the opportunities for a more solidified EU offered by current challenges.

Embrace coalition building

The May 2019 European Parliament elections gave the EU a more fragmented legislative body. The center-right European People's Party (EPP) and the center-left Progressive Alliance of Socialists and Democrats (S&D) lost their combined majority for the first time even if they remain the two largest parties. Euroskeptic, far-right, and national-populist parties did not secure a watershed result, but they did establish themselves as a fixed point on the European political stage. At the same time, the center has also been strengthened thanks to gains made by Renew Europe (formerly the Alliance of Liberals and Democrats for Europe) as well as the European Greens. The prospect of coalition building at the EU level sounded cumbersome and many were quick to foresee the disaster of never-ending negotiations that may fall apart at any time. Nevertheless, coalitions are an inevitable step in building EU institutions based on proportional representation. A more diverse representation within the European Parliament and less dominance of the main EPP and the S&D are signs of institutional maturity and do not necessarily spell instability.

There is nothing terribly new or frightening about this prospect of European coalition building. Analysts of EU institutional design would find a wealth of knowledge in the research of coalition formation experts at national level. We could already be ahead of the game by actively engaging with the prospect of "minority Commissions", much as minority governments have slowly, but surely, been accepted in the scholarly literature as a rational outcome of interparty negotiations. In fact, the EU already runs on coalitions at different levels and EU representatives automatically use their national experiences in building them. They should be good at it. The challenge, much like in the debate surrounding the imperative mandate of elected officials, is deciding which interests to serve: should participants in European coalitions serve their national constituencies or Europe?

Enjoy having enemies

While the current wave of Euroskepticism and nationalism is a challenge for the European project, this also presents the EU with an opportunity for further consolidation: the EU now has clear-cut internal "enemies". More so than an abstract sense of purpose, enemies provide a strong incentive to unite. "Nativism versus multiculturalism" and "progressive liberals versus social conservatives" are the main dividing lines that pit generations one against the other and mark an urban–rural divide. These contests continue to take place at the national level and are exposed by national elections. Brexit is the example of how internal problems have been pinned on the EU. At the time of the Brexit referendum of 2016, the EU failed to rise to the challenge and campaign against its British detractors and negative campaign. In the aftermath, the EU Commission President Jean-Claude Juncker accepted that he "was wrong to be silent at an important moment". Since then, the idea of "more Europe" is increasingly being offered as a solution to fight nativism and isolationism while nationalists no longer shy away from using Euroskeptic rhetoric. The stage is set for ideological confrontations after years of doctrinal diffusion between political families. The struggle for the meaning of Europe will be at the center of it.

It is also useful to be clear about who the "enemy" is not. The EU was built on a desire to make war impossible among European nations. Post-1989 eastward enlargement geographically extended the area where this applies. These states benefited extensively from EU enlargement, but we forget too easily how young these democracies are. Scholarly investigations and EU policy are still permeated with the wishful thinking of a linear diffusion of democracy in this region. Both sides cut corners during the fast-forward accession process. Both were aware of this at the time. Encountering pushbacks from these new members should not come as a surprise.

Elite-driven challenges to the rule of law are an opportunity for the EU to demonstrate the many economic and political advantages that enforcing the rule of law can offer. In doing so, EU institutions can maintain and even reinforce their strong appeal for the public in the region. EU intervention worked at important times in recent history (as during Romania's constitutional crisis in 2012). EU inaction was also exploited (as during Hungary's constitutional reform of 2010). However, the incomplete nature of the democratization process in new member states and weak national institutions also means that they are more malleable to change. In many policy areas, the EU *acquis communautaire* filled an institutional void and did not encounter formal resistance. The challenge moving forwards is for formal reforms to govern the behavior of policy-makers and bureaucrats and to dominate over informal norms and practices. This takes time. Solidarity with newcomers is in the long-term interest of old members states.

Act like Europe has always been there

Much like the nation state, Europe is not a natural product; it exists through action and not by default. One of the distinguishing features of a novel institutional project is that it can be so easily invented. "European citizenship" is a political construct. Ascribing meaning to a political construct requires deliberate action. For this to be achieved, European elites are slowly coming to terms with the understanding that the benefits of a pan-European institutional liberal-legal order need to be defended and are not self-explanatory. On 4 March 2019, French President Emmanuel Macron addressed the "citizens of Europe" and presented a project of "European renewal". He focused on institutional remodeling with a purpose of further integration. More importantly, between the lines, he rekindled the idea that "European interest" should trump "national interest". This is a programmatic meaning required for the success of pragmatically crafted institutions. The resurgence of federalist movements revitalized by younger generations is another example of engaging with the idea of a unified Europe.

Selling the EU product more aptly means engaging in a continuous strategic communication with European citizens who need to be reminded of the advantages of the EU. That we were all Europeans before we became Spanish or Czechs is not a tough case to make. Europe has always been there in some sense, even if the institutions of Europe are more recent creations. Pro-Europeans should take a page from the nationalist playbook and narrate the story of Europe more convincingly. Such strategies have history on their side.

Conclusion

The great transformation of national identities into a European identity is a work in progress. The institutions, norms, and habits that have so entangled European citizens give the texture of the EU. Tangible outcomes of European institutions – multinational families, companies running on €30 flight plans from Bologna to Vienna to Bucharest, transnational climate protests – defy the rhetoric of isolationism and are safeguards against disintegration. And yet the greatest threat remains resistance to change. The great challenge moving forwards is to step away from the institutional models that worked in the past and adapt to contemporary demands for ever more permeable borders; to pick up on the echo of the nation state and see the loss of national sovereignty not as a tragedy, but as a strategy. Europeans cannot meet the substantive challenges they will have to face without Europe as a framework for action and identification.

PART V

REFLECTIONS ON EUROPE'S WORLD ROLE

40

THE WORLD AS INVENTION
Benjamin Bennett

The world is a European invention, and Europe's task in the twenty-first century is to take responsibility for it. It is true that every large cultural unit, now or in the historical past, can be said to have a "world" of its own. It is perhaps even true that every human individual has his or her own "world", in the sense of a particular way of organizing the data of experience. But the world, the familiar globular entity, both physical and intellectual, which ever-increasing numbers of people, over the past six or seven centuries, have been persuaded to accept as a universal human environment, was invented (although we still say "discovered") by European explorers, experimenters, and thinkers.

A principal characteristic of this world is that it is not organized, that it always turns out to be more than we thought it was, more than we can fit under the dominion of God or Fate in any form, that it always turns out, paradoxically, to be different from itself. Indeed, the inventors of this world, and we in their wake, set a positive value on its infinite elusiveness. We insist on respecting hard facts, which always means new facts, since old facts by definition are soft, corrupted by the devices we have applied in understanding them. We insist on the uncharted, the unknown, even the unimaginable, as a field for our activity. In other words, this new world – which we thus follow those European pioneers in recreating – is designed to be out of control. Its whole character – as world, as "reality", as fact, as a field for activity – is always to be at least one step beyond all our abilities to control it.

Out of control

If you want a world of infinite possibility, therefore presumably of infinite promise, you have to accept a world out of control. It took until the twentieth century for the second half of this bargain to become fully clear to us. The world has been out of control ever since its invention; but only recently have the most disastrous consequences of this condition forced themselves on our awareness. For our original intentions in world creating, and even many of their early consequences, were not by any means bad. Even European imperialism, to give the project its commercial and military name, did not take too long to start exporting all sorts of cultural and political products by which the new universal world would be given a shape that promised much for the future: the institution of the nation state, for example, with its tendency to break down tribal and caste divisions; and above all, the idea of democracy.

It is true, if we believe Hannah Arendt, that the politics of nation states inevitably produces the possibility of totalitarianism, and if we believe Michael Mann, that democracy inevitably produces the possibility of ethnic cleansing. But these are just possibilities. Are they not outweighed by the demonstrable benefits of those European exports? Or to take another example, do the benefits of modern experimental science not outweigh the possibilities it opens for wholesale death and destruction?

The trouble is that our world as a whole is designed from the outset to be out of control, which means that there is nothing to prevent the worst conceivable possibilities, like totalitarianism or ethnic cleansing, from becoming realities. Does the case of thermonuclear war mark a turning point? That war is definitely a possibility but seems unlikely ever to be realized. Have we triggered a control mechanism here, which, in spite of our world's design, prevents suicide? Is there any evidence that such a mechanism is operating with respect to the slower but equally sure world suicide of climate change? Another characteristic of our world is that it likes to think about itself, to watch itself operate. Do we therefore simply prefer a suicide we can savor while it is in progress? In the 1960s, we watched *Mondo Cane* and its imitators. Now all we need to watch is the news. The creators of that quasi-documentary called their subject matter a "world". My point is that they were correct in doing so.

Spectators

Media theorists, and others, might be inclined to argue that our spectatorial attitude toward the world is itself a major part of the problem that piques it. But the only conceivable alternative to watching the world would be to live in it, which in a strong sense is impossible. In order to carry on our public and private lives in a reasonably orderly way, we require a reasonably orderly social, cultural, and political environment. The world out of control I have been talking about is of no use to us in this regard; we must confine our living to organized fragments or segments of that world, in the form of states, societies, and cultures. The only exceptions to this rule, as far as I know, are diasporic peoples, peoples driven out of their homelands who have no place to live as the peoples they are except, precisely, the world. Diasporic peoples of course also live as committed citizens of the cultures they inhabit. But there is always a second side of their living which is situated in the great elsewhere created by early modern Europe.

The Jews have a special place among such peoples, for precisely Europe is the place where huge numbers of them settled. This fact, in the present context, affords us a useful perspective on Hannah Arendt's arguments about the political irresolution of European Jews from the eighteenth to the early twentieth century, arguments for which she, and her memory, have endured much undeserved and mostly unanswered obloquy, as if she had accused us of complicity in our own extermination.

She suggests, it is true, that we might have known better. The lives of European Jews, in the typical diasporic situation of combined local citizenship and world citizenship, were further complicated by the vague but inescapable recognition that the world is itself a European invention. And it is hard to see how, under the circumstances, we could have failed to put two and two together and make Europe into a kind of homeland for us as diasporic Jews. Which was a mistake. For it is relatively easy, in hindsight, to see how the conceptual slipperiness of that move (involving the differences among Europe, its individual countries, and the world), plus the impossibility of control on the level of world, made the eventual response of extermination practically unavoidable.

Responsibility

But what of the future? If the past is a guide, we can expect in coming decades that the disastrous part of our world bargain will occupy ever more territory, both physical and intellectual. Is there a way of coping with this state of affairs, or must we simply accept it? Can the problem we are faced with, now including even natural catastrophes, be regarded as a security problem? "Security", as far as I can see, in modern international parlance, is a euphemism for "control". And control is out of reach, as absolutely and inherently out of reach for the United States or China or the United Nations as it is for the smallest Arctic or Pacific island society that is even now being swallowed by the ocean.

The only possibility for coping that occurs to me, since taking control is out of the question, is taking responsibility. The fundamental problem with our world is that it is a particular kind of invention, and responsibility can be taken for inventions. And if we ask who, or what agency, is to take responsibility in this case, there is only one possible answer. For you cannot take responsibility for something unless you are responsible for it. Which means the agency we are looking for is Europe.

Our Europe is of course not the same Europe that invented the world. It is, among other things, that Europe minus most of its Jews. But I think it may still be Europe enough. It still occupies the same little corner of land in which the speakers of who knows how many different languages and dialects are pressed up against one another. And it is now much more organized, economically and even politically, as Europe, than ever before; although that organization is now, as ever, endangered.

But the question remains: what can we possibly mean by "taking responsibility" in this case? I do not know the answer to this question, but I know that the answer, if it is found, will not look like an answer, will not settle anything (which would be a form of control). And I think there are people who may know more on this point than I do, for example Jürgen Habermas in his book, from 2011, *Zur Verfassung Europas* (*On the Constitution of Europe*).

If things are out of control, perhaps it is time to shake things up yet further. Perhaps the sociopolitical garment we have been wearing all these centuries, constructed of well-known relations among concepts like nation state and democracy, needs to be turned inside out and worn the wrong way round. Europe may already be well ahead in this regard. But in any event, the world is utterly out of control, and Europe's task in the twenty-first century is to take responsibility for it.

41

DEFENSIVE INSTITUTION BUILDING

Shawn Donnelly

Questions about Europe's future are best answered by making reference to three key trends: the increasing pressures from the international system that challenge Europe to adjust in the economic and defense realms; the domestic preferences of Europe's most powerful countries in determining how to respond; and the continued use of non-EU institutions by powerful member states to solve deadlocks in the European Council and Parliament. These three trends have become increasingly visible over the last decade of EU politics, and add to it developments of the broader international system based on the domestic ambitions and priorities of China, the United States, Russia, and the UK as the key challengers of European interests, and the countries that are bound to put the EU under the greatest strain.

This chapter explores Europe's response to these developments through principles of realist institutionalism (rather than standard integration theory). Realist institutionalism has three premises: that great powers are interested in upholding interdependence; that they pay attention to distributive gains in the institutions that provide this; and that they select, abandon, reshape, create, and nest institutions as required to secure those gains, in ways that cost the least (borrowing from historical institutionalism). Unlike classic EU integration theory, non-EU institutions are an expected outcome when there are strong threats to European interdependence, when distributive outcomes of a Council compromise would threaten a powerful country's interests (in the narrow, unenlightened sense), and when they ensure strong control over future choices.

Given the challenges it must face, the EU will continue to develop institutionally, becoming more important. But it will do so in the context of other institutions outside the EU that are led by Germany for the eurozone and by France for European defense. Such institutions provide elements of government rather than governance that the EU cannot, given the diversity of domestic political preferences across EU member states.

SHAWN DONNELLY

External pressures on Europe

Europe lives and evolves in a world that is becoming increasingly realist. That world will continue to challenge the EU and its member states to grow as a community. The United States, China, the UK, and Russia have a considerable impact on the pressures that Europe faces in order to develop. Each of these country's foreign policies are driven by its own domestic politics in ways that can be sketched with some degree of probability.

For example, the United States will experience a lasting realignment of the political party system that places Republicans in the protectionist corner and Democrats in favor of managed globalization. This translates into a more fragile, fluctuating willingness to play a leadership role in global affairs generally. Government oscillates on trade issues between unreservedly protectionist Republican administrations and Democratic ones that use discrimination in the treatment of environmental and social standards to create a form of market protection that is consistent with its own Green New Deal. Attempts by Democrats to consolidate a formal agreement with the EU will falter on divided government, particularly when there is Republican control of the Senate during Democratic presidencies. The same ambivalence will continue to sap strength from the World Trade Organization and the American commitment to European security through NATO. The dollar will continue to be the dominant global currency for trade, investment, and reserves, and market participants will continue to view the dollar as a safe haven. While the euro will be a strong currency, it will remain regional. The Chinese yuan will move into second place.

China will follow its domestic interest in globalization with Chinese characteristics to double down on expanded trade and investment with the rest of the world, but underpinned by bilateral agreements (creating hub-and-spoke relationships) and Chinese-led institutions that expand beyond investment (like the Asian Infrastructure Investment Bank) to eventually encompass political and security relations. China will consolidate its influence across Asia and Africa and to reject the constraints of international law (particularly of the sea). The yuan will develop as a fully international currency (which is how it will become the world's number two currency for trade, investment, and reserves). EU–China trade agreements will remain elusive.

Other trends can be projected into the future as well. For example, Russia will continue its role as regional spoiler, containing and destabilizing the EU where it can. Economically unimportant, and politically inept, it will seek to ally with China where it can. The United Kingdom is likely to break up, losing Scotland, but not Northern Ireland, leading to renewed violence in Ireland that the EU has to contend with, and that spreads to England. This continues until a second Good Friday Agreement is bundled with England's renewed membership bid in the 2040s.

Europe as an economic and monetary power

The eurozone will enter another crisis in the 2020s, pitting Germany, together with the European Stability Mechanism, against Italy. This confrontation will turn out to be a decisive victory for the hard currency preferences of Germany. The European Stability Mechanism will continue to be the only backstop for the eurozone, despite periodic, prolonged calls for fiscal union. Germany will use Italian financial difficulties in the 2020s to reject those calls and demonstrate that the European Stability Mechanism can orchestrate the restructuring of a major eurozone economy.

Decisions within this new economic arrangement will be politicized and volatile. Italian politics will resist any new form of external constraint. But movements to shift to fiscal union will shatter on German and Dutch resistance to treaty change. Instead, Germany will force through other changes to Europe's EMU, including the banking union, which Italy has resisted in exchange for allowing assistance. Other eurozone governments will complain about having their subscriptions called up (to a total of €700 billion), and the German Bundestag will complain about the European Stability Mechanism taking out loans (totaling a further €300 billion), but the specter of fiscal union's greater immediate and direct costs will get them to follow German government proposals. Pressure from the IMF and the ECB will bring no substantial change to the German government's position. In contrast, the Eurogroup will agree to expand the European Stability Mechanism's borrowing capacity to increase the fund's maximum firepower from €1 trillion to €1.5 trillion. Once that is accomplished, the Eurogroup will declare that neither a fiscal union, nor eurobonds are necessary.

Should this scenario come to pass, it will have two results. First, the eurozone will not only continue, but strengthen its trajectory as a hard currency area. Domestic, demand-led growth will remain low by global standards, but the euro will gain popularity as a strong reserve currency. Europe's desire to focus on price stability, and the lack of a fiscal union, will keep the volume of euros in circulation lower than that of the dollar or yuan. For this reason, the euro will not become a threat to the dollar's position as the leading world currency for trade, investments, and reserves.

Europe as a military and security power

Europe's external security threats look set to intensify over the next decades, as Russia continues its attempt to contain the EU's influence, destabilizing Europe's eastern and southern flanks. As American political willingness to deter attacks through NATO declines, incidents in which Russia contests European air, sea, and land control of the Baltic and Black Sea theaters become more frequent and daring. Ukraine remains a low-conflict war zone that flares up periodically, making it difficult for the country to capitalize on its Association Agreement with the EU.

In this context of Russian threats and American fickleness, France is likely to exploit a military crisis involving close calls or clashes involving Russian and European forces to push for further development of its European Intervention Initiative (EII) as a French-led security alternative to both a European Defense Union and NATO. This new EII will remains outside the EU, and will encompass the development of a strategic doctrine for Europe, staff officer training, weapons planning and development, and force generation.

In building up its EII and placing itself in the effective position of Europe's strategic leader, France will secure ready support from most of the EU quickly, particularly its Eastern member states. Italy and Spain's support can be won with promises to protect the Mediterranean. Border control capacities will prove critical on the Irish/Ulster border as well. Germany's support will come, despite considerable reluctance, in exchange for promises that Europe's strategic posture will remain defensive. Collaborative projects to generate combat clouds, missile defense, and overall combat capacity will take place outside the EU, replacing American equipment and leadership. With France leading strategy and force generation outside the EU, the EU itself pursues the more technical aspects of implementing decisions taken in Paris. In the wake of these institutional developments, Paris will become the place for Moscow, Beijing, and Washington to call on defense matters.

Conclusion

Europe's big challenges over the next few decades will be more than trivial. In many respects, they will be existential. And they will create deadlock in the Council as competing political priorities collide over how to proceed. The principles of realist institutionalism suggest that France and Germany, as powerful countries in Europe, will build up institutions outside the EU to overcome deadlock in the security and economic fields respectively. This development will mean a shift to non-EU institutions for critical, authoritative decisions typical of government, while the EU specializes in governance within the terms set by these new arrangements.

42

THE EU AND SOUTH–SOUTH COOPERATION
Shengqing Zhang

> The EU can best learn about its own flaws and potentials and become
> a meaningful utopia for its own citizens by "bringing the outside world
> back in".   (Nicolaïdis & Howse 2002: 769)

When she spoke as candidate for the presidency of the European Commission
before the assembled members of the European Parliament on 16 July 2019,
Ursula von der Leyen articulated Europe's global challenges as follows:

> None of these challenges will go away. But there have been different
> ways to react to these trends. Some are turning towards authoritarian
> regimes, some are buying their global influence and creating depend-
> encies by investing in ports and roads. And others are turning towards
> protectionism. None of these options are for us. We want multilateral-
> ism, we want fair trade, we defend the rules-based order … We have to
> do it the European way.

In her speech, von der Leyen delivered a clear vision of a *sui generis* collective
European position. But reality often tells another story. Consider European development policy in Africa. For decades, the EU has undertaken several important
steps in realizing its goals of European integration. During the 2000s, the EU
passed the Paris Declaration on Aid Effectiveness and began forging a new consensus on development. Now the EU is working to shape international development cooperation in accordance with its agenda to promote human rights,
good governance, and democracy. One challenge for the European Commission
has been to "produce a statement on EU development policy, a sort of Brussels
consensus to counter the Washington consensus" (Carbone 2007: 54–5). With
the establishment of European External Action Service in 2010, moreover, the
EU is emerging as a major actor in the field of global development.

Nevertheless, there are a number of obstacles to the creation of a common European position on development. Internally, the EU has not overcome the conflicts of interests and competing policies among the member states. Externally, the EU is still facing challenges dealing with stakeholders at the local level in African countries where European interests and colonial legacies often become entangled. Increasingly, moreover, Europe is not the only player. As a result, the emerging "Brussels consensus" on international development confronts new approaches from emerging powers like China, India, and Brazil. Of these, China is far and away the most important influence beyond Europe.

China's new approach

The growing influence of China in Africa reflects the changing landscape in international development. Although China has a long track record of involvement in Africa, the scale of its activity has increased dramatically with the Belt and Road Initiative. The Chinese government has pledged €60 billion in new assistance for Africa during the 2018 Forum on China–Africa Cooperation Summit. The initiative focuses on a different pattern of development that places greater emphasis on South–South commercial interaction and far less emphasis on conditionality than is the norm with European assistance. By implication, China asks for few concessions in the protection of fundamental human rights and the promotion of basic democratic principles. Instead, China operates on a "no strings attached" policy that emphasizes the importance of non-interference and the principle of national sovereignty. Joshua Cooper Ramo, a vice president with Kissinger Associates, refers to this new approach as part of *The Beijing Consensus* (2004), in contrast to the influence of Washington or Brussels. The "Shenzhen model" is the formula for successful development that recipient countries are encouraged to emulate.

The growing influence of China in Africa has had a broad impact. To begin with, it has leveraged the existing balance of power and triggered more intensive economic competition with other donors by offering an alternative option of development assistance. This new offer is attractive for many African countries since it can meet their urgent needs for investment while at the same time strengthening their bargaining power relative to more traditional donor organizations and countries. In turn this has lowered the effectiveness of conditional lending in influencing the policies pursued by governments that receive development assistance. Moreover, the EU has been slow to respond either by strengthening its common policy framework or by tightening the coordination across the member states. This suggests that there is still considerable room for improvement at the EU level in order to reinforce Europe's political will and capacity of performing joint action.

190

Second, China's new approach challenges the normative foundations of the world economic order. This challenge is very different from the influence on the African countries themselves. It emerges from China's celebration of "win-win" competition in the commercial area and from China's self-portrayal as "friend and brother" of developing countries against the "hegemony" of Western countries and Western values. The EU finds it hard to respond to this normative challenge in part because of European difficulties dealing with migration and in part because of the rise of populism. Europe's soft power or civilian power is diminished in Africa as a consequence.

Western institutions have adapted in response. At the global level, for example, the IMF has shown signs of moderating its fiscal requirements in order to compromise with China's approach. In part this is because of a change in the broader consensus among European and American governments about the relative effectiveness of IMF conditionality; in part, though, it is because of the relative power dynamics between the IMF as an institution dominated by Western powers and those development banks promoted by China. Indeed, there is even some evidence to suggest that institutions like the Asian Infrastructure Investment Bank are becoming appealing for some European states. If true, this may undermine the collective role of the EU still further.

A European response

If Europe is to respond effectively to these challenges in development policy, it is going to have to shift its mindset and narrative from imposing values in a paternalistic way to addressing the real demands of local communities. This shift does not have to come at a normative cost. On the contrary, many European norms are actively pursued by powerful elements in the civil societies of developing countries. Europe will simply have to work harder to act as a norm entrepreneur. Europe should also invest more in promoting credible and effective forms of regional integration that can carry this entrepreneurship even further.

Such a reconsideration of the European approach to development assistance is also a chance for the EU to exercise better coordination with other fields of foreign policy, especially in the light of the growing agenda to build an energy union and security union in Africa. Such a broader approach would build upon geostrategic considerations rather than relying exclusively on the economic interests of the member states. At the same time, Europe can explore more opportunities to construct a broader dialogue and to exchange ideas with China while reinforcing both the pursuit of UN SDGs and the strengthening of global governance.

China's rise as a global actor challenges both European development strategies and the established Western-driven normative structure in the global arena.

This challenge is manifest both on the ground in Africa and across the globe. This chapter has briefly discussed the potential risks and opportunities China may bring about for the EU's ambition to map a collective development policy. Europe's future as a leading player in the field of international development will depend upon how effectively the EU is able to respond.

43

THE ENDURING PROMISE OF THE EU

Harris Mylonas

Europe's biggest achievement may be that it always found ways to overcome collective action problems at the local and the continent level and address the problems confronting the population. From the Roman Empire to the nation state as the optimal governance unit, to the creation of the EU, Europeans have been at the forefront of political and social innovation. These institutions served as vessels for expressing societal demands and formulating policies that ultimately solved – in whole or in part – thorny issues such as economic inequality, social immobility, or the tragedy of the commons.

Reassessing Europe's threats

Today's public debates about the future of the EU focus mostly on nativist or far-right parties, immigrants and refugees, and the rise of populism. All trend lines run into the negative. Truth be told, these problems currently do operate against further EU integration, but they are easily and consistently overstated. A clear-eyed look at the data finds hardly any nativist or far-right party in government in the EU and the number of refugees and immigrants in Europe is rather small and politically manageable. Populism's threat to liberal democracy appears to be operative in one case only. A sober assessment of Europe suggests that the state of the Union is strong. Much as they have for the postwar decades, Europeans continue to achieve many of their core political and economic goals through the EU and solely *because of* the EU.

For the issues that Europeans find threatening, and that loom ever larger in the future, the EU presents a unique set of institutions and skilled professionals for combating them. Namely, climate change, automation of labor and its implications, and population aging with whatever that means for pension systems and the welfare state as we know it. The EU has decades of experience in dealing with transborder issues that affect all states, and that cannot be resolved successfully by any one of them individually. Regional integration allows the EU to become an agenda setter on a global scale and influence norms and behaviors on a wide range of issues.

Looking around the world today, the international system operates very differently than it did during the Cold War, the geopolitical context that gave birth to the EU, or even the early post-Cold War period, when many predicted the EU's demise. Global solutions during the Cold War had to be vetted by the two superpowers in a competitive bipolar system where almost every state had to choose a side. In the period following the collapse of the Soviet Union, the US was a global hegemon: intervening where it thought it was necessary, reconceptualizing NATO's reach, and dominating international institutions. The rise and fall of US's "unipolar moment", as Charles Krauthammer called it, has now given its place to Fareed Zakaria's "post-American world".

US unilateralism, which proved unsuccessful in the 2000s, gave way to multilateralism as a way forwards. However, the limitations of multilateralism soon became clear. While the US will remain the world's undisputed military, economic, and technological superpower, fatigue with involvement abroad and growing inequalities at home have resulted in US withdrawal from the trenches of global problem solving. The US will not take the lead. Beyond the US we find a significant number of regional powers without global ambitions. Given these realities, the EU appears to be the only institution that could bring about cooperation in global affairs and has the ambition to do it.

The EU contains about 7 per cent of the world's population but constitutes approximately 25 per cent of global nominal GDP. Maybe even more important from the perspective of global problem solving, the EU is both the largest exporter and importer of goods and services in the world. These facts about the EU are indicative of the influence that it can have on a global scale, through its example, its weight in the international markets, and its position as a norm setter.

The EU as guarantor of peace

But the enduring promise of the EU lies in guaranteeing peace in what we forget is a conflict-ridden part of the world. Yuval Noah Harari recently claimed that during the past century "famine, plague and war have been transformed from incomprehensible and uncontrollable forces of nature into manageable challenges" (2016: 1–2). Arguably institutions like the EU made this possible, at least for the European continent. In fact, research on nation building in south-eastern Europe suggests that in order to prevent minority discrimination and violent, exclusionary policies we need to increase interstate alliances through regional integration initiatives and international and regional institutions such as the EU and the Association of Southeast Asian Nations (Mylonas 2012: 10, 198–9). States participating in vibrant regional integration schemes, such as the EU, are less likely to be revisionist, more likely to be in an alliance with their neighboring states, and consequently expected to accommodate their non-core groups. It follows that in countries in regions with stable security configurations, multi-cultural arrangements are more probable.

Regional integration efforts enhance the success of conflict management and often prevent it from escalating into deadly violent conflict. To an extent this is the result of normative and socialization effects, but it could also be understood as the result of interdependence through movement of people and trade relations, as the French philosopher Montesquieu would expect. The EU serves as an example of regional integration, and others (like the African Union) are following its steps. Similarly, the EU project provides evidence that supranational identities can become compatible with national ones. Europe may be the first place where this is happening in a non-coercive manner, albeit slowly. Moreover, as we can tell from the eastward expansion and the enlargement of the EU, it is possible to change the norms and politics voluntarily.

But on top of regional schemes, cross-regional cooperation is key. For instance, the transatlantic dialogue model between the US and the EU can and should be exported. According to this line of reasoning, the inability of any one power to confront global challenges will ultimately lead responsible powers into the fold of cross-regional cooperation. This way, every state will ultimately become a stakeholder in the international system through regional integration accompanied by cross-regional cooperation. We have a long road ahead.

Re-establishing its purpose: the EU as a global agenda setter

Ultimately, the EU has an important role to play at the global, systemic level as well. It is common knowledge that whether we inhabit a unipolar, multipolar, or bipolar world has important implications for security and prosperity. Keith Darden and I have applied this logic to third-party state-building efforts (Darden & Mylonas 2012). For example, in a bipolar international system, the efforts of one pole to intervene in a conflict are likely to be undermined by the other pole. In a unipolar world, the hegemon may have a freer hand to pursue its goals; while in a multipolar world, the legitimacy of such an intervention could be more contested. The existence of a strong EU pooling together the resources of several states and turning it into a formidable pole in the international system guarantees that no other pole will dominate the system and impose their values on the planet. The EU as a regional leader can operate as focal point that listens, persuades, and inspires insiders, while coordinating with or balancing outsiders. This is not a traditional spheres of influence system utilizing coercion but rather a system based on reassuring security umbrellas and mutually beneficial trade blocs.

What if there were no EU? Borders between current EU member states would be consequential, visas would be required, labor market inefficiencies would be magnified, transaction costs would grow, nine million Erasmus students would not have enjoyed this process, the biggest single market would not exist, nor would the biggest development aid provider, and cohesion funds would not have led to convergence across very different economies. The Paris agreement on climate would probably not have emerged and neither would the EU neighborhood policy. All EU countries on their own are small, together they are a pole in the international system. That said, European integration is not a one-way street: we can choose to go back in time and relive the interwar years.

The EU may need to re-establish its purpose. It has always been, first and foremost, a project of peace, cooperation, and mutually beneficial exchange. In the process of securing peace, the EU has managed to find ways to bring about cooperation among diverse nation states and to tackle important problems. It is in this connection that the recent difficulties of the EU in dealing with the relatively small numbers of immigrants and refugees are worrying both EU citizens and outsiders. Pessimists would argue that if the EU cannot deal with this relatively minor problem what would it do in the face of climate change, automation of labor and its implications, and population aging? Deepening this regional integration project is a way forwards. It will allow the EU to continue being an agenda setter on a global scale, influence norms and behaviors on a wide range of issues, and balance existing and aspiring poles in the international system is critical points in time.

PART VI

FINAL THOUGHTS

44

RICHIE HAVENS, BEETHOVEN, AND
THE MUSIC OF REVOLUTIONS

Steven Johnson

Music has long been famed for its power to emblematize human experience. Western writers from Plato onward have pondered this phenomenon and most of us, whether we have read the philosophers or not, have witnessed how even a short passage of music can encapsulate a moment in time, or the texture of an era, or even in special cases the soul of an epoch.

Examples of this power were plentiful 50 years ago, in Europe, America, and elsewhere, too, at a time when Western society was being ripped apart by social revolution. The revolution pitted the so-called "establishment" against a "counter-culture generation" that raged against racial inequality, overly narrow social structures, corporate greed, and "immoral" wars like the one in Vietnam. The anger of the younger generation was most often expressed through music, in part because the main types of popular music in this age – rock and rock and roll – happened to align themselves against the establishment.

For specific examples, one could identify many songs that embody the spirit of the era – Barry McGuire's "Eve of Destruction", perhaps, or any one of several Bob Dylan songs, or one that for me at least perfectly condensed the rage of youthful protesters: Neil Young's "Four Dead in Ohio". In the end, though, I choose Richie Havens' "Freedom", which he improvised on the spot at the very beginning of the Woodstock festival. We also know now that the festival attained legendary status almost immediately, because everything associated with it – the timing (1969), the difficulty of launching the event, the national and international pilgrimage it created, the sheer size and scale of the event, its peacefulness, and naturally its music – effectively turned it into a counter-cultural shrine. Havens' song – and particularly his performance of the song, marked by the wild abandonment of his guitar strumming and his primal screams of "freedom" – stood out as a venting of the counter-culture's collective spleen and thus became perhaps Woodstock's most powerful anthem.

Freedom

Watershed moments like this one, with music linked symbiotically to culture, happened in earlier times, too. Perhaps the most powerful example occurred in the early nineteenth century, when the era's greatest composer, Beethoven, and his most revolutionary work, the Symphony No. 3, were joined together with the most profound social revolution of the modern age. In that momentous time, revolutionaries were engaged in a dire battle with the *ancien régime*. Their struggle was carried out in print and speech through most of the 1700s, as they worked to replace the old order – and its system of divine-right rule, hereditary privilege, and state-sponsored religion – with a new set of ideals built upon Enlightenment liberalism. In essence, the liberalists demanded representative government, equality before the law, and the right to speak and publish and assemble and worship as they wished. Their central concepts were freedom, liberty, and the sanctity of individual human rights and, as we now know, they remain core values in our society to this day.

Several factors explain why Beethoven's music matched up so well with this cultural tidal wave. For one thing, his development as a man and artist synchronized well with the Enlightenment generally, because the American and French Revolutions had occurred during his youth – the latter one broke out during his impressionable nineteenth year – and because he had grown up in the midst of the electoral court in Bonn, where Enlightenment ideals were often discussed and supported. Second, he just happened to reach artistic maturity in about 1800, right when Europe was beginning to respond with greater intensity to the consequences of the Enlightenment. Indeed, if timing is everything, his timing could not have been better. Third, Beethoven saw music not as a product designed for entertainment but as a quest for philosophical and moral truth. Even back then, people listened to Beethoven differently than they listened to, say, Rossini. And finally, Beethoven as a man and artist was acutely aware of his own individuality. Because he lived in this particular era, because of his natural temperament, and because of the social isolation brought about by his deafness, he thought more deeply about the nature of artistic uniqueness than did his contemporaries. This point is crucial, I think, because Beethoven's dogged determination to express the strands of his inner being – and to work out his personal issues through art – aligned perfectly with a Europe that was beginning to valorize the notions of individuality and uniqueness.

However, Beethoven was hardly the first to embrace this principle. In his *Confessions* (1765–70), for example, Jean-Jacques Rousseau took one of the great first steps toward Romantic individuality. In the opening paragraphs of that book he boasted about the uniqueness of his plan to expose every facet of his being: "I will present myself ... and loudly proclaim, thus have I acted;

these were my thoughts; such was I." Rousseau wrote the book in the years just before Beethoven was born – remarkably early in relation to the Romantic age, which would not dawn for another 40 years – but it actually came out to the public years later, when Beethoven was a teenager. In Germany a preoccupation with individuality appeared in the 1770s and 1780s in the novels and plays of Goethe and Schiller. For example, Goethe's *Sorrows of the Young Werther* (1774) – which came out in a second edition when Beethoven was 17 – prioritized personal feeling and railed against the oppressive restrictions of the *ancien régime*. Schiller's plays, much admired by Beethoven, were filled with social criticism and calls for personal freedom.

These important works were harbingers of a movement that was taking shape at the turn of the century. Perhaps the best verbal account of the new deification of the individual, though, came from William Wordsworth in 1800. In his preface to the *Lyrical Ballades* – a collection of poems by himself and Samuel Taylor Coleridge – Wordsworth delivered a quiet manifesto for a new kind of poetry. He argued, for example, that works of art must involve spontaneous overflows of powerful emotion, that they must draw their subject matter from inner feeling, and so must be written in the first person. He also emphasized that a work needed to be organic, that it must proceed "from seed to plant" (this point came from Coleridge), and that it must present the formation of a self. In other words, it must take its audience on an interior psychological journey.

Expression

Indeed, in searching for a single work of art that embraces these principles and, in the process, emblematizes the spirit of this age, one might well choose Wordsworth's poem "Tintern Abbey", or perhaps Goethe's *Faust*, or maybe even *The Third of May 1808*, the powerful Goya painting that cries out against tyranny. But it would be hard to find a work that better represents this epoch than Beethoven's Symphony No. 3 (1802–4). The famous backstory of the work underscores its power as a political and social statement. Beethoven originally planned to dedicate this work to Napoleon, because he saw Napoleon as a shining beacon of the Enlightenment. However, when Napoleon declared himself emperor, the composer saw this as a betrayal of liberalism and, according to an eyewitness, tore off the dedicatory page. Eventually he changed the title from "Bonaparte" to "Eroica" and rededicated the symphony to the memory of a great man.

But it is the music itself – not the backstory – that makes the symphony so powerful an anthem for this historical moment. Beethoven's first two symphonies had mostly followed the manner adopted by his predecessors Haydn and Mozart (although to be sure his rebellious personality peeks through in a few places). In the third symphony, however, he strikes out in a new direction from the very beginning. Listeners could hardly miss his repudiation of the eighteenth-century symphony and its *ancien régime* protocols.

Many commentators, then and now, have noted how the first theme of the first movement begins simplistically, then darkens into complexity, and then recurs again and again, intermixing with all sorts of other materials, transforming itself into a variety of different emotional states, until near the end – at the place musicians call the recapitulation – it unfurls a new victorious character. Knowing the symphony's backstory and the age in which it was written, it is hard not to hear this moment as the triumph of an individual self. It is a self that, after overcoming great adversity, has reached a promised land, where freedom, equality, and brotherhood reigns.

I would argue that the symphony's power of encapsulation might even be better expressed by the two chords that start the work out. These chords don't simply set up a context for the following themes. Unprecedentedly assertive, they signal by themselves a momentous shift in the place where music comes from. Composers before Beethoven had certainly used music to communicate emotion, of course, but they did so from a third-person perspective, in an objective manner detached from their own private psychology. Mozart, for example, is well known for his way of stringing together passages of contrasting emotional character. In a single piece, for instance, he may start in a lyrical song-like manner, then continue with a turbulent passage channeling the spirit of *Sturm und Drang*, a style popular in his time, and then continue with a passage that references, say, hunting music, or perhaps some other well-known style. The point is, that these styles were objectified types: they were categories of feeling rather than personal expressions of an artist's inner psyche.

The situation at the beginning of Beethoven's Symphony No. 3 is fundamentally different, for in fact the first two chords signal a seismic shift in the nature and source of musical expression. In a single instant, Beethoven has shifted musical language from the objective to the subjective, from the third person to first person. As a unit, these chords function less like a musical motif and more like a stern call-to-order. They almost approach the verbal, as if Beethoven were commanding his listeners to "HEAR. ME." When he directs the first violins to play four notes of each chord at once, making them roll their bows rapidly across the strings, he generates a friction that translates into intense and focused energy. What is more, the precise rhythmic character of the chords, combined with their loud-but-not-too-loud dynamic level, reinforces the sense that they are there to start an auspicious personal conversation.

Like the main theme, these chords take their own epic journey. They return frequently in the first movement, changing personality, sometimes coming back underneath or on top of other themes, sometimes turning lyrical, and sometimes rising up at moments of high tension, where they hammer out painful dissonances. Whatever the case, their narrative embodies Wordsworth perfectly: drawing on deep inner emotion, they trace a spontaneous overflow of emotion, they grow organically into ever newer states of being, and – perhaps most significantly – they narrate the formation of a self. They encapsulate the age of individuality more succinctly than any other thing I can think of.

Transformation

Obvious similarities connect Beethoven's *Eroica* symphony with Richie Havens' "Freedom." Both championed the values of individual liberty and both, benefiting from timing and context, became anthems for a new generation. But there are differences, too. The counter-culture revolution of the 1960s was relatively short-lived and, arguably, it changed Western culture in only minor ways. By contrast, although it did not happen tidily or all at once, the early nineteenth-century shift from the *ancien régime* to the next political and social order produced profound, long-lasting, and systemic changes. Beethoven's championing of the self was equally systemic, transforming the way artists viewed their work.

Years ago, I interviewed John Cage, an experimental composer legendary for his opposition to the traditional rhetorical systems of European music. Drawing on principles from Dada and such non-Western philosophies as Zen Buddhism, Cage in the 1950s tried to suppress artistic subjectivity by letting his sounds appear randomly, in an order determined by chance. In the middle of our interview he suddenly launched into a rant against Beethoven, denouncing him for having ruined music. While listening dutifully, of course, I could not help marveling that Cage's denouncement in reality served as proof of the epic scale of Beethoven's achievement. Whether Beethoven "ruined" music or not, he certainly did fundamentally transform it. And he accomplished this in a major public performance, in the midst of a European society that was itself being similarly transformed.

45

THE DREAM OF EUROPE: CAMELOT IN THE TIME OF MORDRED

Erik Jones

T. H. White (2015) wrote *The Once and Future King* during the Second World War. It is a story of King Arthur and the knights of the round table in five volumes and with two endings. The first ending comes at the close of the fourth volume. Arthur prepares to go to battle with Mordred with the help of a page boy, named Thomas. In a moment of reflection, Arthur tells his page to leave the battlefield. Thomas' mission is more important than combat. It is to carry the idea that nations should use their might for justice and not for conquest. He knights Thomas – Sir Thomas Mallory – and sends him away to ensure that the dream of Camelot remains alive. When the collection was first published in 1958, only four volumes were included and so this ending was definitive.

The revised collection, published in 1977, added that fifth volume back in and so included the second ending, in which Arthur agrees a truce with Mordred to divide up the kingdom between them. The decision is difficult for Arthur, but he accepts compromise as better than endless warfare. He meets with Mordred on the battlefield to finalize the new arrangement. Before the deal can be done, however, an accidental movement by one of the soldiers reignites the conflict. Both Arthur and Mordred are slaughtered in the ensuing violence.

White wrote his collection as an argument against war and in favor of peace. He also wrote it as a statement on the human condition. Camelot falters not because the idea of justice is unworthy or impractical, but because it is governed by people; even great people – people of legend – make mistakes of judgement and action. The lesson is that we should keep the ideal alive but also that we should prepare for misunderstanding. At its finest, European studies embraces this obligation, promoting an ideal of Europe as a civilizational power or normative superpower, but accepting that Europeans are human and so pushing back against their great potential for violence and misunderstanding.

The last century of European history follows a pattern very close to White's story of Camelot (Jones & Menon 2019). The century starts in horrific violence and bloodshed that threatens to bring an end to civilization; it then moves into an improbable and in many ways unprecedented period of peace, prosperity, and justice. Just as the dream of a Europe whole and free appears close to realization, however, Europeans start to take their project in different and competing directions. They revive old jealousies and divisions, in some cases even to the point of violent conflict. History, it seems, never really ended. Europe is less exceptional and more prone to relapse into misunderstanding than Europeans might have thought.

Improving the study of Europe

This new sense of fallibility can only be good for improving European studies. That is what emerges from Part I in this volume. What that fallibility means in practical terms is that students of Europe have to work across disciplines, they have to think critically about the lessons they have learned – particularly those lessons that emerge from the canon of Western civilization – and they have to compare insights with scholars from different countries, including most importantly those working outside of Europe. This new pattern of inquiry will not be easy. Disciplines are called that because they are rigid, and connecting them is hard work. Culture is more than just books or symbols; it is values and priorities, which imply both privileges and obligations. The process of building a more inclusive study of Europe will challenge strongly held identities; it will create frictions, confusion, and even conflict.

The advantages of building a more inclusive study of Europe are nevertheless worth the effort. Greater inclusivity and openness not only promise to generate new insights, but also to redress past injustices in the way traditional narratives or lines of inquiry have excluded important groups or covered up real grievances. It will make Europe, as a subject of inquiry, more relatable, because it will paint the story of Europe in the same contrasts that Europeans perceive in their own life experience. Moreover, a more open and inclusive study of Europe will make European studies more attractive to a wider community of scholarship. Once Europe ceases to be exceptional, European experience becomes less exclusive and more relevant to scholars working on other regions.

A more diverse, open, and inclusive study of Europe will also mirror more closely the recent changes in the governance of European higher education. In doing so, it will reflect the advantages of diversity and inclusion that exist across all areas of inquiry. It fosters a sense of shared experience and common purpose, and it will provide a model for strengthening the training of future generations that can be shared with countries and regions outside Europe. This is the ideal, at least. The practice will be messier, but that does not make the struggle for openness and inclusivity any less worth pursuing.

Lessons to share

Europe has always been a work in progress, both as a grand ideal and as a series of different projects. Liberal democracy is a good illustration. The ideal of liberal democracy has significant attractions but the practice is always challenging. It is even more challenging when it is married to fluctuations in economic performance, changing patterns of industrial organization, and real-world problems related to the distribution of wealth and income. Moreover, what is true within a liberal democracy is also true within other patterns of political and economic organization. Western Europeans should be more attentive to the lessons they can learn from the Iberian peninsula; they should also pay closer attention to the experience of Central and Eastern Europe.

Europe's other projects offer important lessons as well, about the nature of citizenship, the politics of market integration, and the impact of regulation. These lessons are important both within countries and between them. They also challenge much of the conventional wisdom held in other parts of the world. The effort to build a multi-country EMU without a corresponding political, fiscal, or financial framework is another rich laboratory for generating insights. The challenge is to communicate this experience in ways that make it both accessible and relevant rather than exaggerating its uniqueness.

Not all of the lessons Europe has to offer are salutary. That much goes without saying (and should never be forgotten). But failure is an important source of insight as well. Europe has a lot to offer in terms of experience with the problems of urbanization. Europe also reveals a lot about how success cannot be taken for granted. For example, the political and economic integration of the middle class was a great European achievement that now needs to be re-established. Indeed, this is an area where the study of Europe and the dream of Europe intersect: social integration has to be explained and valued if it is to be achieved, even as a work in progress. Moreover, this insight applies not only to "Europe", but warrants close consideration from one European country to the next.

But what is Europe and who are the Europeans?

The difficulty with studying Europe and drawing lessons from European experience is that the subject is constantly evolving both socially and demographically. Europeans' perceptions of themselves and of one another are also changing. European identity is not a stable construct, either as a concept in analysis or as a concept in practice. That instability is evident in the rise of nativism at the national level and in the resulting politicization of Europe; it is also evident in the changing attitudes that Europeans have toward migration, both within and across national boundaries. Of course, this difficulty is not unique to Europe. Other parts of the world also experience the challenges associated with social change and identity politics. What sets Europe apart are its geographic position, and its political and economic ambitions.

Other parts of the world do not experience the tension between cross-border institution building and the nation state to the same extent, particularly in the movement of labor and the management of migration. The practice of collective decision-making collides with the reality that not every country is equally attractive to potential migrants and not every country is equally exposed to migration. The economic, social, and political challenges that migration represents tend to vary from one country to the next as well. The implication is that any increase in migration tends to exacerbate national differences and to encourage politicians at the national level to retreat into the language of "us versus them". It is conceivable that Europeans will learn to transcend this dynamic, much as countries of migration have done elsewhere in the world, but such a transformation is far from certain no matter how desirable it might be in normative terms.

Illustrations within European countries serve to highlight both the cross-border and the domestic consequences. The isolation of Bosnia as a container for unwanted migration shows what happens when Europeans do not come together to solve complex problems. It also shows how destructive the lack of political agency can become. The experience of an open, cosmopolitan city like Berlin is very different. Although there are clear tensions in German society, the possibility for immigrants to exercise political agency offers a source of release. The prospect that social movements will emerge to help address problems that governments would otherwise ignore shows the importance of political agency more generally.

Europe is what Europeans make of it

This notion of political agency underscores the importance of thinking about Europe as a project, and about European identity in a more aspirational form. Looking to the future of Europe is necessarily a speculative enterprise, but the speculation can be bounded by the strength of European aspirations. This is the figurative candle that King Arthur gave to Thomas Mallory.

What is striking across the contributions in this volume is that they leave no doubt but that Europe has a future, and that Europeans will make it. That future may be more or less optimistic, or more or less conflictive, but it remains distinctly "European" in the sense that there is some kind of project that will shape the experience of all those who live there. Moreover, that project includes some kind of EU. It will be more diverse, perhaps. It may be larger or smaller in terms of membership. But it will continue to show the influence of its foundational movements and formal institutions. It will also reflect the political aspirations of future generations. In other words, it will continue to be a work in progress rather than a destination.

This Europe will have an important role to play in the wider world as well. The question is whether that role will be reactive or proactive, and hence whether Europeans will follow where they used to offer leadership. This sounds like a loaded question, and from the European perspective perhaps it is. Why would Europeans aspire to follow? Perhaps the answer lies in a return to classical realism, where Europeans equip themselves to be a military power in response to great power competition, because Europeans lack the capacity to inspire something different. This is that ending of the Camelot story that sees King Arthur trying to finalize his truce with Mordred.

The promise of Europe is something different. It is symphonic, majestic, inspirational. For Europeans to live up to that promise, however, they will need to know their own history and culture. For others to be inspired by Europe, they will need to understand the lessons of European experience. The community of scholars studying Europe share in the responsibility for ensuring that such understanding is possible. Europe is an idea as well as a place and a people. To borrow from White, it is a once and future dream about the potential for a people to achieve something better than their nature that needs to be given the widest possible audience.

REFERENCES

Ahrens, P. *et al.* 2018. "Politics and gender: rocking political science and creating new horizons." *European Journal of Politics and Gender* 1(1/2): 3–16.

Alba, R. & N. Foner 2015. *Strangers No More: Immigration and the Challenges of Integration in North America and Western Europe*. Princeton, NJ: Princeton University Press.

Anderson, B. 1983. *Imagined Communities: Reflections on the Origin and Spread of Nationalism*. London: Verso.

Atkinson, R. & C. Rossignolo 2008. *The Re-creation of the European City: Governance, Territory and Policentricity*. Amsterdam: Techne Press.

Barrett, B. 2017. *Globalization and Change in Higher Education: The Political Economy of Policy Reform in Europe*. London: Palgrave Macmillan.

Bekemans, L. *et al.* 2019. *Europe 2025: A New Agenda*. Berlin: Social Europe.

Berman, S. 2019. *Democracy and Dictatorship in Europe: From the Ancien Régime to the Present Day*. New York: Oxford University Press.

Blank, S. 1974a. "Council for European Studies." *International Studies Notes* 1(1): 36–8.

Blank, S. 1974b. *Western European Studies in the United States*. New York: Council for European Studies.

Boucher, A. & J. Gest 2018. *Crossroads: Comparative Immigration Regimes in a World of Demographic Change*. Cambridge: Cambridge University Press.

Brubaker, R. 1992. *Citizenship and Nationhood in France and Germany*. Cambridge, MA: Harvard University Press.

Bündnis 90/Die Grünen 2016. *Volles Programm Berlin: Stadt Der Möglichkeiten 101 Ideen Für Berlin Wahlprogramm Zur Abgeordnetenhauswahl 2016*. Available at: https://gruene.berlin/sites/gruene.berlin/files/b90g_berlin_vollprogramm2016.pdf (accessed 9 October 2017).

Cappano, G. & S. Piattoni 2011. "From Bologna to Lisbon: the political uses of the Lisbon 'script' in European higher education policy." *Journal of European Public Policy* 18(4): 584–606.

Carbone, M. 2007. *The European Union and International Development: The Politics of Foreign Aid*. London: Routledge.

CDU Berlin 2016. *Starkes Berlin: Das Regierungsprogramm Der CDU Berlin 2016 - 2021*. Available at: http://cduberlin.de/image/inhalte/file/Wahlprogramm_final-Screen.pdf (accessed 9 October 2017).

Committee for the Study of Economic and Monetary Union 1989. *Report on Economic and Monetary Union in the Community*. Brussels: Committee for the Study of Economic and Monetary Union.

Corbett, A. 2005. *Universities and the Europe of Knowledge: Ideas, Institutions and Policy Entrepreneurship in European Union Higher Education, 1955–2005*. London: Palgrave Macmillan.

Council for European Studies 1974. *Newsletter: European Labor and Working Class History* 6.

Council of Europe 2008. *Report of High-Level Task Force on Social Cohesion: Towards an Active, Fair and Socially Cohesive Europe*. Strasbourg: Council of Europe.

Darden, K. & H. Mylonas 2012. "The Promethean dilemma: third-party state-building in occupied territories." *Ethnopolitics* 1 (March): 85–93.

De Bellis, M. 2019. "Europe's shameful failure to end the torture and abuse of refugees and migrants in Libya." *Amnesty International*, 7 March.

Díez Medrano, J. 2020. "National identity and the citizens' Europe." *Research in Political Sociology* (forthcoming).

European Commission 2017a. *My Region, My Europe, Our Future: Seventh Report on Economic, Social and Territorial Cohesion*. Brussels: European Commission.

European Commission 2017b. *White Paper on the Future of Europe: Reflections and Scenarios for the EU27 by 2025*. Brussels: European Commission.

European Commission 2019. *The Gender Pay Gap in the European Union*. Brussels: European Commission.

Eurostat 2019. *Urban Europe: Statistics on Cities, Towns and Suburbs*. Brussels: Eurostat.

Fabbrini, S. & V. Schmidt 2019. "Imagining the future of Europe: between multi-speed differentiation and institutional decoupling." Special issue of *Comparative European Politics* 17(2).

Filiz, A. 2018. The Corner at the Center: Migrant Labor, Difference, Relationality and the Making of Berlin. PhD dissertation, Emory University, Atlanta.

Fischer, J. 2000. *From Confederacy to Federation: Thoughts on the Finality of European Integration*. Brussels: European Commission.

Fligstein, N. 2008. *Euro-Clash: The EU, European Identity, and the Future of Europe*. Oxford: Oxford University Press.

Foner, E. 2019. *The Second Founding: How the Civil War and Reconstruction Remade the Constitution*. New York: Norton.

Gancia, G., G. Ponzetto & J. Ventura 2018. "Globalization and political structure." Barcelona GSE Working Paper Series, No. 878.

Gest, J. 2016. *The New Minority: White Working-Class Politics in an Age of Immigration and Inequality*. Oxford: Oxford University Press.

Giuffrida, A. 2018. "Pope Francis adviser decries Matteo Salvini's 'co-option' of crucifix." *The Guardian*, 26 July.

Greenfeld, L. 1999. "Is nation unavoidable? Is nation unavoidable today?" In H. Kriesi *et al.* (eds) *Nation and National Identity: The European Experience in Perspective*, 37–53. West Lafayette, IN: Purdue University Press.

Guisan, C. 2011. *A Political Theory of Identity in European Integration: Memory and Policies*. Abingdon: Routledge.

Hansen, P. & S. Jonsson 2014. *Eurafrica: The Untold History of European Integration and Colonialism*. London: Bloomsbury Academic.

Harari, Y. 2016. *Homo Deus: A Brief History of Tomorrow*. New York: Random House.

Havel, V. 1985–6. "The power of the powerless." *International Journal of Politics* 15(3/4): 35–40.

Huseinović, S. 2019. "Egzodus iz Bosne i Hercegovine." *Deutsche Welle News*, 5 July.

Jeftić, A. 2019. *Social Aspects of Memory: Stories of Victims and Perpetrators from Bosnia-Herzegovina*. Abingdon: Routledge.

Jones, E. & A. Menon 2019. "Europe: between dream and reality?" *International Affairs* 95(1): 161–80.

Judt, T. 1996. *A Grand Illusion? An Essay on Europe*. London: Penguin.

Kuhar, R. & D. Paternotte 2018. *Anti-Gender Campaigns in Europe: Mobilizing against Equality*. Lanham, MD: Rowman & Littlefield.

Lamont, M. 2009. *How Professors Think: Inside the Curious World of Academic Judgment*. Cambridge, MA: Harvard University Press.

Lamont, M. 2012. "How has Bourdieu been good to think with? The case of the United States." *Sociological Forum* 27(1): 228–37.

Lamont, M. 2013. "European Studies as an intellectual field: a perspective from sociology." *Perspectives on Europe* 43(1): 41–5.

Maas, W. 2007. *Creating European Citizens*. Lanham, MD: Rowman & Littlefield.

Maas, W. 2016. "European governance of citizenship and nationality." *Journal of Contemporary European Research* 12(1): 532–51.

Maas, W. 2017. "Free movement and the difference that citizenship makes." *Journal of European Integration History* 23(1): 85–101.

Martin, C. 2018. "Imagine all the people: literature, society and cross-national variation in education systems." *World Politics* 70(3): 398–442.

Martin, C., O. Nijhuis & E. Olsson 2019. "Working like a dog: literature and the evolution of industrial relations systems." Unpublished manuscript.

Marx, P. 2019a. "Should we study political behaviour as rituals? Towards a general micro theory of politics in everyday life." *Rationality and Society* 31(1): 313–36.

Marx, P. 2019b. "Anti-elite politics and emotional reactions to socio-economic problems: experimental evidence on 'pocketbook anger' from France, Germany, and the United States." IZA Discussion Paper No. 12342. Bonn: Institute for Labor Economics.

Matthijs, M. & M. Blyth 2018. "When is it rational to learn the wrong lessons? Technocratic authority, social learning, and euro fragility." *Perspectives on Politics* 16(1): 110–26.

Mylonas, H. 2012. *The Politics of Nation-Building: Making Co-nationals, Refugees, and Minorities*. New York: Cambridge University Press.

Nicolaïdis, K. & R. Howse 2002. "'This is my EUtopia ...': narrative as power." *Journal of Common Market Studies* 40(4): 767–92.

Parsons, C. & M. Matthijs 2015. "European integration past, present, and future: moving forward through crises?" In M. Matthijs & M. Blyth (eds) *The Future of the Euro*, 210–32. New York: Oxford University Press.

Pew Research Center 2017. *Europe's Growing Muslim Population*. Washington, DC: Pew Research Center.

Ramo, J. 2004. *The Beijing Consensus*. London: Foreign Policy Centre.

Schmidt, V. 2019. "The future of differentiated integration: a 'soft-core' multi-clustered Europe of overlapping policy communities." *Comparative European Politics* 17(2): 294–315.

Shnabel, N. & A. Nadler 2008. "A needs-based model of reconciliation: satisfying the differential emotional needs of victim and perpetrator as a key to promoting reconciliation." *Journal of Personality and Social Psychology* 94(1): 116–32.

Shonfield, A. 1969. *Modern Capitalism: The Changing Balance of Public and Private Power*. New York: Oxford University Press.

Shore, C. 2000. *Building Europe: The Cultural Politics of European Integration*. London: Routledge.

Smirnova, J. & W. Cai 2015. "See where women outnumber men around the world (and why)." *Washington Post*, 19 August.

Smith, A. 1992. "National identity and the idea of European unity." *International Affairs* 68(1): 55–76.

Thomas, D. 2001. *The Helsinki Effect: International Norms, Human Rights, and the Demise of Communism*. Princeton, NJ: Princeton University Press.

Ushkovska, M. 2019. "European Union integration and national self-determination." *New England Journal of Public Policy* 31(2): article 7.

Van Middelaar, L. 2019. *Alarums and Excursions: Improvising Politics on the European Stage*. Newcastle upon Tyne: Agenda Publishing.

Waters, M. 2014. "Nativism, racism, and immigration in New York City." In N. Foner et al. (eds) *New York and Amsterdam: Immigration and the New Urban Landscape*, 143–69. New York: New York University Press.

Werner, P. 1970. "Report to the Council and the Commission on the realization by stages of Economic and Monetary Union in the Community." *Bulletin of the European Communities*, Supplement 11/1970. Luxembourg: Office for the Official Publications of the European Communities.

White, T. 2015. *The Once and Future King*. London: Harper Voyager.

ABOUT THE COUNCIL FOR EUROPEAN STUDIES

The mission of the Council for European Studies (CES) is to produce, support, and recognize outstanding, multi-disciplinary research on Europe through a wide range of programs and initiatives. These include fellowships, grants, publications, awards, conferences and meetings, public lectures, and symposia, as well as direct research and artistic collaboration. CES is particularly committed to supporting research that can play a critical role in understanding and applying the lessons of European history and integration to contemporary problems, including those in the areas of global security, sustainability, environmental stewardship, and democracy.

Every year, CES awards dozens of fellowships, grants, and prizes; publishes fascinating research guides and journal issues; hosts its renowned international conference; sponsors cutting-edge research; and enters into important partnerships.

INDEX